THE CULTURE GAME

TOOLS FOR THE AGILE MANAGER

Daniel Mezick

The Culture Game: Tools for the Agile Manager

Revision Number: 2.1

ISBN (978-0-984-8753-0-6)

Dedication

To Roberta,
for taking good care of me,
and for being a friend like no other

May 2012

Table of Contents

Table of Sidebars

Table of Figures

Foreword

At Zappos Insights, we have the pleasure of introducing thousands of people to a values-based culture where workers actually enjoy their Monday mornings. Because we have created a great work environment while still delivering outstanding service and increasing revenue, we attract many authors and experts who like to study our culture. One of those is Dan Mezick.

Dan and I met when he was on tour, and asked hard-hitting questions to get to the source of what makes our culture tick. He asked it like a curious kid, fascinated by this new world. We continued to have conversations in the months to follow, and it started with me giving him information about Zappos, but it quickly changed to me learning from Dan about how culture really works.

Dan provides an ideal perspective because he has experienced corporate culture for himself (at Aetna), started a company (and managed over 70 people), and immersed himself in vigorous academic study (of the social sciences and system dynamics). The result is knowledge + experience = wisdom.

Before meeting Dan, I had not realized all the different dynamics of culture that are at play. And the key word here is “play” because Dan not only identified the games within our culture that I was unaware of, he actually helped us create new ones. I hired Dan to learn about team dynamics through an Agile framework. My intention was to learn Scrum, but what I really learned was how fundamental safety is to innovation (and many other seemingly unrelated connections). And rather than giving long lectures, Dan engaged us in games that experientially drove these points home.

While this book was in Dan’s mind before we met, I pushed him almost forcefully to create a body of knowledge he could pass on beyond his epic 1-to-1 interactions. And I am happy to say that rather than a long-winded, academic approach to culture change, Dan has provided high-leverage techniques to improve a culture almost immediately.

This can instantly work for you; though let me give you a fair warning because you may be in for an unpleasant surprise…

My favorite book on personal organization is *Getting Things Done* by David Allen. And let me tell you, the first time I read it I hated it. The second time I read it, I got it. And the third time I read it, I lived it. Why did it take me so long? Well, the cold hard truth is that the first time I read it, I wanted to get organized, but I didn't really *want* to get organized. I didn't realize it at the time, but I was more committed to keeping my life as it was, and all the comforts that came with it, than really taking on a deep change.

So honestly, I won't be surprised if you read this book, and say, "You know what, I don't like it, and it's not that good." And then I won't be surprised when the book seems to stare at you, look at you, begging the question – "Are you ready yet? Are we going to try this? Do you really want things to just continue as they are?"

But here is the good news – you don't have to implement the whole book. You don't even have to read it all. If you fully get just one piece of it, and run with it with full commitment… you'll see a huge shift. And even better . . . you'll probably have fun while you're doing it.

Rob Richman

The topics in The Culture Game are just now beginning to rock and roll in our world. In a little while, say 25 years or so - call it a generation – mighty changes will have been wrought. Perhaps you will then recall reading this book, back in the day, and maybe you will look back with satisfaction on the path upon which you thereafter walked.

After 25 years or so, all these various innovations around culture design and their relatives will have been through many refining iterations and changes. Then, there will come a time when all these innovations will have truly done their work: they will have catalyzed great movements. They will have caused, struggled with, and ultimately absorbed and made productive all the upheaval and tumultuous change that started with their very inception. Perhaps then, at that late date, you will remember this book, the wonders you encountered herein, and what steps you took as a result.

And when the whole great, epic cataclysm of magnificence wrought by the eventual success of culture design practices and their progeny has come to pass; when the fullest possible triumph of cultural engineering and culture hacking has finally been attained – and when the full cultural fruit and flower of Reason and Beauty are utterly manifest in all our daily lives, well, we can hope that you will then remember the sense of promise you may have first felt when you read these pages.

The Culture Game is about the work of cultural pioneers and innovators, and about the newly burgeoning trend of culture design. Moreover, The Culture Game is a kind of promise, and a call to a certain kind of future, a future for which the pioneers described in this book have made a down payment on all our behalf. This future – one we can all safely anticipate only to the extent we are willing to help create it - is a future wherein we will have fully designed all the aspects of the various cultures we daily inhabit, and made them all maximally supportive of our humanity, and of our possibility for interpersonal connection.

If you consider just for a moment the life you might live in an accidental cave you stumble upon versus the life you might live in the Palace of Versailles, you get a sense of the difference we contemplate between undesigned and designed cultures. The difference between lives lived in a designed culture to support us in all our human needs, desires, and dreams versus the random and accidental cultural dystopia in which we today conduct our daily struggles is an almost inconceivably vast and hugely beneficial difference.

That such a future beckons us now is an underlying premise of this book. Many of you may feel something of a call as you read these pages. As we have. This thing, this great change, is surfacing only now, and The Culture Game is evidence of that phenomenon. Hundreds and then thousands will help create the great change. Then millions and, finally, billions. That you are reading this book now may bode well for you. You may be feeling early what is now a tug for a few, but what will ultimately be an irresistible compulsive energy to the many. Perhaps if you pay attention to the least little inclination now, it will repay you manifold over the years to come.

When all that is now clearly foreseeable in culture design has come to pass; and moreover, when much that is not now foreseeable at all but descends from what is at hand, when all that has as well arrived, then, at that moment, in the fullness of time, many of you readers of *The Culture Game*, Dan Mezick's early book on the topic, may well trace your happy involvement in the tremendous events that followed your reading it. You may even recall this audacious little introduction, which, perhaps you found encouraging, and which was written just for you by…

Jim and Michele McCarthy
In May of 2012

Part One: Preliminaries

Chapter 1 - Introduction

What is the culture game? It is a game you win by upgrading your company culture to value continuous organizational learning. Because of the current pace of change, organizations that learn fast can repeatedly outflank and outperform their so-called peers. New companies can seemingly come out of nowhere to develop and dominate new opportunities and prosper. The pace of change bestows nearly immediate rewards on the most adaptive company cultures. To be adaptive as an organization, that organization must intentionally engage in continuous learning. Organizational learning is by no means random but rather, a highly intentional act. Getting there is a game. . . and culture is the name of the game.

The culture found in typical organizations is ripe for substantial improvement. The typical company culture does not encourage high levels of group learning. Instead, all sorts of artifacts clog company culture, including policies, practices, and procedures, some written and some unwritten. This clog reduces learning flows by discouraging experimentation, an essential raw material of organizational learning.

Developing a New Culture of Learning

Culture in a company exerts a powerful force on the participants. The observant need not look further than the career histories and current behaviors of respected leaders to get a clear understanding of what is actually valued in the organization. Those who get ahead are not giving lessons in the rules of the current game. Instead, participants typically must figure out company culture for themselves. Wiser participants rapidly learn to pay attention to what is *done* while discounting what is *said*.

This arrangement works against development of a culture conducive to group and organizational learning. Those who advance in the culture learn the game and perpetuate the current cultural arrangement. A few "win" by choosing to play by ***the rules***, while the majority becomes disengaged. Meanwhile, the business environment, driven by technology, changes rapidly and effectively punishes low levels of group and organizational learning. Our company cultures are typically closed systems that respond slowly to change.

We are at a tipping point for management. Managers occupy unique positions to engage in the intentional shaping of culture in the direction of more adaptation. As a manager, you have the authorization to convene meetings, deploy budgeted funds for expenditures, and occasionally hire people. As a manager, you can encourage a new culture of learning by implementing learning practices proven to work at the group level. When your people learn as a team, they become more adaptable and achieve much better results, especially when the pace of change is fast. Teams that learn quickly are more adaptive than teams that don't. Adaptive teams are teams that can get better results, by rapid response to change.

Culture Hacking and Software Hacking

Prior to the late 1970s, it was difficult to gain access to computing power. Mainframe computing power resided behind glass walls in data centers; only a privileged few were able to gain access. That all changed when hardware manufacturers began creating small, inexpensive computers in the late 1970s, when the cost of computing power began to decline. In response, ***software hackers*** starting writing computer programs for personal use, and the era of ***software hacking*** was born along with the birth of the personal computing revolution. These applications often improved the quality of life by automating routine tasks and creating forms of entertainment like games. Before long, tech-curious people were programming small, inexpensive computers and building software applications for personal use.

As time passed, the microcomputer software industry was born, and the rest is history. The early software hackers created that industry.

That industry changed the world.

We are now facing a similar tipping point in the domain of company culture. For computers, the disruptive influence was the advent of the microprocessor, which made personal computers possible. In the culture space, the disruptive influence is the pace of change, driven by the widespread influence of technology in every aspect of society. Technology is accelerating the pace of change in business.

This acceleration of change is mandating an increase in (and more frequent) adaptation on the part of businesses, if they are to cope. Traditional corporate cultures are no longer adequate to succeed in the new world of business. Cultures that originated in the era of the industrial revolution are obsolete, precisely because they discourage learning at the level of organization. There is huge demand for a new culture of learning in our organizations. At issue is where to find tools to create this culture.

Culture Hacking Tools

With the advent of the computer revolution, it became standard practice for businesses to launch projects to develop software for their internal use. Dedicated, in-house information technology (IT) departments became the norm for most successful organizations. It was also typical that software design projects would fail, because software development is a complex process. This failure came at enormous cost.

Advanced forms of teamwork became necessary to deliver working software consistently. ***Agile methods***, essentially team-learning practices, emerged in response to the enormous cost of failed software projects. For IT, the harsh complexity of software development became a laboratory for the development of repeatable team-learning practices. Pioneers like the signatories of the Agile Manifesto[1] developed techniques such as

---

1 Beck, K., Beedle, M., Van Bennekum, A., Cockburn, A., Cunningham, W., Fowler, M., Grenning, J., Highsmith, J., Hunt, A., Jeffries, R., Kern, J., Marick, B., Martin, R. C., Mellor, S., Schwaber, K., Sutherland, J., & Thomas, D. (2001). "The Agile Manifesto." Retrieved from Manifesto for Agile software development website: http://agilemanifesto.org/

working in small iterations, inspecting frequently, and collecting continuous feedback from end-users. Agile processes harnessed change for the customer's competitive advantage.

In the end, technology essentially created the crisis of rapid change, as well as the solutions for coping with it. Agile software development methods are in fact group-learning techniques. The sixteen practices described in Part Two were derived from Agile software development. They are in fact ***culture hacking tools***: practices that, if implemented correctly, can immediately raise the level of learning inside a team and the wider organization as a whole. It is now possible to apply these practices inside any organization that needs to become more adaptive.

Culture Hacking is a Bottom-Up Approach

Culture hacking is a bottom-up rather than a top-down process. Managers can deploy culture hacking tools, such as Agile methods, to alter the way the culture works inside a small team or a department. Such alterations to the culture are local in scope: when team or department members venture outside, the wider organizational culture will continue to dominate the thinking (and learning levels) of all participants. Even so, bottom-up culture hacking holds the promise to develop more effective teams and departments. And when managers who are engaging in culture hacking actively coordinate their efforts, the impact on the wider organization can be very impressive.

Culture hacking tools include new forms of structure for interactions, new forms of meetings, and new organizational designs. The building blocks of these culture tools include specific interaction protocols and specific fundamental social structures, such as ***triads*** and Scrum.[2]

Just like the computer software hackers of the late 1970s and early 1980s, the culture hackers of the early 21st century are building the tools needed to construct their ***programs***, but instead of computer programs, culture hackers are rewriting the culture in organizations. Figure 1

---

[2] These building blocks are described in detail in later sections of this book.

compares the software hacking of the 1970's and the culture hacking of the early 21st century:

Figure 1.Software Hacking Compared to Culture Hacking

Disruptive Influence	**Computer Software Hackers**	**Company Culture Hackers**
Advances in technology	Microprocessor, driven by science	Rapid change, driven by technology
Platform to construct operating systems and applications	Microcomputers	Business Organizations
Timeframe to emerge	1975-1985	2010-2020
Platform building blocks	Machine language code, low-level functions, and software structures	Cultural codes, interactions, meetings and related social structures
Operating Systems	CPM, MS-DOS, Windows	Yet to be determined, still emerging
Engineering Practices	Software architecture and design	Cultural architecture and design
Early thought leaders	Donald Knuth, and others in the domain of software development	Jay Forrester, and others in the domain of organizational development
Nature of the coding task	Create new code from scratch, using ***homebrew*** tools	***Refactor*** or modify existing cultural codes, using ***homebrew*** tools

The early computer programming hackers had to create all-new application code for all-new platforms. These platforms for software applications included the early microcomputers such as the Altair. In the present day, culture hackers do not create new code from scratch. Instead, they modify the existing cultural codes, mostly by tinkering with meetings and interactions. Instead of an all-*new* platform, the platform is the *existing* organization. Culture hackers are actually in the business of *refactoring* existing cultural code on existing platforms. In computer programming, *refactoring* is the restructuring of existing code so that the overall system displays more robust performance, and so that new levels of performance are more easily extended . . . and maintained.

Efforts to refactor the culture of an organization have the same goal.

Summary

Culture hacking is the active, intentional and iterative modification of existing cultural norms in your existing organization, with intent to create a stronger culture of learning. *The Culture Game* is a handbook for managers who want to alter the culture of their teams and departments. The Tribal Learning Practices found in Part Two are a set of tools for your toolbox as you embark on the journey of hacking your culture.

Everything is changing, and changing more rapidly than ever before. The rate of this change is increasing *like never before*.

- In 1978, Chris Argyris & Donald Schön published *Organizational Learning*.
- In 1990, Peter Senge published *The Fifth Discipline*.
- In 2001, a tribe of pioneering people in software published *The Agile Manifesto*.
- In 2008, Dave Logan, John King, and Halee Fischer-Wright published *Tribal Leadership*.
- In 2011, Jane McGonigal published *Reality is Broken*.

In 2011, I put these pieces together, and wrote this book as a manifesto. It is a manual containing specific practices and principles for increasing group learning inside *tribes*, groups of about 20 to 150 people. This book is a concise how-to manual of sixteen essential learning practices that you can use right now to encourage a greater ability to respond to change inside your teams, inside your personal network, and within your entire organization. What's next is up to you.

Who Should Read This Book

This book is for anyone working in an organization, especially *managers* who want to help their organization respond to challenges more effectively.

This book is a self-help manual for people in organizations who want to improve, be more effective, and make a bigger impact in the world.

This book is also for organizational coaches, executive coaches, and Agile coaches who deliver coaching to organizations in pursuit of great results.

This book is for anyone who wants to influence the development of a *learning culture* in their organization, and leverage faster learning to obtain great results.

This book is how-to manual to develop a more effective, responsive, and adaptive enterprise.

This book is for people in organizations who want to influence how their organization thinks, how it speaks, what it says, and how it behaves.

This book is for people in those organizations interested in helping their *tribes* become great.

If you fill one or more of the following roles in your organization, and want to obtain better results with others, then this book is for you:

- A member of a team
- A manager of people
- A convener of meetings
- A director of an organization

- An executive of an enterprise
- A leader

The last role is a very important one to understand well.

What is a Leader? Who is a Leader?

Leader is a term that means many things to many people. When we think *leader*, some of us think of a ***hero*** who is a visionary who overcomes great obstacles to create a new world full of great results. Others may think of an *autocrat*, someone who imposes their will on the world (and those around them) to manifest results.

Usually, when we think of l*eader* we think of charisma, that special quality that few people have, the quality that helps one person influence a great many people. The reality is that almost anyone can *choose* to be a leader, with or without the quality of charisma.

In this book, I define a *leader* as follows: *Anyone* who influences *anyone else* in a social setting, such as a team or organization.

Regardless of positional authority, every person has more influence than s/he typically believes s/he has. *Influence* in this book means the various processes that affect the thoughts, words, and actions of others. These definitions of influence and leadership mean that literally everyone already has some power, opportunity, and capacity to exercise leadership in their organizations.

As you will see, this book provides specific tools for anyone who wants to help their organization manifest results more effectively; it is a how-to manual for leaders of all kinds, who seek specific, actionable techniques to create results through more and better learning within their organizations.

Chapter 2 - Agile Origins

The Learning Organization and Agile Software Development

In 1978, Chris Argyris & Donald Schön published the book *Organizational Learning*[3], which went largely unnoticed outside of academia. Argyris & Schön pioneered investigation into how groups of people learn together.[4]

Peter Senge of MIT later wrote a book on the very same subject that has since become very popular. It has been over 20 years since Senge's book, *The Fifth Discipline: The Art and Practice of the Learning Organization*[5], hit the bookshelves in 1990. The book introduced Argyris & Schön's concept of organizational learning to a generation of managers. Senge's book described the characteristics and properties of the *Learning Organization.* This type of organization can rapidly integrate new information and turn it into organizational knowledge. This knowledge in turn feeds the organizational ability to respond to change – and to be extremely adaptive.

Since that time, many other books about organizational learning have been written. *The Fifth Discipline Fieldbook*[6], written by Senge and others and published in 1994, provided some early guidance on how to foster actual learning to take place in organizations. Between 1990 and 2001, very few genuine learning organizations could be identified in

---

3 Argyris, C., & Schön, D. A. (1978). *Organizational Learning: A Theory of Action Perspective.* Reading, MA, USA: Addison-Wesley Publishing Co.

4 For a good description of Argyris and his work, see: http://infed.org/thinkers/argyris.htm

5 Senge, P. M. (1990). The Fifth Discipline: The Art and Practice of the Learning Organization. New York, NY, USA: Doubleday/Currency.

6 Senge, P. M., Roberts, C., Ross, R. B., Smith, B. J., & Kleiner, A. (1994). *The Fifth Discipline Fieldbook: Strategies and Tools for Building a Learning Organization.* New York, NY, USA: Currency Doubleday.

mainstream business. It became obvious that manifesting a learning organization was far more difficult than describing one.

Key Agile milestones followed the turn of the last century.

- 2001: Pioneers in new software development practices created the *Agile Manifesto*[7], a document detailing 4 values and 12 principles that encourage greatness in software development teams. Agile methods turn teams into small learning organizations.
- 2011: Agile practices are considered mainstream. For those willing to implement genuine Agile, the team-learning problem is conquered. Agile figured it out.

Enter Agile Software Development Practices

During this same period, pioneers in the teamwork of software development started experimenting with new ways of working. Practitioners like Dr. Jeff Sutherland and Ken Schwaber began formulating Scrum, a team-organizing framework for software teams. Kent Beck and others started developing and collecting specific technical practices under the banner of Extreme Programming. The social practices of Scrum paired with the technical and social practices of XP substantially raised the level of discipline in software development.

At the time, software development as an engineering discipline was very under-developed. Most software teams were approaching software development as a manufacturing challenge, usually with dismal results. Software development is more like product design than product manufacturing. As such, it is a complex undertaking where agreement on the final product's feature set is seldom clear. In software development projects, there is usually considerable uncertainty regarding the cost, quality, delivery date, and features. Unless and until the team achieves collective clarity, software projects see little success.

The Scrum framework provided an empirical process control structure for teams building software. As a result, teams could more

---

[7] See footnote 1

effectively develop and deliver highly complex software products. Scrum and the Agile Manifesto articulated the values, principles and practices that software development teams needed to embrace to take a shot at greatness.

Software development is a notoriously complex undertaking. The end product is an abstraction – bits of *code* that are stored magnetically on a disk. The architecture of even moderately complex software systems is daunting to comprehend. To deliver a functional system, every member of a software team must reference the same *shared mental model* that every team member understands.

Software Development as a Teamwork Laboratory

A software team is a special kind of team. Almost every software product is a unique creation. Everyone involved in the team's work must hold a shared mental model of the system to work on it together. The software development environment is very harsh and demanding for teams. They must communicate, coordinate, and collaborate very effectively to reach the goal of delivering a working system. Software development is a kind of rich learning laboratory for exploring shared vision, mental models, team learning, personal mastery, and systems thinking – the same five disciplines of the learning organization described by Senge in 1990.

Agile software development frameworks such as Scrum encourage and enable team learning to take place. Agile teams are in fact small learning organizations. The lessons learned by the Agile community become the road map and action plan for creating a genuine large-scale learning organization. This book describes these lessons and provides a specific how-to manual for mapping them to the wider enterprise.

The Agile Manifesto of 2001

In 2001, pioneers exploring teamwork in the software development space convened in Snowbird, Utah and formulated the Agile Manifesto, a statement of 4 values and 12 principles that launched a team learning revolution in software development worldwide. Most of us did not know it at the time, but the Agile Manifesto provided a values-and-principles structure for organizational learning at the *team* level. Agile practices enhance, encourage, and help manifest genuine team learning. These lessons in team learning come from software development laboratories, and can map to entire enterprises who want to become learning organizations.

Most organizations that dive rapidly into Agile find cultural norms already in place that tend to constrain progress and to hold them back. Likewise, most attempts at becoming a genuine and authentic learning organization fail for the same reasons. The root causes of these failures are the same. An Agile organization ***IS*** a learning organization as described by Senge. Genuine & Authentic Agile teams are very small learning organizations. The challenge really is to harvest these small-team learning behaviors and then apply them to the wider enterprise at scale. This book provides a "bottom-up" roadmap for doing exactly that.

Agile and Scrum Values

From about 1998 to 2008, software developers rapidly embraced the Agile Manifesto and Scrum for organizing and executing the delivery of software. Jim McCarthy likes to say, "software stubbornly refuses to ship until the team is aligned." Scrum's five core values, along with the Agile Manifesto's four values and twelve principles, provided the guidance software teams needed. Notice the focus on interactions and collaboration with customers. This is a hallmark of Agile practices[8].

Figure 2. Agile Manifesto's Four Values[9]

Individuals and interactions .... over processes and tools

[8] If you are new to Scrum, you can become familiar with it by referring to the overview of Scrum found in the Appendix. Since Scrum is an important influence in the development of the Tribal Learning system, knowing more about it is also important.

[9] Note: Adapted from Agile Manifesto's Four Values, downloaded from http://www.agilemanifesto.org/iso/en/

Working software................ over comprehensive documentation
Customer collaboration........................ over contract negotiation
Responding to change................................over following a plan

Figure 3. Scrum's five core values[10]

1. Respect
2. Commitment
3. Focus
4. Courage
5. Openness

Let's take a look at the Scrum values in depth.

Respect denotes both a positive feeling of esteem for a person or persons, and also specific actions and conduct representative of that esteem. Scrum absolutely supports and encourages respect. Without respect, there is no meaningful positive communication. Instead there is high potential for miscommunication, disrespect, low (or NO) communication frequency, and hurt feelings. *Genuine & Authentic Scrum requires respectful interactions.*

Commitment is the act of binding yourself to a course of action. Scrum encourages commitment. If you cannot commit, you cannot act. You are in a state of do-nothing limbo, a state of inaction. Scrum binds you to commitments. Genuine & Authentic Scrum displays high levels of commitment. *Genuine & Authentic Scrum is not possible without everyone involved paying attention to and keeping commitments.*

Focus is the concentration of attention. Scrum encourages focus. If you cannot focus, you are not paying attention in a meaningful way. If you cannot focus, you cannot learn to any meaningful level of depth. *Genuine & Authentic Scrum is always focused, all the time. Scrum encourages and requires focus to be effective.*

---

10 The Scrum values first appeared in the book, *Agile Software Development Using Scrum* from Ken Schwaber and Mike Beedle. (1996)

Courage is a quality of spirit that enables you to face danger or pain without showing fear. Scrum supports courage. When no one has the courage to say it, the truth about reality is obscured. Often, teams feel unsafe to describe reality honestly in the workplace. They are afraid of losing their jobs or suffering some type of harm for saying what everybody knows. Courage is necessary in Scrum. It takes courage to call out problems, identify impediments, ask for help, receive help, and offer help. In a Genuine & Authentic Scrum implementation, courage is evident in the way people behave. We honor and encourage Courage in Scrum. Scrum without courage is Scrum that only goes so far. *Genuine & Authentic Scrum requires courage.*

Openness is characterized by an attitude of ready accessibility (especially about one's actions or purposes), without concealment, or being secretive. Scrum strongly encourages openness, and expression of the whole truth. Instead of asking, why should I share this information? Ask, why wouldn't I share this info? Genuine & Authentic Scrum generates a high level of *transparency*. Everyone knows everything about the work in a Genuine & Authentic Scrum implementation. *Genuine & Authentic Scrum reveals a huge level of openness on the part of everyone participating.*

Mapping the Lessons of Agile to ANY Enterprise

This book maps the lessons of Agile software development from teams to the enterprise. The book distills the lessons of the Agile software development revolution, and provides a how-to manual that can help you to map the lessons of Agile to your enterprise. The result is a handbook that any organization can use to enable enterprise-wide learning. These lessons can apply to any company that wants to leverage organization-wide learning as a competitive weapon.

In software development, team learning is an absolute and essential requirement for success. That is why the essential lessons from Agile practice are so important. These lessons can be extracted, generalized, repurposed, and scaled up to enable enterprise-wide learning. The lessons of Agile team learning do scale, although many Agile practices do not, as you will learn from this book. The Agile revolution in software development contains all of the keys to fostering wide-scope, enterprise-wide learning.

The Agile revolution of the past 10 years answers three questions. What is the best way to initiate team learning? How do we actually make it happen? How do we DO it?

The Scrum Framework

One of the lessons of Agile software development is that *structure matters*. The roles, meetings, documents, and rules help determine the results we get. Organizations are social systems. What is valued and how authority is distributed are materially significant to a healthy system. Scrum is a team framework that encourages group-level learning.

Scrum employs three personal roles and three types of meetings to engineer effective interactions by and between team members. Scrum is built on a set of values that distributes authority in specific ways.

Scrum encourages the periodic examination of experience through a meeting called the ***retrospective***. The Scrum framework encourages experimentation, proactive management of boundaries, and a high degree of structuring with respect to interactions.

Scrum encourages everyone to focus his or her attention. That is why someone facilitates all Scrum meetings; the convener who is in authority during the meeting uses a facilitator (the "Scrum Master") to keep the meeting on track.

Teams that ***do Scrum*** learn well that they perform better when coached, and when team members have become very good at *paying attention collectively*. Teams display their visual artifacts such as task boards, diagrams, and charts prominently on the walls of their workspaces. Ideally, the entire team occupies and shares the same workspaces.

Scrum is a Good Game

The practice of Scrum is a root of the Tribal Learning Practices. Scrum is a teamwork-and-learning framework to build complex products using teams of knowledge workers. Scrum encourages and helps create a total team-learning environment, or *safe space*, for knowledge creation.

The Scrum framework qualifies as a game. As long as people opt-in, rather than being forced to play, Figure 4 demonstrates that Scrum has all the essential elements of a good game.[11]

Figure 4. Scrum is a good game

Good Game Properties	How Scrum Implements a Good Game
A clear GOAL	Scrum defines the Sprint Backlog and Sprint Goal as part of the game
A clear set of RULES	The Scrum Guide is the de facto rule book for Scrum
A way to receive feedback (a way to know the SCORE)	Every Sprint, the team shows the work just completed and declares the work DONE
Optional participation by all players	In Genuine & Authentic Scrum, all the people in all the roles consent to participate

Tribal Learning

Tribal Learning is the social learning process that takes place inside medium-sized groups – tribes that contain fewer than 150 people. It involves learning not just about the work, but also about the people *doing* the work. Tribal Learning is what happens when you use the set of tools described in this book. Tribal Learning is the act of learning taking place

11 Scrum is now mainstream, and many organizations are using it. A significant problem is that the people involved are not opting in. This actually kills the game of Scrum by removing the essential sense of control. I have written a blog post that drives deeper into this idea. Agile and executive coaches may want to take a look. See: http://newtechusa.net/agile/the-recipe-for-botched-agile-adoptions/

at the level of *tribe* – in groups from about 20 to about 150 people. The Agile software revolution has taught us how to manifest *team* learning. The *lessons* of Agility now provide the basis for learning at the next-wider scale – *Tribal Learning*.

Why aim to achieve Tribal Learning – that is, learning in groups of about 20 to about 150 people?

First, such learning helps foster a more nimble, agile organization overall. Tribal Learning helps an organization to identify opportunities, threats, environmental changes, and risks more quickly. Such learning helps an organization respond to its environment with very small delays. This is a distinct competitive advantage.

Second, genuine Tribal Learning, while being quite fun and satisfying, is also a hallmark of great organizations. Great organizations enjoy a level of performance far in excess of their peers and competitors.

Agile software development has taught us how to generate extensive team-level learning. The lessons are there and are described concisely in Part Two. Now you can apply these lessons across your entire enterprise. This book describes how.

Scrum creates the potential to achieve substantial levels of happiness and enjoyment. Figure 5 depicts how it creates a *sense of control*, a *sense of progress*, a *sense of belonging*, and a *sense of high purpose*. There is a lot going on in Scrum. Teams that do Genuine & Authentic Scrum exhibit and display many of the Tribal Learning behaviors described later in this book[12]. Of organizations that have adopted an Agile methodology for their software development, over 70% reported the use of Scrum as their framework for organizing teams. [13]

---

[12] Chapter Six lists and explains all of the Tribal Learning Practices

[13] See Jeff Sutherland's blog describing Agile and Scrum at: http://scrum.jeffsutherland.com/2011_02_01_archive.html

How This Book is Organized

This book is organized into four Parts.

Part One introduces all the ideas in this book. It also provides important preliminary information on essentials of Tribal Learning, including extensive coverage of a core concept – *psychological safety*. Everyone reading this book needs to examine Part One.

Figure 5. How Scrum delivers happiness

Four Requirements for Happiness	How Scrum Delivers Happiness
A sense of CONTROL	Per the rules of Scrum, only the Team is authorized to select WHAT work they will do, and HOW they will do it.
A sense of PROGRESS	Per the rules of Scrum, the Team and the Product Owner cooperatively define a definition of DONE. When the Sprint is complete, they use this definition to measure the work. Teams declare victory after every Sprint.
A sense of BELONGING to a group and being CONNECTED to others	In Scrum, Teams are authorized to self-organize in any way they see fit. Teams are cross-functional, and team members share work equally. Individuals identify with their Team as they bond to each other.
A sense of HIGHER PURPOSE and VISION	In Scrum, service to the product vision (expressed as the Product Backlog) is the purpose of the Team. The Team is competent to face a difficult goal based on a clearly articulated product vision.

Part Two provides the bottom-up tools that anyone in any organization can use to encourage more Tribal Learning. Most of these tools are simple and free. You simply need some willingness to try them for yourself. These tools are best utilized within a small group of people who are working together to ***tip*** the culture in the direction of more learning and more fun at work.

You do not need to ask permission to use these tools. You do not need to obtain a budget to use them, and you need no authorization to use these tools. You can simply do these practices with other like-minded people in your organization, and you will tip the culture towards more Tribal Learning. Part Two is a toolkit populated with tools you can use to develop more Tribal Learning. By doing so, you will help to develop a more nimble organization that can respond to opportunities, threats, changes, and challenges. The focus here is on your team, your department, and your local sphere of influence. You can use these tools inside your sphere of influence to alter the way in which people interact and learn as they work together.

Part Two provides you with immediately actionable Tribal Learning Practices that you can do RIGHT NOW to manifest more learning in your organization. These practices are quick, effective, and inexpensive. Most of them do not cost a dime. When you do any one of them, you encourage other people to use more of them. When you do any one of them, you manifest more learning. Most of these patterns and practices originated in the Agile software development community. All of them are quick to implement, and can help your organization learn faster, leading to more adaptability, a resilient culture, and better results.

Part Three contains specific information and guidance on how to socialize Tribal Learning in your organization. The primary technique is to use triads as described in the groundbreaking book on the subject, *Tribal Leadership*[14]. This section provides you with the concepts and

---

[14] Logan, D., King, J. P., & Fischer-Wright, H. (2008). *Tribal leadership: Leveraging natural groups to build a thriving organization*. New York: Collins.

facilities of the Tribal Leadership system as applied to socializing Tribal Learning immediately in your own organization.

Part Four is a rich Appendix with reference material, tutorials, and related information that supports your integration of all the material in this book. Part Four includes a rich bibliography as well as links to more material, that you may want if you are planning to put the concepts of this book into practice. Part Four is designed to support your implementation of the ideas found in the book.

Chapter 3 - Tribal Learning Overview

Tribal Learning Explained

Technology in general (and *software development* in particular) is a specific and powerful *driving force* in our society and culture. In the same way that the Medici bankers influenced culture during the Renaissance, technology and software development are influencing the period we are living through right now.

A perfect example is the Agile software development community, which continues to be a learning laboratory for *teamwork*. Designing and publishing software is a complex process. When teamwork on software teams is weak, it results in slipping schedules, cost overruns, failed projects, and very unhappy investors and end-users. The Agile community has figured out that teams must first become skilled at learning as a group. After this happens, the team produces high quality software. The Agile community has done the hard work of studying teams and teamwork, and now has the expertise to repeatedly create and re-create *teams* that rapidly learn. The result is working software that ships on time.

These teams are in fact small *Learning Organizations* as described by Peter Senge in his book *The Fifth Discipline*. The knowledge of how to create teams that learn is now available to any business leader who studies the available Agile software development literature.[15]

Scaling Agile to the Enterprise and Non-Technology Domains

There is a big demand to apply Agile techniques to non-technology domains like sales, marketing, finance, even executive leadership. The Tribal Learning Practices found in this book are intended to empower you to achieve this. These practices are distillations of specific Agile practices. For example, the Agile framework Scrum is based on iteration and very frequent inspection of results. The Tribal Learning Practices of

---

[15] See the Bibliography for a list of Agile-related books, links, and papers if you are new to Agile software development methods.

{Inspect Frequently} and {Examine Your Norms} derive directly from Scrum. Likewise, Scrum prescribes a short set of meetings, and every one of these meetings has a designated facilitator. Tribal Learning extracts the practice of {Facilitate Your Meetings} and generalizes it for any team engaged in work that is complex and changes frequently. It is easy to apply Agile principles to non-technology domains by implementing the practices found in the Tribal Leadership framework.

Everyone wants to scale Agile from the team level to entire enterprises. However, for typical organizations, scaling these Agile learning practices to the level of *enterprise* is a non-starter. Few (if any) organizations exist that currently serve as legitimate examples of enterprise-wide Learning Organizations as described by Senge. Fortunately, examples of teams that learn are very plentiful, thanks to the Agile software development community. This worldwide community, through trial-and-error, has learned how to develop and sustain teams that learn. The worldwide Agile community has solved the Learning Organization problem for a small and very specific organizational unit: the *team*, consisting of about 5 to 9 members.

Safe Space - for Learning

The problem is that Agile practices that work at the *team* level do not scale to the level of ***enterprise***. Why? The primary reason is that Genuine & Authentic Agile teams operate in ***safe space***. Creation of ***enterprise-wide safe space*** is a non-trivial problem to solve. This is the main reason that scaling Agile results to the level of enterprise is so difficult to achieve. Creating safe space for a team is *easy*; creating safe space inside an entire enterprise is *hard*.

Safe space is essential for group-level learning. *Safety* is a property of a ***social space*** where it is safe to take interpersonal risk. Safe space is a social space that welcomes the best idea, regardless of the source. Safe space encourages high levels of interpersonal risk taking, such as asking for help. In work-oriented groups like software teams, safe space creates a bias towards engaged, active, group-level experimentation with many possible solutions.

The creation of safe space is achievable inside software teams of 5 to 9 people by using Agile values, Agile principles, and Agile practices. Safe space creates the potential for very high levels of rapid, group-level learning. We know how to create teams that learn; the key is the creation and maintenance of safe space. The larger question is how to engineer the creation of even wider safe spaces – *at larger scales* – inside our organizations.

Tribal Learning is the next step, the application of powerful team learning practices in the sweet spot – *above* the level of team and *below* the level of enterprise. The Tribal Learning framework is a set of specific ***interaction practices*** that any manager can immediately deploy in pursuit of great results inside his group of direct reports. Tribal Learning effectively scales Agile results to the next level – the *departmental* level, the *next* level up from teams. This is where managers have the greatest formal and informal authority, and influence. This is the sweet spot – where wider-scope cultural change is achievable and can happen quickly.

Tribal Learning is a set of tools and techniques any manager can use to influence culture in an organization intentionally. One manager using Tribal Learning can make a difference. Several managers, each with direct reports, working together – as a ***tribe*** – can strongly influence the *entire* culture of the enterprise.

Tribal Learning is most powerful when deployed by tribes of aligned managers and their direct reports. ***Tribes*** are groups of about 20 to about 150 people who hold a shared mental model about the tribe, the work, and the culture. Managers who work together to deploy Tribal Learning are, in fact, creating a mid-sized Learning Organization – a ***learning tribe***. Multiple informal ***learning tribes*** can tip your entire culture in the direction of genuine, enterprise-wide learning as described by Senge.

This book is a how-to manual that provides you with everything you need to deploy Tribal Learning in your organization.

The Three Essentials of Tribal Learning

The beauty of Tribal Learning is threefold.

First, Tribal Learning builds on the well-documented success of Agile principles and practices for teams. You leverage these proven principles and practices inside the Tribal Learning framework.

Second, you need no permission or budget to implement Tribal Learning in your organization. This means you do not have to appeal to ***higher-ups*** for permission or request a budget to get started. You just start to do it, right now. If you are a manager, you have *already* been authorized to implement Tribal Learning in your group. You do not need to ask permission. This means you can start using Tribal Learning Practices immediately. Most of the practices involve simple, small changes to the meetings that you currently convene.

Third, the Tribal Learning strategy builds on the strong social structure of informal triads, which are three-person social structures.[16] In a triad, three people function with aligned *values*, where each person is responsible for the quality of the relationship between the other two. In *Tribal Leadership*, the authors describe how to create, maintain, and sustain triads to informally organize work around shared objectives and build on their underlying shared values in pursuit of great results.

Tribal Learning is a set of tools for creating safe space, a lot of play, a lot of learning, and great results inside groups of 20 to 150 people. Tribal Learning is easy to learn, easy to explain, and easy to do. When aligned managers engage in implementing Tribal Learning together, they can tip the entire culture towards more safety, freedom, learning, and amazing results.

Figure 6 depicts the three-part framework for Tribal Learning, where managers can create safe space and group-level learning. This operational space exists just above the level of *team* and just below the level of *enterprise*. Tribal Learning is a *learning framework* that any manager can deploy today – alone, and with others – in pursuit of great results that will effect corresponding cultural changes. Tribal Learning

---

[16] as described in the best-selling book, *Tribal Leadership* – see footnote 7

builds upon a foundation of Agile practices, automatic authorization, and mid-sized, informal social networks known as tribes.

Figure 6: The Tribal Learning Framework

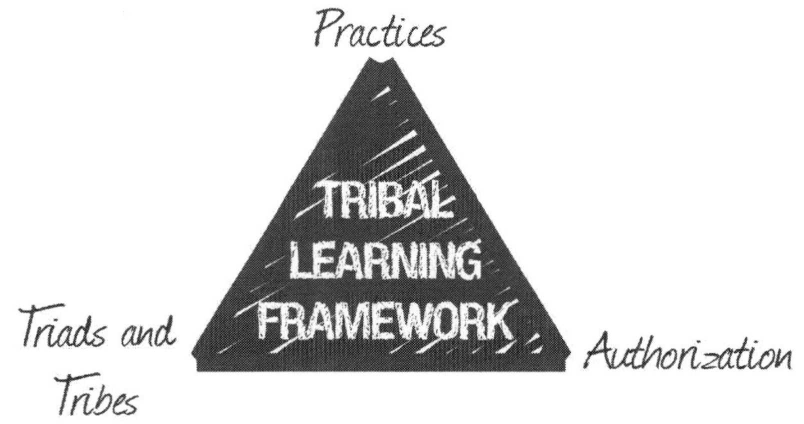

Tribal Learning, Part 1 – The Practices

The first component of Tribal Learning is the ***set of patterns and practices*** that are all rooted in the Agile software development community. These practices are all group-level behaviors exhibited by the very best Agile software development teams that I have observed. Most Genuine & Authentic Agile teams display ***all*** the Tribal Learning Practices, and thus support elevated levels of organizational learning. Effective software teams usually contain 5 to 9 people[17]. Tribes are groups up to 150 people. *Learning tribes* tend to do many of the Tribal Learning Practices.

The Agile community figured out how to convert typical, low-engagement teams into engaged, high-performance Learning Organizations, through outstanding work habits. Some of these habits, such as {Inspect Frequently}, are identical to standard Agile practices, while others developed because teams were doing genuine Agile and

---

17 The phrase ***Seven, plus or minus two*** is common in Agile

Scrum. For example, {Be Punctual} is a significant behavior that is a consequence of doing good Agile.

Agile practices and frameworks like Scrum encourage patterns of group behavior, like *managing your boundaries*, *paying explicit attention*, *being punctual*, and so on. These practices, such as facilitating your meetings, encourage very high levels of team learning. These practices are the first of the three essential parts of Tribal Learning.

Here is an example. You may recall from Figure 2 in Chapter 2 that the *Scrum* framework has five *values*. They are Focus, Commitment, Openness, Courage, and Respect. By implementing Scrum in a genuine way that honors these values, people doing Scrum begin to be more *punctual*. This is because punctuality strongly reinforces three of the five Scrum values: Respect, Focus, and Commitment. {Be Punctual} is a Tribal Learning practice that aligns with and supports Scrum values.

Tribal Learning, Part 2 – Automatic Authorization

The second part is automatic authorization. As a manager, you have people on your staff who report to you, and you have the authority to convene meetings. You typically invite your staff and others to meetings that you convene. Your supervisor is the source of the authority delegated to you. It may also be a cultural norm to convene meetings if you are a manager in your culture, meaning that a known, customary cultural norm is granting you at least *some* authority to convene meetings.[18]

A key feature of the Tribal Learning framework is that most of the practices in the framework do not require any additional permission from your boss. You can simply choose to ***change a few things around***. When you choose to implement the Tribal Learning Practices, you are choosing to encourage, maintain, and sustain more group-level learning inside your staff and inside your meetings.

---

18 It is a worthwhile exercise to examine exactly where your authority to convene meetings comes from, since your authority is always granted to you from somewhere or someone. Note that you can "authorize yourself."

Note that, as a practical matter, it is essential for you to notify your people about your plans. You need to explain to them any policy changes, however small, so they will be comfortable and can situate themselves within your organization and inside your meetings. You are being respectful when you do this, because notification is a form of respect.

There are many definitions for authorization. The one I like the best is ***the right to do work***.[19] As a manager, you already have authorization to convene and run meetings. This means you may run these meetings as you wish. You probably already convene and execute these meetings according to current cultural norms in place within your wider organization. It may currently be normal for people to arrive late at the start of meetings. If it is typical for meetings to run later than planned, in effect you hold all the attendees as hostages until the meeting is over.

One of the tools in the Tribal Learning framework is the practice {Be Punctual}, which you may choose to implement in the following way:

1. **Your meetings now start on time**. You are always present five minutes before the start time.
2. **The door closes at the start time**. People who are late must open the closed door and then close it behind them.
3. **Your meetings now end on time**. You always organize the meeting content so this happens. You now never, *ever* end a meeting after the stated end time.
4. **Your meetings used to last 60 minutes or more,** and are now 50 minutes long, so that those attending have some time to get to their next meeting (if they have one) on time.

---

[19] This definition comes from the Group Relations community. Click the FAQ menu item on the home page: http://www.akriceinstitute.org/displaycommon.cfm?an=1&subarticlenbr=34

As to the question of who authorizes you to make these changes, the answer is simple: *you do*. The authorization comes with your role as a manager, and by virtue of your role as a convener of meetings. You have *automatic authorization.* You are *pre-authorized.* This is an essential feature of the Tribal Learning approach. You can implement Tribal Learning in your organization immediately, right now, precisely because you are *already* authorized.

Authorization is an interesting subject. We often use the words *empowerment* and *permission* to refer to aspects of authorization. In this book, I define *authorization* as the right to do work, borrowing from the Group Relations community. This community actively examines the roles of leadership and authority in groups, conducts conferences, and publishes research on these topics.[20]

For an excellent discussion of authorization, I suggest you examine the paper *The BART System of Group and Organizational Analysis* by Zachary Gabriel Green and René J. Molenkamp.[21] This paper provides an excellent framework for deconstructing boundary, authority, role, and task in a way that is useful for anyone who wants to make sense of the processes of innovation and change-making in organizations.

Authorization is often constrained by limitations that are undocumented or are otherwise unclear. The BART paper provides excellent coverage of these dynamics, breaking down authorization into various types such as *personal authority*, *formal authority*, *informal authority*, and so on. A major strength of the Tribal Learning framework is that it leverages your formal, positional authority as a manager to direct your staff, convene meetings, and so on. Don't ask permission!

---

20 You can learn more at the website: http://www.akriceinstitute.org/

21 Green, Z. G., & Molenkamp, R. J. (2005). *The BART System of Group and Organizational Analysis, Boundary, Authority, Role and Task*. See: http://akri.affiniscape.com/associations/8689/files/BART_Green_Molenkamp.pdf

You can start to generate substantial group-level learning in your organization simply by deploying the Tribal Learning Practices by yourself, with your own direct reports. This is powerful and can contribute to immediate results. The next step is to implement the Tribal Learning framework with other managers, in effect by collaborating with them to manifest change in your organization. (This subject is the focus of the next section.)

The same issue of authorization applies to budgeting. Since most Tribal Learning Practices revolve around interactions and meetings, there is no additional budget required, although the practices {Get Coached} and {Socialize Books} do cost something and you may have to request a budget for them. Other than these two exceptions, no Tribal Learning Practices cost a dime, and that means you do NOT have to ask for funding of any kind.

Tribal Learning, Part 3 – Triads and Tribal Leadership

The third part of Tribal Learning is *tribal leadership.* Tribal Leadership is a collaboration and leadership framework described by the authors Dave Logan, John King, and Halee Fischer-Wright in the book of the same name. In that book, the authors describe how three-person groups known as ***triads*** can transform teams and entire organizations.

A single manager can deploy the Tribal Learning Practices in this book with good results. As a manager, you can choose to deploy some of these practices inside your group. The Tribal Learning Practices create safe space and encourage elevated levels of group-level learning. As elevated levels of learning occur within your group, they may influence other groups that attend your meetings. This is the first level in implementing the practices.

The next level of implementation is encouraging other groups to try the Tribal Learning Practices. The best way to do this is to identify other managers who are willing to try it. The key is to *identify* and *align* with other managers who share *values* with you. Starting small is the right idea here: to get started, identify and align with just *two* other managers around Tribal Learning. This three-person structure is known as a ***triad.***[22] It consists of three people with aligned *values*, where each person is responsible for the quality of the relationship between the other two.

Since all managers have direct reports and all managers convene meetings, the result is that three managers influence a large group of people. Over time, the people using the Tribal Learning Practices see the *results*. Many of these people begin to value openness, respect, and continuous improvement. They begin to value (or more strongly value) acts of focus, commitment, and courage in individuals and in the wider organization. They begin to *align* their values. The people who hold these values and feel this alignment are in fact becoming a *tribe*.

The entire purpose of implementing the Tribal Learning Practices is to build a *learning tribe*. A learning tribe can easily respond to change and adapt. A learning tribe thinks, notices changes, and quickly adjusts. A learning tribe can design, build, and deliver great products on time every time.

A Note on Open Space and Tribal Learning

One of the Tribal Learning Practices is {Open the Space}. This is an important practice to generate an increase in organizational learning along several important dimensions. The Open Space meeting is a special type of facilitated meeting. The Open Space meeting begins with a large circle of chairs arranged for opening the meeting and ends when the facilitator closes the meeting. In between, participants convene small group sessions around the stated meeting theme.

The Open Space meeting format is very *tribal* and engaging. This type of meeting is specifically designed to be open, and maintain safe space. The closing circle presents the opportunity for participants to describe their Open Space experience, and close the meeting. Participants in the closing circle often report feelings of high learning, high play, and high engagement with others.

---

22 See footnote 14

Use Open Space to create safe space, enable smooth organizational transitions, mix perspectives, and re-mix the learning. I advise you to create a recurring date each year that includes an Open Space meeting ritual. This recurring cultural event can generate a re-telling of the current story of your organization and ***re-hydrate*** the cultural values of openness and honest communication in your tribe. Use Open Space to mix and re-mix the Tribal Learning, to punctuate organizational transitions, and generate learning.

Beliefs, Behavior and Results

All change in organizations is *belief change*. A good example of change takes place with the introduction of Agile practices inside software teams. Agile teams start working as soon as they have enough actionable guidance to begin. This is the opposite of the ***waterfall*** approach, which encourages extensive up-front planning and a sequential series of steps. Early in a project, the Agile method is empirical while the waterfall focuses on study, planning, and prediction. Each approach requires a set of underlying beliefs. The waterfall method assumes that prediction of all variables is possible, while the Agile approach does not.

Assumptions, Beliefs and Mental Models

We know the world through our *mental models*. We construct them and then we use them to navigate the world. Mental models are a collection of assumptions about how something works, like a toaster, an automobile, a team, or an organization. For example, you have a mental model of how this book is organized and what is in it. When you think about this book, you refer to your collective set of assumptions about it, including the topic, the length, and the organization of the material. You might hold some assumptions about me, the author. Collectively then, this set of assumptions constitutes your mental model of this book. The assumptions are actually *beliefs*.

Assumptions

What we commonly called *assumptions* are actually very strong beliefs, so changing them is a non-trivial operation. Our mental models contain all sorts of beliefs that form the overall model. Each belief in a model is essential but not sufficient in itself, as they function as a group or a set. The *complete* set of assumptions is what makes the model tick. A change of just one belief in the set may break the model, and then we need to question all the beliefs in the model. Since all change is belief change, this is what makes all real change genuinely hard to implement.

Personal Mastery and Belief Change

All learning is change, and all change is belief-change. When you learn, you modify (software people might say *re-factor*) your beliefs. People who are always learning are constantly changing their models. They have become adept at responding and adjusting to new information and knowledge as it becomes available to them.

Figure 7. The role of belief models

Note: In this model, Individual ↔ Models (Filter) ↔ The World

From Figure 7, you can see the rub: ***we interact with our models***, not the world per se. This means we *filter our experience of the world through the models* - through the collection of assumptions and beliefs we currently hold. These assumptions and beliefs literally frame and contain our reality. Our models literally determine what we pay attention to and do not pay attention to, what we see and do not see, what we hear and do not hear, and what we perceive or do not perceive. The ***how it happens*** when something *occurs to us* is a function of how our models *filter* the information around us.[23] Teams and organizations filter their input in big ways.

We know the world through our models. When our models are working well, we feel comfortable and at home in the world. When they do not, we experience discomfort and often feel a crisis or forced awareness.[24] The steps work like this:

1. Some kind of change occurs in the environment that invalidates our model;
2. The actual change-event itself does not occur to us, because we are filtering the input through our now-invalid model;
3. More events occur in the environment, which we do not perceive at all, so we do not recognize their importance.

---

[23] For a great practical discussion of how things ***occur to us***, and the relationship between our language and our models, see: Zaffron, S., & Logan, D. (2009). *The Three Laws of Performance: Rewriting the Future of Your Organization and Your Life.*

[24] The term ***forced awareness*** is borrowed from the book *The Disciplined Trader: Developing Winning Attitude.* by Mark Douglas. (1990). Douglas describes his experience with bankruptcy, and how he subsequently lost everything, all due to a set of limiting beliefs. After the forced awareness, he embarked on journey to identify and hold new beliefs and a new, more valid model of the world he works in, which is the world of commodity trading and speculation.

4. Eventually, the evidence of multiple events becomes overwhelming, and we notice changes. We also notice that what we currently believe is not working well anymore.
5. We experience a forced awareness or crisis that mandates our explicit examination and inspection of current results.
6. We realize that our assumptions are incorrect, that things do not work the way we thought they work. Only then, do we make changes to our assumptions and update our mental models.

Now we can see the problem; all change is belief change, and all belief change is difficult, because beliefs interconnect to form complete models. A crisis of forced awareness occurs when you realize that your model is not working. Forced awareness causes you to begin the hard work of examining your assumptions. The work is difficult because making even one small change in even one of your assumptions has ripple effects throughout the inter-connection in your mental model.

Chapter 4 - Keep it Safe

Overview

For organizations to learn, they must develop and sustain a safe environment. By safe, I mean a climate in which people experience no discomfort or fear to call out problems, suggest solutions, conduct experiments, make mistakes, process differences, et cetera. This *psychological safety* is one of (if not THE) most important aspects of developing a Learning Organization.

Patrick Lencioni, in his book, *The Five Dysfunctions of a Team*, states that the first dysfunction is *Absence of Trust*. While trust is a big deal inside teams, it probably does not tell the whole story. People work together to co-create a space. The space created by teams (or any group) is not physical but social. Ikujiro Nonaka[25], Professor Emeritus at Hitotsubashi University Graduate School of International Corporate Strategy, calls it the ***ba***. [26]

A team's members create and hold the space in common. The team, in turn, exists inside a wider context, such as a department, division, or entire organization. Trust is important at each level, but it is more important to express explicit commitments both to respect people and also to improve continuously.

Safety depends on trust and respect, which are related concepts. Lencioni writes that "In the context of building a team, *trust* is the confidence among team members that their peer's intentions are good,

---

25 For a bio on Professor Nonaka, see: http://en.wikipedia.org/wiki/Ikujiro_Nonaka

26 See: "The Concept of Ba: Building a Foundation for Knowledge Creation" by Nonaka and Konno found at: http://home.business.utah.edu/actme/7410/Nonaka%201998.pdf

and there is no need to be protective or careful around the group."[27] Figure 9 shows these relationships as the safety *Stack.*

Figure 8. The Safety Stack

Note: The Safety Stack depicts dependencies on respect and trust

In this book, I define respect as *a positive feeling of esteem for a person and specific actions and conduct representative of that esteem.* The operative word in this definition is *representative*. People watching your behavior interpret outward respectful conduct as a sign and signal. Your behavior is *representative* of that esteem. It is a form of *signaling.* This essential sign and signaling concept is developed in more detail later in this section and in Part Two, {Announce Your Intentions}.

Without respect, no meaningful positive communication can occur. Instead there is a high potential for miscommunication, disrespect, low (or NO) communication frequency, and hurt feelings. *An authentic Learning Organization maintains and sustains respectful interactions by and between its members.*

---

27 Lencioni, P. (2002). The five dysfunctions of a team: A leadership fable, p, 195.

Respect is a key ingredient of the Learning Organization. Respect generates higher levels of psychological safety. With that safety comes the ability for individuals to relax with their teammates in ***the space***, while learning about the work and each other. For typical teams who do repetitive work, relatively low levels of safety are not optimal but are acceptable. However, to do complex product development or develop software, teams need to explore problems and solutions in a sustained safe climate. Only then can *team learning* take place. If learning at the team level is low, the ability to solve complex problems will also be low or even suppressed completely.

Figure 10 depicts how a single event can destroy psychological safety. Points A, B and C depict positive events, such as working and socializing together. Over time, respect and safety grow. Point D depicts an episode of demonstrated disrespect, or conflict. Such episodes can destroy carefully cultivated safety levels very quickly and abruptly. *Safety can decay exponentially*. For this reason, people correctly sample safety levels very frequently. This has implications for authority figures in organizations.

Figure 9. Exponential Decay in Psychological Safety

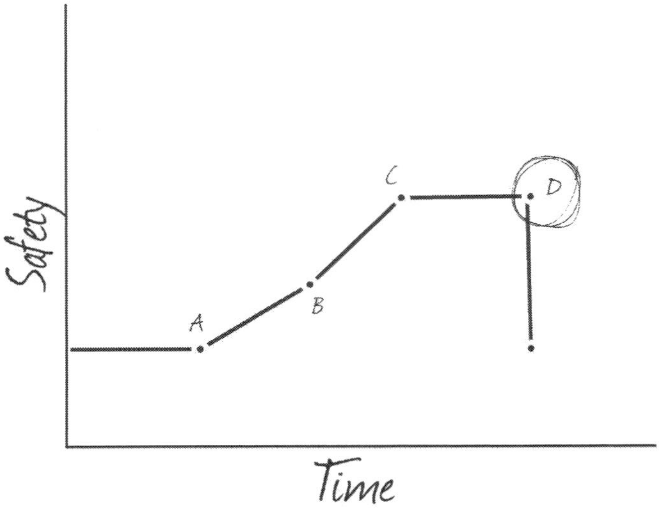

Respect for People and a Commitment to Continuous Improvement

Matthew May[28] is an author and consultant who spent several years teaching for Toyota University, and arm of Toyota that taught other organizations how to get great results. Regarding the essence of organizational improvement, Matt says, "I do not care what you call it . . . whatever the technique is called, if it is a good one, comes down to two things: a commitment to *respect people*, and a commitment to *constantly improve*."[29]

If you are reading this book and already have some knowledge and experience with Agile practices like Scrum, I want you to notice something. If your organization or team is *not* committed to respect for people, and likewise *not* committed to continuous improvement, the organization has no real shot at sustained improvement. Agile practices encourage respect for people and continuous improvement, but there is no guarantee that these values will develop on their own. Therefore, "if you already lack a commitment to respectful interactions and improvement, Scrum and other Agile practices cannot really help you." On the other hand, if your organization already has made these two essential commitments, you are in great shape in terms of embarking on the journey of becoming a Learning Organization.

Organization Learning Requires Safety
to Make Mistakes and Deal in Differences

Team learning is largely the result of mistakes and differences. Organizations that learn engage in what appears to be frequent and risky experiments. Experiments frequently do not work out as planned. If an organization cannot accept the need to experience occasional ***failed*** experiments and mistakes, the level of experimentation will be low and so will the team learning. Likewise, organizations that learn quickly tend

---

28 To examine Matt May's blog, go to http://matthewmay.com/.

29 Matt has written several books, one of which figures prominently in my thinking. *In Pursuit of Elegance: Why the best ideas have something missing*. It is a book on elegance.

to have a culture that encourages and even celebrates differences. ***Differences*** are a tremendous source of team learning. If the culture of the team or organization does not encourage members to process and discuss their differences, then less team learning will take place.

Learning Organizations encourage teams to learn using the ***raw materials*** of low-cost mistakes and processing of differences. However, to do so, the ***space*** in which the team or organization lives must be safe to do so. This is easier said than done because safety is ***fragile***; it must be made fresh daily.

Fight or Flight

Psychologists say that our feelings of safety are wired to and animated by our survival instincts. Since we derive our livelihood from work, any threats to that livelihood generate a fight/flight response. These feelings of fear trigger some of the most primitive and oldest parts of our brain, the so-called ***reptilian brain*** represented by the amygdala. As such, these instinctive fearful responses are difficult to manage. Fear focuses our attention toward the object of our fear and away from everything else, reducing our awareness of the wider environment. When someone or something threatens your paycheck, you can expect to become fearful and act in ways that are largely unconscious to you. This dynamic plays out in teams and organizations.

Safe Space

As introduced above, you feel no threats in a psychologically safe space, and you are at ease to take interpersonal risks in activities. However, since psychological safety is fragile and can decay quickly, we continually test and sample the environment for safety. This is because of the fragile nature of safety, which we instinctively know can decay very quickly. We ***check in*** with peers and superiors to validate our beliefs that ***we are good***, meaning ***I am safe here***. Since reduced levels of respect are a first sign of trouble, we frequently inspect the space for signals about levels of respect. These ***check-in*** patterns are wired to our need to survive. Unless you are independently wealthy, you can expect to display largely unconscious behavior related to the strong and instinctive desire to survive. For the most part, we sample the space for signals and signs from authority figures.

The Role of Signals From Formal Authority in Creating Safe Space

In organizations, it is perhaps ironic that we perceive ***authority*** as a constant threat to our individual survival. ***Bosses*** and higher authorization individuals have the potential to threaten us directly and indirectly, including our positions, our levels of organizational respect, and even our livelihoods. For this reason, we scan continuously for ***signs*** and ***signals***.

Signs and Signaling from Leadership

Semiotics, the study of signals and signs, provides some clues about the critical importance of unambiguous signal and signage with respect to human happiness. We navigate the world via signals and signage.

By definition, signs and signals have meaning. Clear signals generate higher levels of psychological safety, and unclear or ambiguous signals generate little or no feelings of safety. To see this in action, consider the act of driving down the highway. As you drive, you make the occasional lane change. If you signal in advance that you intend to move left, those around you assign meaning to your signal. They assign the meaning that *this vehicle intends to move left*. This provides a level of actual safety, as other drivers then feel that the movement of your vehicle is predictable.

The next step, after you signal and allow some time for others around you to notice, you begin to move left. Now you are being both predictable and reliable. This builds trust. Those driving around you experience the reality that you are predictable and reliable. These properties build the trust necessary for group safety.

Now consider the act of making a lane change without signaling. When you act in this way, you will reduce both the real and perceived safety of those driving near you. You will cause the other drivers to scrutinize your movements more carefully. Why? Because without your explicit signal, they must GUESS what you might do next. You are not acting predictably, when you avoid the use of the clear signaling mechanisms available to you.

The same exact dynamic plays out in your organization. Leaders who signal early and often are easy to adjust to and *follow*. Leaders who send mixed signals, or signals that are otherwise ambiguous, require their followers to guess. Guessing requires followers to divert attention and energy away from the work at hand. The omission of clear signals compels people who are following to guess, thus adding a burden to their work, and reducing their levels of psychological safety.

Psychological Safety Is Made Fresh Daily

Psychological safety needs to be refreshed constantly, because it is not durable. It can and does change quickly. The theory is that below the levels of our consciousness, we all ***know*** that our membership in the group increases our chances of survival. We actively look for signals and signs to validate our membership status. We watch how others behave for clues about *where we are, what to do,* and *how to be*.

In this book, I define leadership as *anyone who influences anyone else in a social setting, such as a team or an organization.* This includes those who are formally authorized, like your direct supervisor. It also includes those who have informal authority via the influence they have with others in the group.

The primary place we look for clear signs and signals is inside the leadership of our organizations. We watch leader behavior for clear signals on what to do next, what to work on, and how to behave. This includes what we are expected to value. In short, we scan the environment for signs and signals, although we primarily anticipate signs and signals from our leaders. This has enormous implications for leaders. It means:

- Followers assign meaning to every little thing that they see a leader do and say.
- Leaders can and do send mixed signals, and signals that are unclear.

- Followers prioritize meaning from what leaders do, not what they say. Followers devalue what leaders *say* when what leaders *actually do* does not match up.
- Leaders are the ***least free*** people in organizations, precisely because followers scrutinize each behavior they do.

The main takeaway here is that everyone in your company can help everyone else get in-sync by engaging in deliberate and intentional signaling. This goes for everyone, not just leaders.

The Tribal Learning Practices include the step {Announce Your Intentions} in Part Two. This is a signaling mechanism to help others understand what is happening and adjust accordingly. This specific signaling technique is covered in Part Two.

Processing Conflict at the Edge of Chaos

Learning Organizations create environments that are safe for learning and knowledge creation to take place. At the root of a safe space is a commitment to respect people and to improve with them continually. This sounds nice and it is intended to, however getting it done is a difficult matter. How conflict is processed is a key aspect of safety for learning. When managers do not actively manage conflict (for example by failing to implement {Structure Your Interactions} as described in Part Two), the potential for chaos is high. Finger-pointing, hurt feelings, and much lower communication frequency can kill team learning.

The Tribal Learning Practices described in Part Two can provide practice in doing some of the behaviors of a genuine Learning Organization. These include examining your norms, paying explicit attention, managing your boundaries, and structuring your interactions. Many of these behaviors support the creation of psychological safety. This safety is a requirement for teams and organizations to learn. If you want to derail the team learning process, simply reduce the level of psychological safety.

Figure 11 depicts a modification of Stacey's Complexity Graph, originally conceived by Ralph Stacey, PhD. The diagram depicts complex work located near the edge of chaos, where conflict, denial and confusion are typical. Complex work at the edge of chaos requires an empirical approach. Complex projects near the edge are best managed with frequent iteration and frequent inspection. Managing this way maintains high levels of psychological safety for everyone involved, often resulting in important and unexpected new learning for the team.

Figure 10. Stacey's Complexity Graph

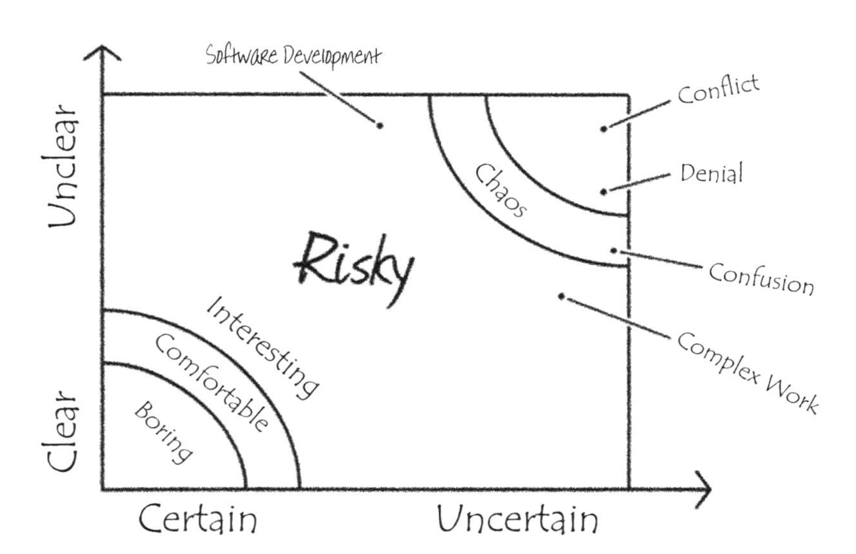

Note: Adapted from *Strategic Management and Organisational Dynamics: The Challenge of Complexity.* (3rd ed.), by Stacey, R. D. 2000, Harlow, England; New York: Financial Times Prentice Hall. Copyright 2000 by Prentice Hall.

Chapter 5 - Game the Work

Overview

The idea of playing a game is a part our collective language. We often use certain language to refer to work as a game. We describe meetings in terms of the ***players*** attending that meeting. We often encourage people to ***play the game***. When someone gains an advantage by noticing a loophole in the rules, s/he is said to be ***gaming the system***.

Games come in all shapes and sizes. There are competitive games, cooperative games, finite games, and infinite games. There are sports games, board games, and drinking games. We play games alone, 1-on-1, and in teams.

Cockburn described software development as a cooperative game.[30] This game requires participants to build shared mental models of abstract concepts such as data flows, process flows, information flows, and workflows. Software development is a game that demands a high degree of cooperation by and between team members. As we saw in earlier chapters, software development teams learned to develop and use Agile methods to ***wise up*** about teamwork. The result was the set of collective behaviors described in Part Two. When your team starts to examine norms, manage visually, pay explicit attention, and manage boundaries, it begins to create the potential to become a Learning Organization, as it engages in a lot of Tribal Learning.

Business in general is a special kind of game, in which we play with others, together and cooperatively, mainly as organizations. In theory, we try to outplay other organizations (we call them ***competitors***) that operate in the same markets. However, in practice, in our daily work, we often receive none of the essential feedback about the quality of our performance.

In the pages that follow, I will argue that everything is a game, but not in the way you typically think about games. Every 1-on-1 interaction is a game. Every meeting you attend is a game. Every social group in

---

30 Cockburn, A. (2007). Agile Software Development: The Cooperative Game.

which you are a member is, in fact, a group of people playing a game. The wider culture of your company is also structured as a game.

Some of these games are well-structured, fun to play, and actually stimulate the pleasure regions of your brain. Good games frequently generate feelings of control, progress, optimism, and persistence. Games that are poorly structured generate feelings of frustration, lack of control, lack of progress, isolation, and despair.

Gaming Games

So, what exactly is a game? A game is a situation that has the following minimal set of features:[31]

1. Voluntary participation
2. A way to receive feedback on your play
3. A goal
4. A set of rules

Let's look at each in turn.

Voluntary Participation

When you are compelled to do something, you lose some of your sense of control, a fundamental ingredient of basic human happiness. Good games are always opt-in; the act of making a decision to do something puts you in the driver's seat and makes you feel good because it provides a sense of control. A sense of control is an ingredient of basic human happiness. Good games are always opt-in.

A Way to Receive Feedback

Having a clear way to understand and track your progress is also a basic ingredient of human happiness. If you have a way to receive feedback on your progress, you gain a sense of control and experience a

31 McGonigal, J. (2011). Reality is Broken: Why Games Make Us Better and How They Can Change the World, p. 21.

sense of progress. Good games always provide very clear feedback on how you are doing.

A Goal

Every game needs one or more goals. A clear goal provides something to focus on, strive for, and pay attention to. Without a clear goal, a game is not fun to play. When a goal is clear, you can organize your attention, thinking, and actions in pursuit of achieving the goal. This makes the game fun and enjoyable.

A Set of Rules

A game always has a set of rules. The rules provide the constraints within which the players are supposed to function, so playing it presents challenges. Clear rules constitute well-defined constraints. Well-defined constraints constitute a set of challenges. When these challenges are surmountable but just beyond reach, we experience a positive psychological feeling, or flow,[32] as we get closer and closer to overcoming them.

Winners and Losers Are NOT In This Definition of a Game

Most games are competitive, for example, backgammon, golf, and tennis. For one player to win at these games, other players must lose. These are types of zero-sum games, because in the simplest form, a winner can only gain at the expense of the opponent. In typical family life, the goals of board games like Scrabble and card games like poker are to win.

We have been conditioned to think of games in this way. For the rest of this chapter, try not to think that way about games. Instead, start to think of a game as an activity, one that is *opt-in*, and has a *goal*, *rules*, and *a way to keep score*. That's it. That is the definition of a game for us here. Winning simply means that a player reaches the goal, whatever it

---

[32] The concept was first proposed by Csikszentmihalyi, M. (1990). *Flow: The Psychology of Optimal Experience*.

is. There does not have to be a loser for you to win. *You* win by reaching the goal.

Tribal Learning is a goal-seeking team game. We play with others in teams. We learn together. We can all achieve the goal of learning and no one has to lose. For the rest of the chapter, try to hold on to this new and simple game definition: a *good game* has *opt-in participation, a goal, rules, and a way to keep score*.

That's it. Let's proceed.

Positive Psychology

Positive psychology is the study of what makes people happier. This is a relatively new branch of psychology. Positive psychology says that we need certain things to be present for an individual to experience happiness or to be happy in a given situation. Happiness is not limited to the level of the individual. Groups can be happy.

Research into Positive Psychology shows that, to be happy, we need at least some of the following elements to be present in our day-to-day lives:

1. A sense of control
2. A sense of progress
3. A sense of belonging and connection, like having membership in a family or being an member of a team
4. A sense of being part of an idea or a cause that is bigger than ourselves

When we have a sense of these things, we feel happier. This explains the astonishing success of the Scrum framework that has a set of roles, meetings, and rules for teams to create software.

Scrum[33] employs ***iterations***, which are short, focused intervals of time when a team performs work. To begin an iteration, the team selects some work to perform from the range of all the relevant and possible work that has been identified for them to do. Then they go to work without any interruptions for 1 to 4 weeks.

When the iteration ends, the team delivers one or more completed work product(s) to the project sponsor. At that time, the team also conducts a meeting called a *retrospective*, during which they inspect the experience of the iteration, and use that information to make small adaptive adjustments in the process they will use to execute the next iteration.

Scrum provides a sense of control – a team is authorized to select their work and to function without interruption during the execution of the work. Scrum provides a sense of progress – when the iteration is over, the team delivers the work, in effect declaring victory on having achieving the work. Then the team gets together to dissect the experience and make any needed adjustments. The team decides together what adjustments to make.

Scrum provides a sense of control, a sense of progress, and a sense of belonging. These feelings help members of Scrum teams feel happier. Scrum has a clear goal, clear rules, and a clear way to keep score. This means Scrum is a very good game, but I am getting ahead of myself. Before we can really make sense of Scrum as a game, we need to understand a bit about the computer game industry.

Online Multi-player Computer Gaming

The computer game industry is a place where the science of human happiness is applied. If a game is not fun to play, no one will play it, so the company selling that game makes no money, or loses money, or even goes out of business. Competing within this business is dicey, because

---

33 See Appendix, "An Overview of the Scrum framework" for more information

there really is no way of knowing how much fun a game will be to play until it is completed. This means that the company creating the game must create an entire game before it can test the market for the game.

These limits require firms in the gaming industry to pay very, very close attention to what makes people happy during game play. This helps ensure success or at least to reduce the risk of failure. Moreover, the computer is the perfect platform for fine-tuning a sense of control and a sense of progress. For example, in a computer game, the goal at each level can be set just a little out of reach, but close enough for a player to achieve it with practice. When a player achieves the goal, s/he then will ***level up*** and the process of striving toward an achievable goal repeats. This ability to fine-tune the goal provides players with a sense of control and a sense of progress. This makes computer games very enjoyable.

The advent of the World Wide Web brought online gaming. This platform provided game designers with a way to create multiplayer, team-oriented games. Games like World of Warcraft®[34] exploit this capability, effectively delivering a sense of control, a sense of progress, and a sense of community and belonging. Playing a game with properties like this is fun and enjoyable.

Jane McGonigal, in her book *Reality is Broken*, describes these dynamics. She explains how and why gamers invest a lot of time and energy in playing games like World of Warcraft®. She describes how the game industry applies research from the science of Positive Psychology to design games that are more compelling and more fun to play.

Gaming Work

Jane McGonigal's book describes something very significant. It details a minimal set of properties that define a game. Players leverage these properties in online games, like World of Warcraft®, to make them enjoyable and fun. The online game industry applies Positive Psychology principles in the architecture of game products. In her book, McGonigal

---

[34] World of Warcraft® is a registered trademark of Blizzard Entertainment, Inc.

argues that the gaming process can be used to change the world, by solving some of the world's most pressing problems. She argues that the solution is to create good games aimed at solving problems. Such games can tap the attention and energy of the existing worldwide gaming community and welcome new players as they come online.

A massive community of online gamers already exists, and millions more people are joining over time. She argues that good game mechanics, like opt-in participation and a clear goal, can attract people to donate small portions of their spare time to the playing of highly intentional online games that are in service to larger causes. This is an interesting idea – the idea that people can construct an online ***game layer*** that can function at a level *over* our current reality, to address solvable problems like poverty and world hunger.

The idea that reality is broken and a ***game layer*** can help fix it is an interesting concept whose time has come. McGonigal is a leader in this space, developing ***good games*** that help to make this emerging ***good game layer*** a reality online. She is one of the first to spread the word that games truly matter, which is why I often refer to her as "Jane the Baptist".

Gaming the Reality of Work

Another way to apply good-game mechanics immediately is to pay attention explicitly to the fact that most of our interactions at work are not fun and not enjoyable, precisely because these interactions exhibit weak game mechanics. Recall that good games are opt-in, have a clear goal, a set of rules, and a scoring/feedback system that tracks progress. This simple structure creates the potential for high levels of group learning to occur. We can leverage this dynamic at work, by intentionally gaming the way we interact in teams, in meetings, and in general.

Work is broken. It is a sloppy game with mandatory participation, fuzzy goals, rules, and scoring. For example,

- when interacting with others at work, we are often expected to happily receive unsolicited feedback

- in many of the meetings we attend at work, attendance is mandatory
- when working in teams, we do not pay attention to the boundaries around the goal, the rules, or the progress-tracking mechanisms

In short, we do play games at work, but they are highly dysfunctional. We can easily restructure these games to be fun and satisfying. Teams that are playing Genuine & Authentic Scrum already experience exactly what I am describing.

As an Agile coach, I teach Scrum *as a game*. I describe the game as opt-in, and playing the game includes a step where each individual gives (or does not give) his/her explicit consent to participate. From there, the clear goal, rules, and feedback system of Scrum provide an enjoyable experience for everyone playing the game. Scrum is a game optimized for teamwork, and it is a *good game*. When we examine Scrum from Jane McGonigal's point of view, it is easy to see how Genuine & Authentic Scrum is a fun and enjoyable game.

Gaming the Interactions

To generate a lot of Tribal Learning, we must structure the group experience as a game. The good-game structure provides safety – participants know where they are, they choose to opt in, and they have a clear understanding of the goals, the rules, and how to get feedback. By intentionally structuring work interactions, we create the potential for a safe space where a lot of learning can take place.

Playing the Happiness Game at Zappos

Zappos is a company famously organized around 10 values. These values play out in interesting ways as the company does business on a day-to-day basis. Working at Zappos has good-game properties. Consider the following Zappos official policy statements:

- A GOAL: Zappos intends to become the best service company in the world[35]
- RULES: Zappos Family Core Values.[36] These are ten guiding values for all employees to utilize while working for the company
- FEEDBACK: Trainees receive feedback continually during training. There is also an opportunity for each trainee to inspect his/her results at the end of each training week. (The training program is 4 weeks long.) Internally, Zappos creates and maintains several feedback loops; employees can actively track their progress via these feedback mechanisms. Externally, the main feedback loop is the company's financial performance, which reflects the *score* of the financial side of the game.[37]
- OPT-IN PARTICIPATION: Zappos includes various tests of willingness into the hiring process. Recruiters select individuals as candidates for hire based on alignment with the Core Values. A subset of those who pass this test then begin a training program. This training teaches the employee about the Zappos culture. Periodically during the training experience, each in-training employee is offered a chance to opt-out. The opportunity to opt-out (to quit) includes a cash payment of thousands of dollars. About 2% of the trainees do opt out by quitting and taking the cash.

A job offer to work at Zappos includes a clearly stated goal, clear rules, and a way to obtain feedback. It also includes voluntary

---

35 Zappos Family Core Values; "Do more with less." See: http://about.zappos.com/our-unique-culture/zappos-core-values/do-more-less ("While our goal is to become a great company, we also want to become the greatest service company in the world.")

36 Zappos Family Core Values; the entire list of ten. See: http://about.zappos.com/our-unique-culture/zappos-core-values

37 Hsieh, Tony. (2010). *Delivering Happiness*. "Tony's social experiments," p. 209.

participation. When we look closely at Zappos, we can see their application and hiring process is actually a well-structured game designed to identify and hire the employees who are best aligned with the Zappos culture.

At Zappos, hiring is a good game.

Gaming the Work

One of the lessons of McGonigal's book *Reality is Broken* is that the entire range of social spaces we participate in are actually games. This is an interesting theory to consider in several dimensions.

1. We have a model for understanding what is going on at work with interactions, meetings, and teamwork. All of these activities are games. We can examine each of them as games.
2. We can examine the game mechanics and tune them to make any activity, such as a meeting, much more enjoyable and much more conducive to Tribal Learning.
3. Via a game mentality, we can actively design psychologically safe space. We know that safe space is a requirement for cultivating Tribal Learning.
4. The Tribal Learning we generate offers many benefits: happier people, doing meaningful work in pursuit of clear goals and in service to a clear purpose. We can game our organizations for learning so that they are more responsive to changing conditions as changes occur.

In describing the social world as a game world, a place where every activity can be structured as a game, we have a framework for creating social spaces where high levels of organizational (tribal) learning can take place.

When viewed in this way, every interaction you have with another person is a game. We can consider the way we do teamwork, the way we conduct meetings, and all of our interactions as broken games, and then restructure each as a *good game* with clear goals, rules, scoring, and opt-in participation. These adjustments will create a social world that is safe for interpersonal risk and elevated levels of Tribal Learning.

Consider a world where:

- The act of making an appointment with another person is a game.
- Every meeting at work is a game.
- Being a member of a team or department is a game.
- Being part of the wider organization is a game.
- Being a citizen of your country is a game.

You might be asking how I can make these assertions. For example, how can a meeting be a game?

Meetings are Broken

Let us consider the act of attending a typical meeting. The meetings where you work might not be optional. They might be (and usually are) mandatory to attend. They might not have a clearly stated goal (they usually do not). They might not have clearly stated rules. They might not have a way to track progress.

This does not mean they are *not* games. It means they are *poorly structured* games. These kinds of games associate with feelings of frustration, boredom, and unhappiness. Restructure that same meeting, and all of a sudden, the game is fun. Make the meeting opt-in, and people *will* have a sense of control. Set up the meeting with a clear goal and a way to measure progress and, all of sudden, that meeting is enjoyable. Set up clearly defined rules for the meeting, and people can locate themselves in that game, play that game, and have fun. A well-structured meeting is, in fact, a game that can be (and is) fun to play. We need to design meetings as good games to make them effective meetings on purpose.

Every good game has opt-in participation, a goal, a set of rules, and a way to keep score. We can apply this good-game concept to every aspect of work, in effect making work much more fun and enjoyable.

Gaming the Interactions

You can leverage this knowledge of what makes a good game to increase levels of Tribal Learning in your organization immediately. View every interaction as an opt-in game designed with a goal, and rules, and a way to track progress. When these elements are in place, you have a fun, enjoyable game. Let us examine the opportunities to ***game the work***. They are quite plentiful.

The following interactions are opportunities to game the work. In each opportunity listed below, think to yourself, how might a clear goal, clear rules, and way to track progress make these interactions more interesting, fun, and enjoyable?

1. As an individual, communicating and working with other individuals
2. As an individual, working inside a team as a team member
3. As a team, communicating and working with individuals and other teams
4. As a team, communicating and working with the containing department or division.
5. Working inside the wider organization as an individual, as a team member, or as a member of a department or division
6. Convening and conducting a meeting
7. Participating in meetings convened by others

When viewed in this way, you can see that work is actually a rich gaming environment. There are many opportunities to engage in gaming at work. The primary way to do this is to explicitly examine your norms and intentionally structure your interactions.[38]

---

[38] See {Pay Explicit Attention}, {Examine Your Norms}, and {Structure Your Interactions} in Part Two

Gaming the Meetings

Meetings are an essential aspect of organizational life and represent opportunities to apply leverage in an effort to cultivate an increase in Tribal Learning. The Agile software development community has done a good job of gaming meetings to make them productive and enjoyable. Books on Agile retrospectives provide guidance on how to design activities and games to generate learning.[39] More recently, books like *GameStorming*[40] and *Visual Meetings*[41] call attention to the fact that meetings are essentially broken. Publication of these books is an indication that the wider lessons of the Agile software community are permeating the wider business community. The Agile community figured out that in order to capture the Tribal Learning, you must first game your meetings.

In her book, Jane McGonigal states that reality is broken, and she is right. Our meetings at work, in particular, are quite broken. Meetings are often a complete waste of time and unpleasant precisely because the game mechanics are so poorly structured. Our meetings are typically mandatory to attend, have ambiguous goals, rules, and feedback mechanisms. Is it any wonder we are often not fully present when ***attending*** such meetings?

Summary

The lessons of Agile software development are clear. We must engage in specific actions and behaviors as a group if we are going to learn as a group. Behaviors such as playing games, examining our norms, paying explicit attention, and managing visually are all Genuine &

---

39 Derby, E., Larsen, D., & Schwaber, K. (2006). *Agile Retrospectives: Making Good Teams Great*

40 Gray, D., Brown, S., & Macanufo, J. (2010). Gamestorming: A Playbook for Innovators, Rulebreakers, and Changemakers

41 Sibbet, D. (2010). Visual Meetings: How Graphics, Sticky Notes and Idea Mapping Can Transform Group Productivity

Authentic Agile teams' behaviors, because they do support other Agile practices. These behaviors are essential to create safe space, build shared understandings, and cultivate high levels of collective learning. Jane McGonigal's book is a manifesto for change-makers and innovators seeking to create a learning organization as described in Peter Senge's *The Fifth Discipline*.

Tribal Learning is a game. As leaders, we can game the learning process by structuring work using good-game mechanics. Any leader willing to do so can create safe space for group learning. This profoundly simple concept can increase business performance and make work more enjoyable by making the learning process more natural and fun in the work environment. Tribal Learning Practices make for a *good game.*

Part Two: Tribal Learning Patterns and Practices

Chapter 6 - Introducing the Practices

The Genesis of the Tribal Learning Practices

The Tribal Learning Practices are actions you can take immediately to elevate the level of learning in your organization. These are actionable steps you can take to today, that do not require attendance at a class, do not require you to understand any theory, and over 80% of the steps outlined here do not cost a dime to implement. Best of all you probably do not need authorization to do these. As such, the practices provide an actionable framework that can help your department, division, and organization become more adaptive by learning faster as a group.

My experience since 2006 includes playing an Agile-coaching role for software teams moving to Agile practices, primarily Scrum and Kanban. I also coach executive teams in how to be great together. What I have noticed over the years is that many of the organizations I coached were not ready for the move to Agile. They often had ***baked-in*** obstacles in the culture that prevented Genuine & Authentic Agile to take root. They often experienced long periods of painful adjustment to what the reality of ***going Agile*** actually meant.

I found myself asking certain questions quite a bit as I gained experience coaching Agile.

- What can I offer to these organizations, which are not really ready for Agile?
- What suggestions can I make to prepare them for a move to genuine Agile and Scrum?
- What steps can they take in preparation to make a move to Authentic Agility?

As I paid more attention to these questions, I noticed some things and was able to bring them into sharper focus.

- First, I searched for cheap, easy-to-understand steps that any organization could take to prepare BEFORE a move to Agile.

- Second, I noticed that many of the most progressive organizations I was coaching were ALREADY doing several of these practices before I arrived.
- Third, I noticed that if an organization used an Agile framework like Scrum, they would, in fact, end up doing many of these practices.
- Last, I began to notice that the truly Agile organization was exhibiting a *flow of learning* that came, in part, from a willingness to do many of these practices. The organizations that are able to implement most of these practices are, in fact, Learning Organizations.

And then it hit me: Agile practices are those that help manifest a Learning Organization as described in Peter Senge's book, *The Fifth Discipline*. The difficulty found in implementing Agile is the same difficulty you encounter when you attempt to increase the quality and quantity of organizational learning. Further, I discovered a correlation between the impediments to Agile adoption and impediments to an organization's transition to a Learning Organization. That is because, by definition, the Agile organization has mastered learning at the level of enterprise.

The Relationship Between Agile Practices, the Tribal Learning Practices, and Organizational Learning.

Think of these practices as pre-Agile practices. If you do them, you start moving in the direction of Agility. As you know from the introduction, Agile software development practices are actually practices that encourage and manifest a lot of learning. By adopting these practices, you can get prepared for an Agile framework like Scrum and then be successful using it.

These practices are also the result of *doing* Genuine & Authentic Scrum. That means that Scrum supplies a structure that helps manifest many of these practices. Mature Scrum teams that actively engage in *paying frequent attention* and *examining what are the norms* find that, through adopting these habits, they increasingly deliver great results, whether or not they use Scrum.

Scrum encourages the practices, all of which encourage increased organizational learning.

Using the Tribal Learning Patterns & Practices

You can think of the practices as *policies,* although the word policy is a loaded term. People tend to associate it with bureaucracy and a command-and-control approach. A policy is simply a rule to guide decisions and achieve intended outcomes. Due to the triggering nature of the word policies, in this book I refer to the policies as ***the practices*** or ***the patterns.***

For the most part, you can implement each of the patterns without spending a lot of money. There is no need to understand theory, take a training course, or make a big investment of time or money. You can simply review the list of patterns and practices, pick those that make the most sense for you and your organization, tailor them, and put them into place. When you have done so, your organization will be better able to face the very substantial challenges of moving to Agility and become a Learning Organization.

If You Are New to the Tribal Learning Practices

Perhaps your organization is already doing many of these practices. Great! Now tune them and tighten them up. More likely, though, is the possibility that you are doing few, if any, of these policies. In that case, select three, four, or five policies that are easiest for you to do. By doing them, you can achieve the following:

- Upgrade the tribe-level learning of your team or organization
- Transfer the lessons of Agile to your wider organization, not just your information technology department
- Prepare for Agility and using an Agile framework like Scrum

If you have issues using Agile Frameworks like Scrum

Perhaps your organization is using Scrum or other Agile practices and getting mixed results. The reality is that Scrum, Kanban, and Lean all actively encourage the practices. Scrum, for example, encourages us to *examine our norms* via the Retrospective meeting, which is clearly defined in the Sprint Review step of Scrum. Kanban, via structured and active visualization of workflow, encourages us to *pay explicit attention* to the flow. Lean, with the *go to the gemba* practice, encourages us to *inspect frequently*.

This is a big deal: the practices of Scrum, Kanban, and Lean all strongly encourage the Tribal Learning Practices. This means that if you can do some of these practices, you are *transcending* Agile, Scrum, Kanban, and Lean. You are already there precisely because you are doing the practices. This means you are in an excellent position to become (and, in fact, BE) a Learning Organization.

The practices are summarized below.

1. **{Be Purposeful}** Everything hinges on leadership. You cannot lead if they cannot follow. State your overarching purpose early and often, using short-form structured speech. Make it easy for those who follow you to understand your vision, your mission, and your statement of short-term intent.
2. **{Facilitate Your Meetings}** Use a page from the Agile playbook and facilitate all your meetings. Facilitated meetings provide space for the convener to observe and reflect. These same meetings tend to have a clear goal, a clear set of rules, and a clear way to track progress. Facilitated meetings are good games.
3. **{Examine Your Norms}** Normal is what you willingly tolerate. Examine your norms, because what you tolerate is a minimal level of what you insist on. What you insist on is more likely to happen. Insist on norms that encourage tribal greatness.
4. **{Be Punctual}** The whole group cannot learn together if the whole group is not present. Punctuality associates with focus,

commitment, and respect; these in turn associate with individual and group greatness. Encourage punctuality to manifest genuine and authentic greatness in your tribe.

5. **{Structure Your Interactions}** Use protocols to clarify essential interactions. Employ structured speech as a tool to clarify the meaning of what you say.
6. **{Announce Your Intent}** Be easy to follow by announcing what you intend to do. Do not fear being blocked by opponents. Instead, rely on your clear signals to attract followers and helpers who align with your intent. Announcing your intent is making a request for help. State what you are doing with purpose.
7. **{Game Your Meetings}** Meeting suck when attendance is not optional, when the goal and rules are fuzzy, and when there is no way to track progress. Make meetings fun, enjoyable, and engaging by gaming them. Use working agreements to give structure and clarity to your set of rules in the meeting-game.
8. **{Conduct Frequent Experiments}** Frequent experimentation means frequent learning. Make learning into a game, by scheduling frequent, cheap experiments. Failing cheap means learning economically. Fail frequently, but never start an experiment until you know exactly how much it will cost.
9. **{Manage Visually}** The books Gamestorming and Visual Meetings are pointing to something. Radiate information and use visual artifacts to define physical space that in turn will influence thoughts and perception.
10. **{Inspect Frequently}** Change is the new normal. Extensive change means high complexity. Use iteration and frequent inspection to make a game of change. Inspect and retrospect frequently as a tribe.
11. **{Get Coached}** Coaching helps the learning process and is a best practice. A coach will see what you do not and cannot.
12. **{Manage Your Boundaries}** Good fences make good neighbors. Be mindful of boundaries for authority, role, and

tasks. Loosen boundaries for inquiry and dialogue, tighten boundaries when deciding and executing. Manage boundaries to create the kind of space your tribe needs to accomplish every kind of work.

13. **{Socialize Books}** Books contain ideas and concepts that you can leverage in pursuit of tribal greatness. Select the right books to reiterate the beliefs, values, and principles you want. Encourage people to talk with each other about what they read.
14. **{Pay Explicit Attention}** Ignorance is ***not*** bliss. Pay attention to what is working and what is not. Zoom in on details and focus on interactions and results. Discuss what you see with the specific intent to be excellent.
15. **{Open the Space}** Open Space meetings are fantastic for managing the integration of transitions, evolution and learning in groups. Stimulate your tribe's development by convening periodic Open Space meetings. These meetings generate opportunities for expression, inquiry, dialogue, and learning.
16. **{Be Playful}** Play games to get work done. Bring in new games and pay attention to existing games you are already playing. Use games for simulation, work, and learning.

You can deploy these practices in any order. You can mix and match what you select to fit your context and ability to execute. Doing just two or three of the practices will make it easy to add more of them, as they all support each other.

Delays are Normal: Understanding Delays and Systems

Delays in achieving good results are common, even when taking steps that have good, long-term characteristics. The opposite is also quite true. Steps you take today that yield an immediate intended result often end up costing you quite a bit in long-term negative effects. The Tribal Learning Practices do tend to have some delays associated with them. Understanding the nature of delays is important when you start to implement the practices.

Good Habits Make You Worse, Then MUCH Better

It is a general fact that good steps taken today usually do not have an immediate positive effect. The truth is that you often get worse before you get better.

Figure 11. The J-Curve

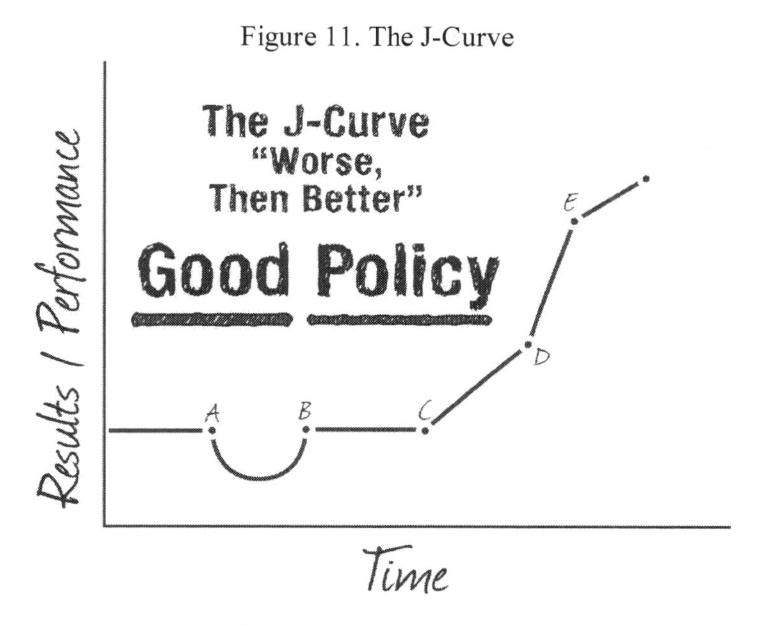

As an example, consider the step of committing to higher education. There is a large body of evidence which documents that higher levels of education are associated with higher levels of income, although there is a substantial delay in obtaining the intended results of a higher income.

Most good habits are like this. Obtaining more and higher education requires substantial time, effort, and money. Over the short term, these results do not appear great. However, over the long run, your income and quality of life can (and often will) substantially improve after a delay. A good habit like paying attention to what you are eating can leave you hungry and irritable, as you make periodic adjustments to your diet. Exercise is another example – short term, it can cause you to feel tired and sore. However, both of these habits are associated over the long term with more vitality, better ability to focus, and a longer life. Diet and exercise are examples of habits that are painful to start, habits that make you short-term *bad* and long-term *great*.

In your organization, good habits like the Tribal Learning Practices can cause short-term pain and long-term gain.

Bad Moves Make You Better, Then MUCH Worse

Alcohol can make you feel good over the short-term yet leave you with a hangover the next day. Habitual abuse of alcohol associates with the long-term results of liver damage and many other problems. Abuse of alcohol is a great example of how you can feel good from something that is bad for you long-term. Other examples include habitual drug abuse and poor sleep habits. These types of habits make you feel good in the short run, even as you are destroying yourself over time.

Figure 12. The Crack-high Curve

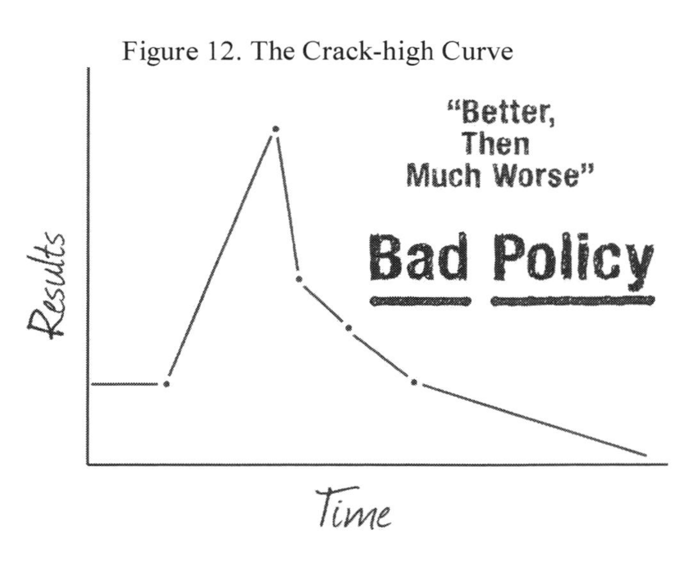

In our organizations, we often institute steps that lead to more of what we say we want to avoid. A good example is adding more people to a late project. In software projects, we know that adding more workers to a project ultimately will make it run even later. We know this, yet we still often do it. This is because at first, it seems to work. At first, we will accomplish more work but, as time passes, we will need to explain things to the new workers, and acclimate them to the project. We need to educate and inform each new worker, as they get deeper into tasks of greater complexity. We will also experience an increase in team-level communication overhead to deal with as we add more people. Each of these longer-term effects conspires to slow the project down. Highly skilled team members start to get frustrated as they realize how much more work they have to do to bring the others up to speed. This tends to chip away at team morale, which is likely to be declining by this point. Little by little, the project slows down as team velocity actually declines. What starts as a good idea with the best of intentions will actually contribute to the very problem that the *solution* was supposed to help solve.

Tribal Learning Practices create results with Little or No Delay

What we really want to do in our organizations is get some good results without waiting very long. This is exactly what the practices are designed to do. Each step produces results after a brief delay or no delay. You should realize that some delays are good, like the delays that come from implementing good habits that will have long-term positive effects.

Each of the practices may have delay associated with it. Examine the description of each step and be sure you understand the potential delays in results that you can expect.

Other Consequences

Each of the practices has consequences. These consequences may include:

1. Delays
2. Explicit examination of norms
3. Role changes

Realize that the practices are going to have you questioning the current habits of your organization. This can be painful to participate in, and even more painful as you experience some delayed results. Try to resist allowing the delays to encourage you to ***backslide*** into the old ways of doing things. For example, developing punctuality around your meetings can be very painful. As your organization notices how difficult punctuality can be to implement, the search for immediate results begins. When those results are not immediate, there is a tendency to return to the old way of being. Although necessary, explicit examination of norms will add to the pain as the organization learns.

Valuing People Over Roles

This pain can increase as people begin to work in new ways, often assuming new roles. For example, when an organization implements Scrum to help promote teamwork in software teams, the rules of the game demand that everyone fit into one of only three roles: ***Product Owner***, ***Team***, or ***Scrum Master***. In organizations that value roles more than they value people, this transition is not a safe one for the people who must abandon their old roles and take up new ones. Awareness of the fact that Scrum is a proven framework to develop great software using teams does not reduce this discomfort at all. People tend to be uncomfortable in new roles and with new ways of working, the very means to achieve improved results. As you incorporate more safety in your organization, higher levels of tribal learning will happen in your organization, often after a painful delay.

Tribal Learning Values

At the root of using the Tribal Learning Practices is a set of ***values***. These values support high levels of learning and a certain playful attitude about work and work-related problems. People doing the Tribal Learning Practices tend to identify with and value the items listed below. These Tribal Learning values derive from the learning frameworks found in the Agile, Scrum and Lean communities-of-practice that exist worldwide. They were derived from two core ideas:

1. Respect for People
2. Continuous Improvement

The Tribal Learning values are:

- Serve Others
- Be Purposeful
- Communicate Honestly with Respect
- Create Relationships
- Increase Learning
- Be Open-Minded
- Adapt to Change
- Create Fun
- Be Focused, Committed, and Courageous

Let's look at each of these nine in turn. These nine values encourage respect for people, continuous improvement, and the Tribal Learning Practices, in the following ways:

1. **Serve Others**: Implementing Tribal Learning Practices serves the entire organization by making it more responsive and adaptive to change. The pace of change is increasing. Implementing practices that encourage tribe-level adaption serves the entire organization.
2. **Be Purposeful**: Change for the sake of change is pointless. Having a clear purpose is associated with greatness in teams and organizations.
3. **Communicate Honestly with Respect**: Honest communication associates with greatness in teams, tribes, and entire organizations. We must value honest, respectful communication to have a significant chance to make learning happen at the group level on a consistent basis.
4. **Create Relationships**: A focus on work, especially creative work, does not bear fruit until relationships are in place that will support respect and continuous improvement.

5. **Increase Learning**: There is no adaptation without learning. Seeking learning at the level of group is associated with greatness, by embracing, identifying, and responding to change.
6. **Be Open-Minded**: Openness is associated with the safe space needed for identifying problems, suggesting solutions, and asking for and receiving help. Always accept the current best idea regardless of the source, and always disclose what you want, think, and feel when working with others.
7. **Adapt to Change**: Openness creates safety, safety encourages learning, and learning creates the potential for adaptation. The pace of change mandates that we encourage the creation of conditions that allow the entire organization to adapt rapidly.
8. **Create Fun**: Playfulness and fun are part of any satisfying game. We seek to game the work, so that we can opt-in, have clear goals, have clear rules, and have a clear way to measure progress. Good games have these properties and are enjoyable.
9. **Be Focused, Committed, and Courageous**: Focus is the concentration of attention. Commitment is the act of binding yourself to a course of action. Courage is a quality of spirit that enables you to face danger or pain without showing fear. These qualities must be present in our groups, to achieve our aim of continuous improvement.

People who are predisposed to the Tribal Learning Practices enjoy them precisely because already they hold most of these values. Those who might not enjoy the Tribal Learning Practices probably do not.

Implementing some of the practices can immediately signal the identities of people aligned with these values and those who are not. Since opting-in voluntarily is a core requirement of any good game, make sure to handle objections in a constructive fashion. Specifically, if you have people in your group who are resistant to participating in the Tribal Learning Practices, it is essential that you continue to be respectful when you interact with them. Do not close the space to exclude dialogue and inquiry, because doing so is counterproductive to group learning and to the Tribal Learning practice {Open the Space}.

It is completely acceptable and normal for some people to resist or be intolerant of what we are trying to accomplish. The main thing is to be sure (*beforehand*) that most of the people in your group are enthusiastic, while you maintain the space open for people to express their thoughts.

With these ideas in mind, we can describe the details of each individual Tribal Learning practice.

Chapter 7 - Be Purposeful

Overview

It is easy to maintain your focus when you have a clear purpose. Endeavor to do everything on purpose and make sure everyone knows what the wide-scope purpose is. A shared and commonly held purpose provides a touchstone and reality check. An explicitly stated purpose informs and connects goal-setting, values, principles, and actions. Having a clear sense of purpose is associated with basic human happiness. Be purposeful.

History and Origins of the Practice

The Agile Manifesto states that, "our highest priority is to satisfy the customer through early and continuous delivery of valuable software."[42] This is the first principle and is fundamental to the entire Agile Manifesto. It clearly states the purpose of the software team. Your highest priority is your purpose - it is what you are here to do. Developing, defining, and ultimately agreeing on a collective purpose will enhance both team and organizational learning.

Scrum's five values (Focus, Commitment, Respect, Openness, and Courage) all associate with the development and articulation of a sense of purpose. Scrum encourages the development of a sense of purpose through these values.

How This Helps

Group learning is enhanced through the creation of a collectively safe space; an important aspect of safe space is the aspect of knowing the properties and characteristics that define ***the space.*** A clearly understood sense of purpose helps with this.

In Japanese, the term describing this space is the ***ba***. The ba not just a physical place but also a social and psychological space. When people in the space cannot name a collective and commonly held purpose, their

---

42 See Footnote 9

capacity for learning diminishes. When everyone understands the purpose well and shares the same purpose, learning increases because everyone knows *the space* by knowing this essential property that helps define it. Agile thinking strongly encourages the development of a sense of collective purpose at the team level. A well-defined purpose contributes to the development of safe space, an essential element to set the stage for group-level learning to take place.

Costs

The {Be Purposeful} practice has a cost, and that cost is *the effort of making hard choices almost every day.* Without a purpose, almost everything is worthy of at least *some* attention. With a clear purpose for the group, the range of what is valued by the group narrows quickly. Expect to invest time and energy in maintaining focus on the agreed-upon purpose of the group. Expect to remind each other, every day.

Results and Related Delays

The results of having a sense of purpose (either individually or with a group) are nearly immediate. When things get fuzzy, reflection on the stated purpose or aim of the group will anchor a discussion, providing focus and clarity. Especially where work is complex and changing, a sense of purpose provides clarity when it is needed. Once you have defined a shared purpose and can name it, you can see the results. Participants in meetings will refer to it when engaging in dialogue, when exploring options, and when making decisions.

Details

A sense of purpose associates with happiness. It takes a big purpose that cannot be achieved alone to give a sense of team and teamwork. Purpose guides goal setting. We can compare goals to the stated purpose and validate them. The goals enable us to close the gap between the current reality of the situation and the future that we want to create. Participation in goal setting also creates a sense of control. This sense of control also associates with happiness.

Purpose informs behavior and actions. We can use the stated purpose as both an anchor and a touchstone to guide action. Tasks that are aligned with goals and purpose become ***meaningful work***. When actions create results, you generate a sense of progress.

Purpose animates and informs values and principles. Clarity of purpose leads to clarity in the explicit definition of values and principles. This clarity in turn makes task definition simple and the execution of those tasks becomes meaningful.

With purpose, values, and principles in alignment, day-to-day activities and planning of work becomes a leveraged activity with a strong focus. Developing a strong and commonly held statement of purpose brings meaning to a group's work.

Challenges

As soon as you explicitly inquire into a collective purpose, you ***open the space*** for that discussion. When that happens, there is an implicit expectation that ***we will follow through***. We will discuss this, inquire into it, and do something about it. If we do not follow through, we will be worse off than before. Once you remove the lid, open the jar, and then discuss a collective purpose, you will have invited people to engage. This is exactly what they deeply want to do. To engage in a discussion about collective purpose brings meaning to work, and contributes to collective happiness. Once you start this discussion, you must follow through. If you do not, you can expect to be in the company of unhappy people.

No matter what, do not dictate or mandate the statement of purpose. If you do that, the others will be unable to locate themselves in the story and will disengage or *check out*. As with most of the practices, make sure people choose to opt-in. Opt-in participation gives a sense of control and is an essential element of any good game.

Steps and Options

Implementation of this practice involves the following steps:

1. **Ask**. Use all available forms of communication to solicit feedback and ideas on what the purpose of the group is. Be sure to include everyone in the discussion.
2. **Listen**. Do not drive the discussion; instead create the space to enable it to happen. As the manager in the room holding the authority, you can either encourage discussions or cut them off. Try to get out of the way.
3. **Meet**. Hold some meetings and make sure you have a facilitator. Since the purpose of a smaller department or group is dependent on the purposes and aims of the wider organization, expect the discussion to question the wider purpose as the context for defining the purpose of this group.
4. **Keep It Light**. Exploring a clearly defined purpose can be very triggering and may evoke strong emotions - potentially negative emotions that express frustration with the organization. Keep the space open for that while keeping it light.
5. **Play Games**. When meeting around developing a sense of purpose, play some games to help generate ideas, movement, and agreement. See the chapter {Be Playful} for more information on the use of games.
6. **Get It Done**. Do not fizzle out!
7. **Keep it Short.** Use short-form structured speech (see {Structure Your Interactions} in Part 2) to create the wording for the stated purpose. Keep it short and easy to remember.

Takeaways: Be Purposeful

- <u>Purpose informs your goals</u>, values, principles, and behavior (actions).
- <u>A clearly stated and commonly held purpose associates with happiness</u>. By providing the space to discuss and develop a statement of purpose, you are creating a sense of control, a sense of teamwork, and a sense of purpose all at once. All of these feelings contribute to happiness.

- The creation and achievement of goals provides a sense of progress, another essential for happiness.
- People learn at a much faster rate when they are happy. Playfulness is difficult when people are worried or unsure. By clearly defining and articulating the purpose of your group, participants can more easily locate themselves within the group space.
- Purpose helps to create an environment for a good game: people will be opting-in to the shared sense of purpose and participating in the development and definition of clear goals, clear rules, and clear ways to measure progress. Good games are satisfying to play and create good learning environments.

Chapter 8 - Facilitate Your Meetings

Overview

*Facilitated meeting*s tend to be focused, organized, and well defined. When you clearly describe who qualifies to attend, what the goal is, what the boundaries are, and how you will manage the meeting, you create an invitation to explore the topic or issue. The convener has the luxury to participate more fully and observe without the additional responsibility to run the entire meeting. Facilitators are there to keep meetings flowing and to end on time. A facilitated meeting requires you to organize yourself in advance of the meeting.

Facilitated meetings are essential if you intend to become great as a group. Meetings are useful only when the objectives, agenda, and duration are all clearly stated and in alignment. Use facilitators to stay organized, complete meeting agendas, and learn faster as a group. Leverage facilitation to attain group focus while pursuing greatness inside your teams as well as in the wider organization. Develop a norm of focused meeting greatness.

History and Origins of the Practice

Scrum is the world's most popular framework for high-performance teams to build software and other complex products. Someone facilitates every meeting in Scrum, and there is a clear reason why. Facilitated meetings tend to encourage learning and the mixing of ideas, because facilitated meetings tend to create a space where everyone gets a chance to be heard, even the genuine introverts in the room.

How This Helps

By establishing a clear goal, a clear set of rules, and a clear way to track progress, you make any game enjoyable. A good game makes for good learning, and meetings are no exception. Facilitated meetings tend to be well planned, have the right participants, and a clear set of rules. Meetings for brainstorming and dialogue are especially well suited for facilitation. The facilitator can defer any movement towards the premature end of a discussion and too early a decision, and keep the space open for inquiry. When the time is appropriate for the group to decide, the facilitator can assist in moving in that direction.

A good meeting serves a stated purpose through its structure. To structure a meeting to be more divergent, focus primarily on generating ideas. Meetings focused on the need for decision-making tend to be convergent. A good facilitator helps by structuring a meeting to match the purpose. When one meeting needs to accomplish both purposes, a good facilitator can help deflect premature movement of the group from dialogue to decision-making.

Costs

There are no hard-money (cash) costs for this step. You can choose to start using facilitated meetings formats immediately. A good practice is to have a person from outside your group to facilitate your meeting. Later you can return the favor, and send over one of the people from your team to facilitate the meetings of the other group. The net cost is zero in terms of time, as you will be swapping people to perform facilitation services for each other. This technique begins to generate a ***facilitation culture*** and creates a mixing of people and ideas and information. This mixing is a form of socialization that further increases sharing of information across departments. Search the web to develop your organization's facilitation skills inexpensively, to get familiar with facilitation techniques, and experiment with them. The International Institute for Facilitation offers facilitation certification credentialing for those who want to dig deeper into specific facilitation competencies and practices.[43]

---

43 Learn more about the International Institute for Facilitation at: http://www.inifac.org/

Results and Related Delays

A well-facilitated meeting tends to have a clear purpose, stays on track, and is productive with just the right level of structure. Facilitated meetings tend to be enjoyable and productive. These benefits tend to manifest immediately.

Details

Facilitated meetings are generally better than meetings that are not. Participants learn to enjoy having someone besides the convener in a role that is responsible only for steering. Breaking out the responsibility for facilitation from the sole authority of the convener will smooth out a meeting and free up the convener to listen and observe.

A decent facilitator can smooth out a meeting by making sure everyone is heard, making sure that loquacious people make space for others, and managing a meeting's sense of progress and tempo. A facilitator can also encourage greater respect inside a meeting by creating and holding space for dialogue. A facilitator can handle making sure that the convener honors scheduled breaks, as well as the start and stop times. This also supports respect, commitment, and focus on the part of all participants.

A skilled facilitator can also make small adjustments that help the group more easily achieve objectives. Sometimes a group of people meeting to make decisions are actually not ready, and are better off continuing with the dialogue a bit longer, before moving to decision-making and action. A skilled facilitator can sense this situation, and encourage dialogue during that meeting.

Challenges

Results can vary based on the skill of your facilitator and the complexity of the meetings you are trying to streamline.

Meeting conveners need to be willing to delegate responsibility to the facilitator to run a meeting. When conveners do this, they are not giving up any authority. You may need to elaborate on this theme with some conveners. ***Facilitators serve meeting conveners***, not the other way around. The convener needs to meet with the facilitator to make these boundaries are explicit and well understood.

The facilitator is ***serving*** the authority in the room rather than ***being*** the authority in the room. A heavy-handed facilitator can unintentionally limit the space for dialogue and turn people off. In general, do not choose an organization's central authority figure to serve as a facilitator.

Steps and Options

Implementing this practice involves the following steps:

1. **Socialize the idea of facilitated meetings.** Send out some emails about the advantages of facilitated meetings. Purchase some books, and make them available and visible.
2. **Identify a facilitator**. The best facilitator candidate is a person who begs you to try it. Facilitation is an art form and a skill grounded in sociology. Listen and watch carefully for the people who willingly opt-in to try facilitation. Watch out for those who seek authority – the facilitator role is that of a servant-leader, not a boss or autocrat. An overly authoritative facilitator can unintentionally limit the space for dialogue and turn people off.
3. **Gather some resources for learning**. The book *GameStorming* provides a great set of meeting facilitation ideas and tools.[44] This and other resources can help you develop facilitation skills and ideas. Investigate the International Institute for Facilitation website and related resources.
4. **Experiment by convening a facilitated meeting**. Start facilitating some of your meetings and inspect the results. Let those who express interest in being the facilitator give it a try.
5. **Inspect the results**. Periodically inspect the results and find out if the participants at these meetings are finding the meeting more valuable. Do not assume they do. Inspect the results.

---

44 See Gamestorming: A playbook for Innovators, Rule breakers and Change makers by David Gray, Sunni Brown and James Macanufo

6. **Develop a culture that includes facilitated meetings.** Offer other managers a facilitator from your group, and then switch. Swap facilitators. If you work in a larger organization, develop a community of practice around facilitation.

Takeaways: Facilitate Your Meetings

- Facilitated meetings help increase learning by creating and holding space where everyone can be heard
- Meeting conveners who delegate to facilitators can engage in observation and participation more freely without the burden of running the meeting
- Facilitated meetings tend to have a clear goal and well-understood ground rules and working agreements. This increased safety transforms a meeting into a good game, and increases levels of engagement.

Chapter 9 - Examine Your Norms

Overview

The activities that you repeatedly do together as a group matter a great deal. How you handle dialogue, brainstorming, meetings, email, and other interactions matter, because great interactions support alignment with purpose, values, principles, and goals. Alignment can quickly dissolve. When that happens, a game goes bad. Ambiguous goals, fuzzy rules, and a lack of feedback can work against your interests and reduce engagement.

When your group makes a deliberate change in habits to increase alignment with purpose and values, it is easy to backslide towards old familiar habits. Constantly examine your norms to make sure that they support your wider purposes and supporting values.

History and Origins of the Practice

Retrospectives are inspection points in Agile practice. There is a natural opportunity at the end of each iteration to inspect and adapt. Genuine & Authentic Agile practice includes reflection and subsequent changes that a team makes in how they will perform future work. Most of the time, the greatest teamwork comes from examining and changing the frequency and quality of interactions.

Agile iterations usually provide some time for reflection and examinations during an iteration, not just after one ends. Reflection and examination of habits is a hallmark of Genuine & Authentic Agile practice and a learning organization. This ***examination culture*** treats everything as an experiment subject to inspection. This frames every activity as an opportunity for learning to occur.

How This Helps

The practice of viewing every habit of the group as something to examine causes the creation of a learning opportunity. If we ***open the space*** for this level of examination, we can inspect habits to make sure they conform to our stated values. When a team's behavior starts to deviate from its stated values, its integrity diminishes and the goals and rules become less clear and, in the worst case, ambiguous. Periodic examination of what is normal helps to maintain alignment of actions with stated intentions, and clarifies and aligns purpose, values, and behavior at the group level.

Costs

Dollar costs are zero for taking action on this step. However, like most of the Tribal Learning Practices, once you open some space to examine norms, the "genie is out of the bottle" and you must follow through. People are naturally comfortable when thoughts, words, and actions align. This is what integrity is all about. Once you open the space for conversations, you must follow through. If you do not, you run the risk of complete disengagement by participants who sense a lack of authenticity. ***Following through*** means that changes that are supposed to take place actually do, and you then actively promote them as the new way things the organization does things – until and unless you *all* later agree upon other changes.

Results and Related Delays

Results happen immediately when you actively examine norms. This is because you create space to make changes immediately. For example, your group might examine their meetings and notice that tardiness has been the default behavior. Your group might then decide to implement {Be Punctual} as the new normal. This would have immediate effects and results. Always be sure to obtain consent from everyone, before you implement such changes.

Details

Explicit examination of what is normal leads to discussion of values and purpose.

Pain points typically include meetings and email.

Examining what is normal is required before you can implement many of the other Tribal Learning Practices. If the group is unwilling to inspect its experience and current habits, nothing can happen. If you are a manager, you are an authority figure and can model a practice to start making it the typical and normal way to function.

Unfortunately, the new normal tends to revert to the previous state. When you examine and then change the concept of what is normal, you are trying to develop new habits at the level of group. Take the necessary time to obtain agreement on new policies and practices, so everyone will be prepared for the change. Expect to have to remind the group about their (opt-in) commitment to the new habits.

You have to be willing to look at everything and make changes. The examination reveals what Jim Collins (author of the book *Good to Great*) calls the ***brutal facts***.[45] This practice is directly related to practically all the other Tribal Learning Practices found in this book.

Inspect the most recent work and the process that created it. The best way to accomplish this is by engaging in iterative work. Iterations provide natural inspection points at the end of each work period.

Challenges

Examining what is normal can be painful. It involves recognizing that we need to improve, and some of it may be interpreted at the personal level, because interactions between individuals are the usual sources of conflict. The first thing to do is create a normal behavior of examining everything periodically. Before implementing this practice, be sure to socialize it and model it. Make it OK to call out practices that hold the group back.

Always be sure to obtain consent from everyone before making changes. Examine what is normal constantly, and always implement change slowly. Make sure that everyone who is affected consents to the changes and is willing to adopt the new way as the new normal. The trap occurs when you to roll out changes without checking in with everyone

---

45 Jim Collins, Good To Great: Why Some Companies Make the Leap – and Others Don't, Chapter 4, p. 65, "Confronting the Brutal Facts"

to make sure they all agree to execute the changed practice. If you go too fast, you can expect ***pushback***. Always make sure that all participants opt-in.

Steps and Options

Implementing this practice involves the following steps:

1. **Identify an inspection point**. Create opportunities to inspect what is going on. Collect data in advance of a discussion.
2. **Perform the inspection as a group**. Convene a formal meeting, ideally one that is facilitated. Make sure everyone present has opted in to attend.
3. **Engage in dialogue about the stories**. Do not jump to suggested solutions immediately. Instead, encourage dialogue so that everyone has the opportunity to be heard. This is the time to listen to the stories people are telling.
4. **Brainstorm**. Develop a set of possible solutions or changes. Consider using the book *GameStorming* for ideas on how to do this. The book *Visual Meetings* is also an excellent resource.
5. **Choose a set of candidate changes**. Narrow down the discussion of changes to three or four ideas.
6. **Pick one and agree**. Obtain group-level consensus to end dialogue and move to decision-making, and then to decide. A good option is to use sticky dots (available at any office supply store). Post the three or four changes on the wall on large sticky notes. Then give two sticky dots to each person and ask them to go up and stick their dots on the ideas they like best. The result will be the general voice of the group concerning next steps and what the group is willing to do.
7. **Monitor participation**. In theory, after the decision everyone will have expressed his/her consent. That is not always the case, so expect to remind people of their commitments to the new policy and practices. Make it a normal practice to remind people.
8. **Track results**. After implementation, pay explicit attention to results that the new habits are generating. Use this inspection

opportunity to inform any additional adjustments to the new habits.

Takeaways: Examine Your Norms

- "Examine everything" is a practice of great individuals, great teams, and great organizations.
- Examining what is now normal mandates an identification of wider concerns. If you have not collectively defined your values and wider purpose, that process is sure to begin immediately after you examine what is the new normal. Examining what is normal begs the question, ***in service to what?***
- Make sure you explain the reason why examining everything is a good practice, and model the behavior yourself. Use your formal authority as a manager to open space to examine and inspect everything.
- This Tribal Learning practice is a core practice upon which all the others depend. Make sure you follow through with agreement and implementation of some changes, and make sure you continue to examine everything periodically. By doing so, you will create an environment in which additional Tribal Learning Practices will successfully take root in your group.

Chapter 10 - Be Punctual

Overview

Being punctual is associated with the values of commitment, focus, and respect. These values associate with greatness in teams and individuals. Stop screwing around. Be great by showing up on time, every time. Respect people and improve with them by being punctual. Model greatness by being there.

The whole group cannot learn if the whole group is not present. When people are late, this delays the start of the meeting or even worse, their lateness requires the meeting to re-start to bring them up to speed. Every meeting has potential for group-level learning. *Punctuality* encourages and supports learning at the level of group. The whole group learns when the whole group is present.

Punctuality is a practice your organization can choose to execute at any time. Implementing this practice does not require any expense, and can be implemented immediately, assuming everyone involved is willing.

Appointments are fundamentally very simple agreements. They are commitments to others, to be in a certain place – or on the phone– at a certain time. As such, punctuality is an important part of strong culture that includes *focus*, *commitment*, and *respect*.

These are three of the five essential values[46] associated with the Scrum framework.[47]

---

46 Scrum is supported by five underlying values. Focus, Commitment, Respect, Focus and Courage. See: Schwaber Ken and Beedle, Mike, *Agile Software Development with Scrum*, p. 147.

47 Scrum Guide. See: http://www.scrum.org/scrumguides/

How Punctuality Encourages Learning Throughout the Organization

If you are punctual, I can strongly argue you are likely also very focused and committed, and respectful in your interactions.

If your entire team, department, or organization can be punctual, you are sure to have higher levels of engagement in your group-level interactions. Higher levels of engagement are essential to group-level greatness. This is the primary advantage of implementing punctuality as a norm in your organization. The behavior helps your organization develop higher levels of engagement.

Pairing punctuality with facilitated meetings is a great way to get immediate results.

Costs

There are no actual costs associated with implementing this policy. You simply decide to do it.

Results and Related Delays

You can expect a delay in compliance on the part of some number of people who purport to understand and agree to the arrangement. Once a majority of people honor the agreement to be punctual, you can expect the benefits to accrue to the entire organization. These benefits include:

- Fewer meetings
- Better and more productive meetings
- Much more attention paid to good time (boundary) management
- Higher levels of focus, commitment and respectful interactions
- More time for reflection in between meetings. Having adequate time to reflect is important for rapidly integrating learning.

"Be Punctual" may seem too rigid in some national cultures and certainly too rigid for some corporate cultures. Further, in the chapter{Open The Space} a meeting format called Open Space is discussed. Two of the principles of this meeting type are ***Whenever It Starts is the Right Time*** and ***When It's Over It's Over.*** Being punctual seems to conflict with these ideas. What gives here?
Like any practice, {Be Punctual} is not applicable to every single situation. You must use your judgment to apply it effectively. Open Space is a meeting format that is intentionally loose in terms of start and stop time. Applying {Be Punctual} to Open Space is a very bad idea. Likewise, some meetings that are strictly about dialogue and inquiry (brainstorming and discussion) need to be looser in terms of start and stop time.
For typical meetings that are a mix of exploring ideas and reaching a decision, {Be Punctual} is useful for encouraging focus, respect, and commitment. Applying

Challenges

The policy of punctuality, like all policies, usually requires that all the people involved opt-in. This provides a sense of control essential to basic human happiness. It is important that the policy is clearly specified, agreed-upon, and adhered to. The ***agreed-upon*** aspect is going to be tough if you dictate it. It is far better for the people to be involved in the decision to implement the policy.

Adhered-to usually requires some kind of negative incentive or sanction in the event the person in question does not follow through on the stated commitment.

Like many of the practices, you will find that implementing the policy is going to force an explicit examination of what is holding you back. This can be painful to acknowledge.

Steps and Options

To encourage punctuality, create a system of positive and negative incentives around the subject of being on time, specifically for meetings. The typical policy is to collect a highly symbolic one dollar from each person

Punctuality to your meetings can make them more enjoyable and focused. Use your judgment.

who is late. The payment symbolizes the valuing of punctuality and the devaluing of lateness.

The pool of collected dollars can spent by the group every month, for example the 4th Friday of the month, at a restaurant or bar where the members can socialize and tell some stories to each other about organizational life and the punctuality policy.

One thing that happens right away when you implement this policy is you get many questions. You get *detailed* questions. Questions revolve around specific details, like:

- If I am late by 1 minute or less, am I late in fact?
- Which clock do we go by?
- What if I only have a 5, 10, 20, or 50-dollar bill? What if I have no bills in my pocket if and when I am late?
- We use Outlook. When invited to a meeting, the options are {Accept}, {Decline}, and {Tentative}. If I do not decline the invite, am I obligated to attend and if I do not am I late? [48]

The bottom line is, when you implement a policy of punctuality, everyone needs to know about all the ***edge cases*** – all of the exceptions to the rule. As an organization, you realize that other things have to change. For example, if the building you work in is a large one, starting meetings at the top of the hour (1PM, 2PM etc.) and running them for 1 hour is no longer an effective way of working. This is because it takes up to 15 minutes to leave the current meeting, optionally use the bathroom,

---

[48] See the sidebar "Punctuality at a SeeEye Corporation" for a discussion on how implementing Punctuality can actually play out. SeeEye is the fictional name of a real organization where a friend worked while I was coaching several Agile teams in her organization.

collect yourself, and use the stairs or elevator to get to the next meeting, etc. If your workplace is in a large building spanning multiple floors, you need to shorten meetings to 50 minutes. For example, start 1:05PM and end at 1:55PM.

This is all part of explicitly examining what is ***in the way***. Jim Collins in the book *Good to Great* calls this ***Confronting the Brutal Facts***[49]. Even a simple policy like punctuality requires a careful and explicit examination of the facts. This explicit examination is itself a very useful exercise for organizations preparing for a move to Agile ways of working.

Implementing punctuality as normal is actually a very small version of implementing Agile in your organization. You immediately notice what is holding you back. Often, these obstacles are cultural. The ***current normal*** is normal at several levels. People are habitually late precisely because there is support for it across the entire organization.

While we are discussing punctuality, now is a good time to mention the use of cell phones and laptops during meetings. These devices severely reduce engagement levels by making it normal and acceptable to be distracted when someone else is talking. This is especially true of the higher-authorized individuals in your company. When a C-level person places starts interacting with a phone during a meeting, the signaling is clear: ***whatever is being said now does not matter***. Even when the phone is being used to take notes, the impression is that the person using the device is distracted, or even worse, displaying disrespect.

Takeaways: Be Punctual

- Punctuality as a norm explicitly devalues lateness and tardiness. It forces the people in the organization to notice how loose the culture is with respect to keeping appointments. It takes openness and courage to establish punctually as a norm.

---

49 *Good To Great,* Jim Collins, p. 65

- Punctuality associates with valuing focus, commitment, and respect. These are actually values associated with the Scrum framework (the remaining two are openness and courage). Focus, commitment, and respect as associated with greatness in individuals and organizations.
- The most common way to implement this policy is to institute a small sanction like a one-dollar penalty for being late.
- Like most policies that require people to adhere, it is best if they opt-in and agree in advance to willingly participate.
- Punctuality as a policy requires an explicit examination of what has to change to make the policy capable of implementation in your organization. Expect to have to make changes that support the new way of working.

Punctuality at SeeEye Corporation

Q: Why are we doing this? I am always on time!

A: Thank you for being on time and respecting others and their time. The hope is to be the change you want to see in others. Hopefully others will follow.

Q: If I arrive late per clock but before the organizer of the meeting, am I considered late and have to pay up?

A: Yes being on time means being there on time per clock. You did not know the organizer was not there yet, but you were aware of running late yourself based on the clock.

Q: If I accepted the invite but decided not to attend that meeting at all, am I late?

A: Yes, if you accepted the meeting you are being expected in this meeting, so decline in advance or missing the meeting will be equal to being late.

Q: If I received the invitation, but never accepted it, does the same rule above apply to me?

A: Yes, unless you decline the invite in advance you are expected at the meeting and will have to pay a fee for missing it or being late.
Q: If the meeting request arrived a minute before the start of the meeting, do I have to pay $1 for not making there on time?
A: No, the organizer is expected to plan at least two core hours (10-4) in advance if possible, otherwise they can't expect you to know about the meeting.
Q: Will there be more exceptions once we start living by this new policy?
A: Yes, we fully understand that as we start living and breathing by this rule, we will find other edge cases and will fine-tune the rules and exceptions. Use common sense. Be on time, and be respectful to others.
Q: All clocks are showing different times, which one should I go by?
A: Let's agree to go by digital clocks in the building or your cell phones. If the clocks disagree go by the one ahead to avoid being late. Don't blame the clock.
Q: I was invited to a meeting, but I already blocked off the time in Outlook!
A: Meeting organizers should not extend invites to someone who has already blocked off the time, but you are still expected to decline.
Q: What if the time for the meeting was scheduled for non-core hours?
A: Presuming you are given enough notice, you are still expected to attend meetings you accept on time and to decline meetings you cannot make.
Q: What if I accepted via tentative status?
A: If you are not sure if you will be going to the meeting and indicate you are tentative, you are not considered to have missed the meeting. Please note that you are not allowed simply to accept all meetings as tentative. You should also use tentative status if you want meeting notes but do not plan to attend - please indicate such when you respond to the meeting invite.
Q: I was late to my meeting. To whom should I give my Dollar?
A: Please deliver the fee to {person name} or {other person name} and we will keep it. If others decide to join, we can reconsider the fund keepers.

Chapter 11 - Structure Your Interactions

Overview

Structured interactions include using *interaction protocols* and *structured speech* to improve communication dynamics and to attain and maintain focus in group interactions.

Facilitated meetings are also structured interactions and are not covered in this chapter. Instead, {Facilitate Your Meetings} is a standalone Tribal Learning practice and is covered in detail by itself. Be sure to examine that chapter.

Protocols are structured interactions between two or more people. Personal interaction mechanics when using protocols includes understanding your role in any interaction.

Structured speech is used in structured interactions. Speech is a form of action. Structured speech is useful for managing how others perceive what you say and the meaning of your verbal and written communication.

Structured interactions are essential for discussing differences, processing mistakes, and making decisions; they are essential when processing the differences and heat generated by conflict.

History and Origins of the Practice

Protocols

The Scrum framework uses a protocol in the Daily Scrum. The participants are required to answer three specific structured questions. There are no discussions during the Daily Scrum about other topics.

Fernando Flores[50] popularized the *speech acts* of John L. Austin.[51] Speech acts include making proposals, greetings, issuing warnings, and inviting. Flores was a linguist and Chilean Minister of Finance who

---

50 Learn more about Fernando Flores here: http://www.fastcompany.com/magazine/21/flores.html

51 Learn more about John L. Austin on Wikipedia: http://en.wikipedia.org/wiki/J._L._Austin

worked with Terry Winograd, a well-known Stanford professor and computer scientist noted for advancing artificial intelligence and natural language processing.

Jim and Michele McCarthy[52] worked at Microsoft in the 1990's and later embarked on a study of teams and teamwork after becoming fascinated with the topic while building software tools at Microsoft. They formulated the *Core Protocols*, a set of structured interactions associated with greatness in teams. The Core Protocols include structured interactions for sending and receiving feedback, investigating a person's thinking, making decisions, creating a shared vision, and other common interactions inside teams.

Structured Speech

Structured speech is speech that has a recurring form or syntax and varying content. In Agile practice, *user stories* represent a practical application of structured speech. Statements in a standard form are used for specifying software requirements. The standard structure is of the form:

As [a user type] I want to [perform an action] so that [specific result]

This standard form is actually a form of structured speech.

Ed Seykota[53], the famous commodities trader who pioneered quantitative market trading methods and trend following in the 1960's, popularized the use of Subject-Verb-Object, present tense syntax (SVO-p) for English language communications in the 1990's.

SVO-p (Subject-Verb-Object, present-tense) is a very clear syntax for communicating clearly and directly.

Nonviolent communication ("NVC") is a form of structured speech that emphasizes empathy and the identification and acknowledgment of the needs of the sender and receiver of communications. NVC is useful for sending communicating with clarity.

---

52 Learn more about Jim and Michelle McCarthy at: http://www.mccarthyshow.com/

53 To learn more about Ed Seykota, see: http://www.seykota.com/tt/faq_index/

How This Helps

Structured interactions increase the potential for Tribal Learning by reducing the possible range of interactions in a given context. When the risk of conflict is high, structured interactions help to mitigate that risk. Such interactions create *containment*.

For example, when delivering feedback on another person's work, the risk of being misunderstood is high. When delivering feedback that is less than complimentary, that feedback might not be well received. Likewise, if you deliver that feedback without explicitly being asked to provide it, you can be perceived as trying to ***fix*** that person, or that person's work. Structured interactions can help here.

Group learning increases when we employ structured interactions, because the structure creates a safe space. When we engage in high-risk interactions in groups, the safety level drops quickly. *Interpersonal risk* skyrockets as feelings of safety plummet. Consider for example a conflict by and between team members regarding a course of action. Without structure, that discussion can tip into a chaotic state where hurt feelings, confusion, and denial are present. That leads to exponential decay in communication frequency about essential work topics.

Situations like this are very common when working in groups. Structured interactions create a *known container* inside of which the interactions take place. That container creates safety. Structured interactions are in fact games with opt-in participation, a clear goal, set of rules, and way to track progress and get feedback. Structured interactions are *good games*. When viewed in this way, it is easy to see how structured interactions work. They create a space that makes crucial conversations possible.

Figure 13. Exponential Decay in Communication Frequency

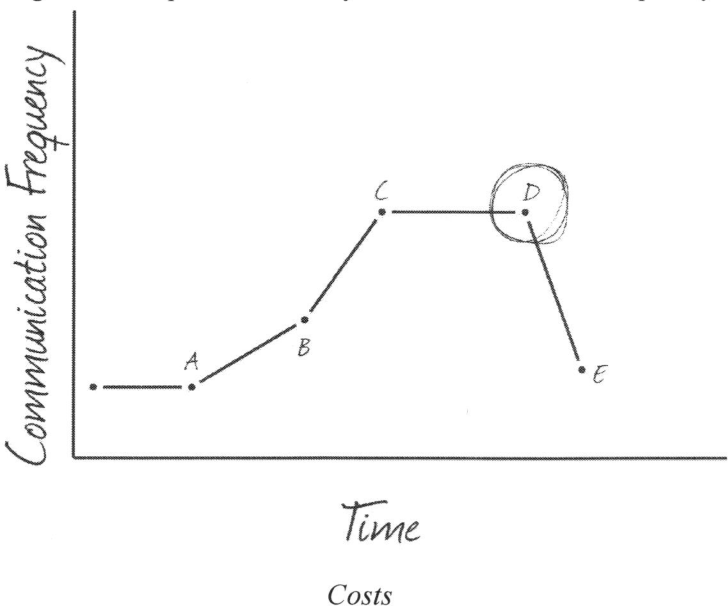

Costs

There are no dollar costs involved in using protocols and structured speech. There are some social costs. For protocols, you absolutely need people to opt-in to using them. Be sure to socialize the idea, get consent, and use protocols as needed. If you install Scrum inside your team, that installation is not complete until everyone opts in to play the Scrum game, including the Daily Scrum with the three-question protocol. McCarthy's Core Protocols require an opt-in of every participant.

Structured speech is another story. Here, you can unilaterally choose to use structured speech during interactions. There is no social cost because there is no requirement to get agreement from others before you use a structured speech form.

Results and Related Delays

For protocols, delays vary based on willingness to agree to use protocols. Often participants say they agree to use protocol-based communication when they do not in fact. Anxiety increases and waste is generated. For situations where stated and actual commitment to proceed are identical, the positive results are immediate. When the team's thoughts, words, and deeds align, the team has integrity. Clarity of purpose, goals, and communication all increase when protocols are in play.

For structured speech, results are immediate. Structured speech increases the clarity of sent communication in both written and oral forms. The fact that Agile practice has settled on user stories is not random. Since you must communicate requirements to develop shared understanding clearly, structured speech is used to contain the content of requirements.

Details on Protocols

Protocols govern interactions, and all interactions are games. For this reason, participants give consent to the use of protocols —voluntary and agreed-upon. The goal of an interaction in a protocol is always well understood. For example, the eleven Core Protocols formulated by the McCarthy's each have a clearly stated goal. A protocol by definition specifies a set of rules and a way to track progress. There is a beginning, middle, and end. All protocols used for human-to-human interaction, and interactions involving groups of people are games. Protocols make important interactions satisfying, purposeful, and fun.

It is important to realize that agreed-upon protocols only have to be used about five percent of the time. The remainder of the time, you may use casual interactions. But when the situation requires agreement and action, the group uses structured interactions (protocols) to discuss, brainstorm, interact, provide feedback, and make decisions. Use protocols when the stakes are high and the group must move to action or a decision.

The Core Protocols

The Core Protocols are a set of structured interactions designed for software teams that intend to be great. These protocols can be used on any team that is building complex products. I have been able to advance the work of teams I have coached significantly by introducing these protocols. The Core Protocols defines a set of commitments that every participant agrees to in advance. There are 11 commitments; the first one is, *I commit to engage with present. I agree to know and disclose what I want, what I think, and what I feel.* [54]

The other 10 commitments follow a similar line of thinking, and strongly support the first commitment.

These commitments support the following individual protocols:

Pass (Unpass)	Decider
Check In	Resolution
Check Out	Perfection Game
Ask For Help	Personal Alignment
Protocol Check	Investigate
Intention Check	

These eleven formal protocols provide structure for investigating another person's thinking (Investigate), for deciding (Decider), for providing feedback (Perfection Game), for questioning another person's intentions (Intention Check), and more.

Please notice that one of the protocols {Perfection Game} is actually the name of a game. The truth is all eleven of these protocols are games. You opt-in, there is a clear goal, a clear rule set, and a clear way to track progress during the interaction. Protocols are a good, satisfying, formal way to ***game your interactions***.

The formality passes after you gain experience with these tools. Protocols provide a structure for respectful investigation into important work that has the potential to generate differences, confusion, and conflict. The protocol structure provides a known container that is well

---

54 You can learn more about the Core Protocols at liveingreatness.com and themccarthyshow.com. You can download the definitive book from Jim and Michelle McCarthy, *Software For Your Head*, in PDF form, here: http://liveingreatness.com/files/Software-For-Your-Head-book-v1.0.pdf

understood. That elevates psychological safety levels and creates the potential for lots and lots of learning at the level of group.

Protocols Summary

Protocols create the following advantages:

- **Better results**. Structured interactions lead to quick and clear communication.
- **A good game**. Protocols are opt-in and always have a clear goal, a clear set of rules, and a clear way to track progress. As such, they are satisfying to use.
- **Much more safety and learning**. Protocols create safe space by their clear definitions and structure. This safety encourages elevated learning levels.
- **Conflict Management**. A protocol like the Core can be used to manage interpersonal conflict and conflict inside the team in general. Once again, structured interactions create safe space. Safe space is very important when conflict is present.
- **More engagement via disclosure**. Notice how the Core Commitment starts with a commitment to disclose what you want, think, and feel. High levels of disclosure associates with greatness in teams and organizations. Disclosure associates with high levels of engagement.

Details on Structured Speech

Structured speech can be used during protocol-based interactions. Structured speech forms such as NVC and SVO-p have the added advantage that they can be used unilaterally; that is, without requiring consent from the receiver. This means when you want to be clear, you can drop into a structured speech form such as SVO-p and start expressing yourself with more clarity.

Everyone is familiar with establishing rapport and basic rapport dynamics. We all know how salespeople deliberately mirror our body language and posture to ***get in-sync*** with us when interacting. The term

somatic mirroring represents a technical term for this phenomenon. Another term for this phenomenon is ***isopraxism***[55]. When you mirror the postures and body language of another, you are signaling that you are not a threat.

A less understood phenomenon is ***verbal mirroring***. This takes place when the sender speaks back to you in the same structured speech pattern you are currently using. If you use structured speech such as SVO-p for more than an hour, you may notice that others speak back to you in the same way. You can leverage this to get clear send-receive mechanics going in your interpersonal interactions. When both persons are speaking in a structured speech form, the likelihood of understanding (and being understood) is elevated.

SVO-p: Subject-Verb-Object, present tense

Indirect syntax can often obscure the subject and encourage the dodging of direct responsibility. Indirect forms of verbal communication can make the intended meaning difficult to figure out.

SVO-p is a syntax of the English language. It is a style of communication in which you always know who is responsible for an action. SVO-p is an active form of language that encourages clear thinking, direct communication, and unambiguous meaning. Using SVO-p can help clarify your thinking.

Communicating in SVO-p always specifies who is acting, what they are doing, and to whom. It requires placing the thought in the present and expressing it in the present tense.

Here are some examples:

Non SVO-p: ***The people who prepare tax forms for others are to be paid.***

---

55 For an excellent discussion of isopraxism, see the Nonverbal Dictionary online, found here: http://center-for-nonverbal-studies.org/6101.html

This sentence defers the payment out to some future moment, and hides the identity of the person paying.

SVO-p: ***I notice the people who help others for free.***

This sentence in SVO-p identifies the actor, and places the action in the now.

Non SVO-p: ***I've yet to meet anyone who has given me a good reason.***

SVO-p: ***People don't give me good reasons.***

SVO-p discourages *passive voice*. Passive forms tend to conceal the subject and avoid responsibility. The use of active voice in the present tense supports immediate action in the present moment.

When you start experimenting with SVO-p in verbal communications, you find that it is necessary to speak and think in simple and direct (SVO) terms. You find that speaking in the present tense keeps your thoughts in the now, and tends to clarify your thinking. SVO-p strongly supports an empirical approach to work and problem solving.

The use of SVO-p strongly supports the reception of iterative loops of feedback in the present. SVO-p maximizes focus on the present, at the expense of the past and future. SVO-p is the best syntax available for communicating very directly in English.

Because SVO-p is so direct, it can be used to engage in disclosure with intent to move into closer intimacy with a person, and it can be used to speak plainly with intent to increase distance and move further away. SVO-p is useful for communicating with great clarity is required.

(Readers from the Agile community may note that the "I want" and "So that" clauses of *User Stories* are in fact formatted as SVO-p sentences. SVO-p is the most direct syntax available in the English language.)

Give SVO-p a try. If it feels uncomfortable, the discomfort may be about the difficulty of making fuzzy, indirect statements in this syntax. You cannot easily make such statements in the SVO-p syntax. SVO-p identifies the subject, makes the action clear, and assigns responsibility for the action. The directness of SVO-p is the greatest strength of the form.

Nonviolent Communication

When specific interactions require clarity, structured speech can help. Another form of structured speech is Nonviolent Communication, or NVC[56].

Speaking to others using NVC includes sending and receiving observations, feelings, needs, and requests. As such, this form of structured speech has some aspects of a strong protocol because it defines both sending and receiving of information. However, there is no need to get agreement from the other person when using NVC, to make it work. You can just use it. When you use NVC, you use it for listening and speaking. NVC works by identifying and acknowledging the needs of others and expressing your own needs. The premise is that most behavior is an attempt to meet various forms of needs. NVC acknowledges this and provides language that helps communicate using this model of human interaction.

Challenges in Using Structured Speech

Using a structured speech format like SVO-p or NVC requires some discipline. As an experiment, try using SVO-p or NVC for one entire morning or one entire afternoon.

Challenges in Using Protocols

Button-pushers and boundary violators do not like to participate in the use of protocols. The inherent clarity, structure, and explicit boundary management repel those who prefer to be unconstrained. Proposing the use of a protocol is a kind of litmus test. Some people may not opt-in.

---

56 For more information on NVC, see: http://www.cnvc.org/. For an excellent explanation of this empathy-based communication practice which has elements of structured speech, see: http://www.cnvc.org/about/what-is-nvc.html

Steps and Options

Implementing {Structure Your Interactions} involves the following steps:

For Structured Speech:

1. **Learn about the various forms of structured speech.** Investigate Nonviolent Communication, SVO-p, and User Stories as employees by the Agile software community. Investigate the underlying theory of speech acts as developed by the linguistics community.
2. **Use these techniques formally or informally**. Informally, experiment with NVC and/or SVO-p. Formally, discuss the use of these structures with your team.

For Protocols:

1. **Learn** about the work of Fernando Flores, linguistics, and speech acts. Examine the book *Software for Your Head* by Jim and Michelle McCarthy. Gain an understanding of protocols in general.
2. **Discuss and socialize protocols**. Make sure the people in your group are opting-in to use protocols.
3. **Experiment with using them**. Use agreed-upon protocols in meetings when deciding, when exploring options, and when moving to action. Since they are rigid, be careful to use the formal Core Protocols only when they are needed. (3-5% of the time for typical teams.)
4. **Inspect the results**. Examine how the group likes using a structured way of interacting.

Protocols provide structure and are "training" wheels for executing on rich and engaging communications about things that matter. Once you gain competence in the basic use of protocols and learn to value and master them, you can relax formalities when meeting face-to-face.

A Note on Web Meetings and Conference Calls

Protocols are especially good when interacting with people who work away from the office. Conference calls and web meetings online encourage disengagement in several dimensions. Using protocols can raise the level of engagement during meetings with remote workers and team members.

Takeaways: Structure Your Interactions

- Structured interactions reduce complexity when the subject matter can be triggering for participants. When deciding, when providing feedback and especially when processing conflict, use protocols.
- The best basic structured interactions you can use are the Core Protocols as described in the book Software for Your Head. Keep in mind these protocols are used less than five percent of the time. Use them when things get sticky.
- A special and more primitive form of structured interaction is structured speech. SVO-p syntax for writing and speaking is structured speech. 'User stories', which have a standard form and syntax are another example of written structure. Use structured speech to engage in sense-making and clarify your thinking when interacting with others.

Chapter 12 - Announce Your Intent

Overview

Announcing intent is perhaps the most important activity of genuine leaders. Leaders and followers who announce intent are doing everyone on their team a HUGE favor by eliminating guessing and information delays and by allowing others to adjust to plans. Announcing intent is almost the same as soliciting help. Soliciting help associates with team greatness. Announce your intentions early and often.

To announce your intent, you must know what you want. This clarity helps everyone around you, and increases safety levels and associated levels of group learning.

History and Origins of the Practice

Teams, departments, and divisions are smaller social groups inside a wide organizational context. These are all *social systems* that engage in substantial levels of self-organization. Software teams using the Scrum framework display very high levels of self-organization precisely because the framework encourages this behavior. It is useful to note that Scrum mandates the announcement of intentions from both the Product Owner role and the Team role.

The Team role, composed of individual members, is authorized and responsible for handling the Daily Scrum meeting. In the meeting each team member is required to answer the question, "what are you doing today?" This amounts to a Scrum requirement to announce intentions daily, regarding work and related tasks. Likewise, a team's Product Owner in Scrum is required to clearly describe the product to be built. The description goes into an ordered list called the Product Backlog. This document amounts to a clear statement of intent for the product.

It is noteworthy that, per the rules of Scrum, the Product Owner and Team members are required to announce their intentions. *Self-organizing* social systems thrive on a lot of timely information. Announcing intentions makes it easy for teammates, co-workers, and colleagues to adjust to your plans in a way that helps you.

Remember the definition of ***leader*** at the start of this book: A leader is *anyone* who influences *anyone else* in a social setting, such as a team or organization. Announcing intent is a powerful way to exercise leadership in a self-organizing world.

How This Helps

Announcing intent is a form of disclosure, and disclosure is associated with greatness inside teams. No one can offer to help you if they have no knowledge of what you are working on, what problems you are facing, or your aims and intentions. Announcing your intent amounts to a passive request for help. You are disclosing information that is useful to anyone who may be able to help you. Such announcements amount to a unilateral broadcast of information that does not require a reply from the reciever. Upon broadcasting the unilateral message, others in the wider social system may choose to either help you or not.

Costs

There are no dollar-costs associated with announcing intent. You do not need to ask for a budget. You do not need to ask permission. You do not need anyone else's authorization. You can simply do it. Scrum is pointing the way by mandating the announcement of intention from the Product Owner and Team in the Scrum game. This is a big tip-off that there is something powerful in this method of increasing levels of information disclosure.

Announcing intent costs nothing and greatly helps the overall efficiency of the working groups and tribes in which you have membership.

Results and Related Delays

Experiment, since delays in results will vary according to the maturity of your group. If the space is safe for learning, you may see immediate results. If the culture supports a lot of information-hiding and information-silos, you may shock some people with your level of openness. Experiment with announcing intent and inspect the results frequently.

Details

Jim and Michelle McCarthy, the creators of the Core Protocols and the authors of the book *Software for Your Head,* discuss how huge quantities of help are available from others who are aligned on your intentions and have proximity to you. [57]

When you announce your intentions, you are creating implicit space for others to either help you, do nothing, or block you (blocking is covered below in a later section). When everyone is announcing their plans and intentions, what is being shared is essential information about the work. Self-organizing systems are *information-bonded,* meaning that information is the glue that holds them together. Announcing intention is a powerful way to influence what is going on inside your group.

According to Jamshid Gharajedaghi, author of the book *Systems Thinking, Managing Chaos, and Complexity*:

> There are fundamental differences between the nature of the bond in mechanical systems and the nature of the bonds in sociocultural systems . . . while the elements of a mechanical system are 'energy bonded', those of sociocultural systems are 'information bonded.'[58]

Social systems such as teams are ***systems*** precisely because the participants share information within them. Social systems are information-bonded. Information is the glue that holds the self-organizing system together.

High communication frequency is associated with greatness in teams. By broadcasting information about your plans, you invite others

---

57 Jim and Michelle McCarthy, *Software For Your Head*, p. 253.

58 Jamshid Gharajedaghi, Systems Thinking: Managing Chaos and Complexity. (2nd ed.). p. 83.

to help you as you increase the level of available and important information in the wider social system. This act encourages and supports more tribal learning, especially if you have some positional authority in the organization.

Figure 14. Concentric Rings of Social System Membership

Jim and Michele McCarthy say this about asking for help when working in teams: "Being great means not accepting the old way of doing things. Being great requires that you intentionally change your behavior after thinking about the ideal way to behave, and then following through with courage."[59]

Leaders, particularly those with positional authority, can become better leaders by experimenting with this. Followers are constantly paying attention to leaders with positional authority. Followers ascribe meaning to even the most random behaviors.[60]

---

59 Jim and Michelle McCarthy, *Software For Your Head*, p. 253

60 signaling by leaders is covered in Part1, see ***Psychological Safety***

When leaders do not announce intentions, the followers often make guesses about what the leader wants, leading to all sorts of waste. Art Kleiner covers this dynamic in some detail in his book, *Who Really Matters,* where he devotes an entire chapter to guesswork, describing how followers want to help leaders. When leaders send either no signals or unclear signals, the followers often engage in guessing.

Organizational theorist Charles Hampden-Turner calls this kind of phenomenon ***amplification***. When you are a Core Group member, a process takes place in which your remarks appear amplified; people hear your statements louder, stronger, and more command-like than they seemed to you when you uttered them. Casually mention a product you'd like to develop someday, and discover, three weeks later, that someone spent a million dollars introducing it. Wrinkle your nose when talking to a new hire and discover, years later, that they have been systematically steered away from attending any more meetings with you. Why does this happen? Because nobody knows exactly what you want. They assume it part of their job to guess. Even if you are that rare kind of boss who displays clear signs that you are eager to be asked for clarification, your subordinates with still tend to guess instead of ask. You would do the same.[61]

We have a name for leaders with positional authority who clearly announce intentions. We call them ***visionary***. The clearest example of a bold announcement of intent from a positional leader was when President John F. Kennedy declared the national goal, "to land a man on the moon and return him safely home before the decade is out."[62] This was a clear, unilateral statement of intent. Announcing intent makes following easy.

---

61 Art Kliener, Who Really Matters: The Core Group Theory of Power, Privilege, and Success, p. 75.

62 before a joint session of Congress in May of 1961, see http://history.nasa.gov/moondec.html

Challenges

Announcing intent in unsafe environments can cause anxiety as you realize that if you tell the truth about intentions, others may block your best efforts. Most corporate workplaces do not value openness and often punish it. Suck it up. Try announcing your intentions in low-risk situations, see what happens, and then inspect your results. Keep in mind that all interactions are games[63], and allow people to opt-in to help achieve your clear statement of intent – your clear goal.

When you announce intent, you set up attraction and repulsion. Some are attracted even as others are repulsed. One thing that happens when you announce intent and follow through is that the very act of announcing becomes part of the landscape. Those in proximity to you adjust, and many incorporate your announcement into their own plans, in effect helping you. In Scrum, during the Daily Scrum meeting, this is exactly what happens. Team members adjust to each other based on what they know to be your intentions for the day.

Steps and Options

Implementing this practice involves the following steps:

1. **Discuss It Openly**. You may choose to discuss the self-organizing power of announcing intent and the attraction and repulsion dynamics openly. By paying explicit attention to the dynamics of announcing intention at the level of group, you can get better results. In unsafe workplaces, where learning levels are low and sticking your neck out is risky, you can openly discuss these dynamics inside your own team. Doing so makes that smaller space safer and more conducive to higher levels of group-level learning. Discussing the communication technique of announcing intentions and then using this is a powerful cultural statement. That statement tends to support higher safety levels inside your group.

---

63 See “Game the Work” in Part One

2. **Announce Early and Often.** Use low-risk opportunities to state your intentions about everything. If you intend to work late, say so. Likewise, you can experiment with stating what you plan to do about lunch, what time you are coming in tomorrow, and what you plan to do tonight. Experimenting with broadcasting low-risk information can give you the experience you need to start really using this powerful technique. When you broadcast your intent to do something, it has great impact. You are asking for help and attracting others to your cause. The power of this technique is proven in Scrum and is always part of what smooth-running, self-organizing teams and groups are doing.

Takeaways: Announce Your Intentions

- All social groups are naturally self-organizing systems; the people in them naturally adjust, and re-adjust, to the actions of the other members.
- Everyone can influence how the system behaves by simply announcing intentions and following through. Over time your statement of intent becomes predictable and reliable as part of the environment; it becomes part of the picture.
- If you are a leader, start leveraging all the attention you are getting by knowing what you want and announcing it immediately.
- Social groups like teams and departments are information-bonded. The more information that is available, the smoother the group can function.
- Lots of information is associated with the feelings of safety that create the conditions for tribal learning. Make the space safer by providing as much information as possible about your current plans and intentions. Scrum points the way by mandating the Team members and the Product Owner to announce intentions explicitly.
- Your organization might not be safe and learning levels might be low. You do not need anyone's permission to start announcing

intentions as a habit. Experiment with announcing intent unilaterally and watch what happens.

- As soon as it makes sense, start discussing how this communication style helps the team by making essential information about the team widely available to itself. Pay explicit attention to changes in the way the team behaves after having these discussions, and work to accelerate increased levels of available information, safety, and learning.

Chapter 13 - Game Your Meetings

Meeting suck energy when attendance is not optional, when the goal and rules are fuzzy, and when there is no way to track progress. Make meetings fun, enjoyable, and engaging by *gaming* them. Use working agreements and roles to round out and give structure and clarity to your meeting. Game your meetings.

Overview

Meetings are a major source of waste. The waste comes from tolerating any behaviors that reduce focus, commitment, and engagement. Meeting can suck your energy when attendance is not optional, when the goal and rules are fuzzy, and when there is no way to gauge the progress of the meeting. Make meetings fun, enjoyable, and engaging by *gaming* them.

Use *working agreements* to round out and give structure and clarity to your set of rules in the meeting-game. In-advance agreement on what's ***normal*** in a meeting makes engagement easy. Establish clear boundaries and ***safe space*** in meetings via *working agreement*s. Use working agreements to raise overall levels of engagement, focus, commitment, and respect substantially.

History and Origins of the Practice

Working agreements are mentioned in the Agile book *Agile Retrospectives: Making Good Teams Great* from Esther Derby and Diana Larsen. This book mentions the establishment of Working Agreements as a good practice for every retrospective meeting. The retrospective is a required Scrum meeting. The worldwide Agile community now uses retrospectives as a standard practice. Working Agreements help define the clear set of rules that are part of any good game.

How This Helps

Establishing a clear goal, clear set of rules, and a clear way to receive feedback makes any game enjoyable. If the participation is optional and opt-in, all four essentials for a satisfying game exist. Meetings are games and by structuring them to be satisfying and enjoyable, more tribe-level learning can take place. This is because the four properties of a good game help create safe space for productive interactions around the objective for the meeting. When a meeting is set up as a good game, each participant can locate himself/herself within the flow of the game and enjoy the experience. This well-defined space creates the potential for high levels of engagement and learning.

Costs

Dollar costs are zero for acting on this step. Examining norms and actively gaming a meeting is a simple. First, pay attention. Notice how meetings that drain your energy are often missing a clear goal, a clear rule set, and clear way to track progress. Second, being willing as a group to make and keep some simple agreements raises the level of engagement at your meetings. The simple agreements (called *working agreements*) are part of the rule-set in your meeting. A meeting with clear rules is more fun and enjoyable because you can locate yourself inside "the story" of the meeting. You know the structure. This contributes to a *sense of control* on the part of all participants. A sense of control associates with happiness.

Results and Related Delays

Results are immediate when you implement working agreements for meetings. Participants typically report a clear sense of being located in the meeting, with feelings of focus and engagement.

Details

Meetings are usually opportunities for learning. Yet it seldom turns out that way. Typical meetings tend to be a low-engagement, energy-sucking waste of time. Low levels of engagement make meetings extremely counter-productive. What gives here?

Normal is something we all co-create. Creating in-advance agreements about what is normal– especially for meetings – helps create safe space and encourages more learning. Establishing the ground rules for meetings helps people feel comfortable.

Remember that work is a big game. A meeting at work is a smaller game but a game nonetheless. A meeting that is not opt-in and does not have a clear goal does not make for a good game. Likewise, fuzzy or missing definitions for the rules of the game do nothing to help people feel good about playing. Working agreements for meetings are in fact the clear 'rule set' that are part of every good game. That rule set contributes to safe space and encourages Tribal Learning.

Challenges

Meetings that are good games have a clear goal, a supporting agenda, clear rules, and a way to track progress. The first challenge as a convener is to state the objective or goal. Always do this. The second challenge is to describe and define the working agreements. If you are just starting out with this, state the start time, stop time, and goal when you send the invite out. Then, inside the meeting, go through the process of getting alignment on a minimal set of working agreements. If you are new at this, expect it to take up to 10 minutes. You want to encourage dialogue around this. For example, if someone needs the cell phone out to communicate with a child who is traveling to a school event, this is sure to generate discussions. Let these discussions flow.

The remaining challenge to game your meetings is the idea of opting-in. Who needs to be there? Who does not? How is this currently handled? If you explicitly examine your current culture in terms of meetings, you may find that this is actually very fuzzy and hard to pin down. Put a stake in the ground by clearly stating who is required to attend and who is optional. Ideally, you want to afford *everyone* the choice of attending or not. This creates a sense of control and generates more happiness. Now the people that are attending actually *want* to be there. What a concept!

Implementing an opt-in meeting requires you to ***examine what's normal.*** This can be painful and the end-result is much more learning.

After dialogue around the topic, people start to realize that they are unsure if they are required to attend meetings they are invited to. They start to realize that they attend every meeting and are not sure why. Participants who opt-in bring engagement to the meeting. They also enjoy a personal sense of control. Take a shot at communicating an opt-in policy for your meetings. Opt-in participation is an essential aspect of a good game (see Part 1 for more details on this concept.)

Working Agreements

Working agreements are exactly that- agreements. Establish working agreements by discussing the following when the meeting starts:

Core working agreements. Are there any previously established, core working agreements that we are not honoring? See below for a description of how to develop core working agreements. These are the default for each meeting with this group of people. Discuss any amendments.

Who must leave? Discuss who in the room must exit before the meeting is over.

Start and stop time. Explicitly state these times.

Cell phone usage. Use of cell phones during meetings reduces engagement. Discuss acceptable cell phone use during this meeting.

Use of laptops. Use of laptops during meetings dramatically reduces engagement. Discuss acceptable laptop use (if any) for this meeting.

Breaks. After 45 minutes, people tend to check out as focus drops. Give people a break of 7 to 12 minutes for every 45 to 50 minutes of sit-down meeting time.

Punctuality. Discuss the end-of-break boundary. Consider agreeing that the door closes when the break is over and by this, I mean the second the agreed-upon break is over.

One conversation. Try to establish the rule that when one person talks, everyone else listens. Discuss prohibiting side conversations and over-talking.

Anything else. Ask the group if there is anything else it makes sense for use to agree to before we start.

Write it down the understandings on a white board or flip chart paper on the wall. Make these agreements very visible.

Figure 15. Sample working Agreements for a meeting

Sample Working Agreement	**Rationale and Purpose**	**Notes**	**Type**
Defined start Time	Manage time boundaries, provide a known container for the work	This one is easy, dictated by room availability	situational
Defined break time and durations	Manage time boundaries, provide a known container for the work	Be mindful to loosen time boundaries somewhat when engaging in dialogue (vs. deciding).	situational
Defined End time	Manage time boundaries, provide a known container for the work	This one is easy, dictated by room availability	situational
Limits on Cell Phones	Increase engagement levels; each individual fully present	When people (and especially higher-ups) use a cell phone when others are speaking, the signal is very disrespectful	core
Limits on Laptops and other devices (iPad for example)	Increase engagement levels; each individual fully present	Same as above	core

One conversation rule . . . no side conversations, no over-talking	Practice respectful interactions; enhance team learning	This working agreement formalizes respectful interactions	core
Leaving the Meeting-protocol	Increase engagement levels; each individual fully present	Some people may have to leave. Open that discussion so they identify themselves and can leave gracefully	situational
Lunch break and duration	Manage time boundaries, provide a known container for the work	Time and duration of lunch create a formal post-lunch appointment to reconvene	situational
Purpose, agenda and roles explicitly stated	Provides clarity and allows each person to locate themselves in the meeting activity.	Facilitated meetings tend to make sure the purpose and agenda are clear	core

With these basic agreements in place, you have a chance at a good and engaging meeting.

Core Working Agreements

Core working agreements are agreements that are the default. Over many meetings, develop and establish the core agreements- the defaults. Put them on a poster and make sure they are always visible. New participants and new hires can align when the default agreements are mentioned and visible.

You end up generating Core working agreements after several meetings, in which you use the same basic agreement. For example, agreements about the use of cell phone and laptops might become part of the core set used at every meeting.

Situational Working Agreements

Agreements that ride on top of the core agreements are situational. These per-meeting agreements might cover things like the time lunch starts, how long the lunch break goes, the timing of breaks, and so on. Always be explicit about all the agreements and always put all of them on the wall were everyone can see and refer to them.

Cell Phones and Laptops

The use of cell phones and laptops reduce engagement at meetings. The usual complaint is that important emails about work might be received during the meeting. Give me a break. Most meetings are 1 hour or less. Even if this were true, how would you feel if I had my cell phone open or was typing on my laptop while you were speaking?

Perception is reality. If the cell phone or laptop is out and I am using it, I am not listening to you. This is associated with disrespect (even more so if I have more authority than you). Likewise, if my laptop or cell phone is out, I can be cruising the web. I might actually be taking notes on what you are saying. It doesn't matter! The perception on your part is that I might be cruising the web, checking email, etc. It makes you feel disrespected. This severely reduces *engagement*. If a few people start using laptops and cell phones, before long everyone is using them.

Define working agreements for cell phone and laptop use in meetings.

Breaks

Participants seated in a meeting need breaks approximately every 45 to 50 minutes. Agree on a schedule for breaks. When you do, the people will throttle their focus in conformance with the upcoming break. And always DO the break and do it on time. In the 1990s, I taught classes in software development. Often I would need to go a little bit longer, with a point to get it in before a break. At times, I noticed people fading as we got close to the break time. As a result, I would often say: "we are taking our break in 10 minutes. I have just two more important points to make about this topic. Please stay with me for just 10 minutes and we will be in good shape here."

When I signaled in this way, the students would perk up and pay attention as I completed the topic. But if I went even ONE MINUTE over, they would completely ***check-out***. The moral of the story is: Always define when the breaks take place, and always take them on time.

Regarding meetings after lunch: in my experience, people automatically glaze over after lunch. For this reason, try to arrange for some kind of activities in the meeting between 1:00 and 2:30PM. Get people talking and moving around if possible. If this is not possible, consider shorter breaks that occur more frequently.

In general, if you are having marathon meetings, inspect that. Why is this needed? Why is this normal? Can we break this meeting up into two smaller meetings? Long meetings are drag. Game your meetings by making them short and adding clearly defined breaks for longer meetings, so people can pace themselves. Be mindful that people can easily check out and disengage after about 45-50 minutes. Provide a pause that refreshes.

Defining Roles

Consider defining roles for your meetings to help support your aims. One of your aims might be to socialize the Tribal Learning Practices.

A useful role for this is the Observer role. Defining this role is useful for socializing what you are doing with the Tribal Learning Practices. You can invite people who express interest in learning more and they attend as Observers. (This technique comes directly from the Scrum framework. In Scrum, the Daily Scrum meeting has an Observer role. Observers who attend are silent and do not speak during the meeting.)

Defining a role includes describing boundaries on behavior and specifically describing what the role is authorized to do. A good definition for the Observer role might go like this:

- The Observer must arrive before the meeting starts.
- The Observer must sit as close to the door as possible.
- The Observer must not speak during the meeting.

Defining a role like this is actually an expression of the Tribal Learning practice {Manage Your Boundaries}. With this role in place, you have created a structured way for those who are interested to learn more about what is happening inside your meetings.

Steps and Options

Implementing this practice involves the following steps:

1. **Describe participation as optional**. Make it plain who is mandatory and who is optional for meeting attendance. Ideally, the meeting is opt-in for all participants and mandatory for the meeting convener. This structure ensures that only the people who are motivated are present. This increases a sense of control in participants and contributes to high engagement levels overall. Try to make attendance opt-in for everyone.
2. **Name the objectives for the meeting**. Describe the objective for the meeting in the simplest and clearest terms possible. Never convene a meeting without naming the objective. The stated objective or goal constitutes a big part of the decision criteria for potential attendees. If you do not name the goal, expect lower levels of engagement. Increase levels of engagement substantially by clearly stating the meeting goals up front.
3. **Be clear about rules regarding behavior inside the meeting**. Be specific. State the working agreements up front. Do not be vague about the working agreements. Hold people to these opt-in agreements when they are in the meeting.

4. **Provide feedback on how the meeting is progressing**. During the meeting, state the progress on the agenda as it unfolds. A good idea is to create a visual artifact that displays progress. This can be a Task Board[64] or a set of agenda items with empty check boxes. Place the poster on the wall and check off the agenda items as they are completed. (You can use Post-It® flip charts that stick to the wall). Never leave attendees in limbo. Make it so anyone coming in at any time can figure out the status of the meeting in terms of reaching the stated goal.

Takeaways: Game Your Meetings

- Meetings are games. Poorly constructed games are mandatory to play, and have fuzzy objectives, fuzzy rules, and no clear way to keep score. Stop that, and game your meetings by paying attention to good-game dynamics. Make meetings opt-in, and have a clear goal and a clear set of rules. During the meetings, use a visual display like a task board or a list of agenda items, and move items across columns, or check them off. Make sure participants have a sense of progress. Create some kind of visual artifact that shows "the score".
- Opting-in associates with a sense of control and higher levels of engagement. Try to figure out how to make it so everyone who attends actually is deciding to be there. Allowing them to opt-out is essential.
- A good meeting is a good game. Good games have clear rules. Establish a set of working agreements that everyone agrees make sense. Be careful when establishing these per-meeting agreements to allow everyone to say what they think. The act of doing this creates safe space and high engagement.
- Factor per-meeting working agreements into a set of basic, core agreements that apply for most meetings.

64 see the chapter "Manage Visually"

- Make sure the per-meeting and core agreements are always visible at each meeting. By this, I mean on the wall or the white board. Seeing is believing. Expect to remind people of what they have committed to. Having the commitments up on the wall is one very easy way to do this.
- Consider defining an Observer role for your meetings and be mindful to define a short set of rules for that role. People can opt-in as Observers, subject to the rules for the role.

Chapter 14 - Conduct Frequent Experiments

Overview

Frequent experimentation means frequent learning. Make learning a game by scheduling frequent and cheap experiments. Failing cheap means learning cheap. Fail frequently, but never start an experiment until you know exactly how much it costs to obtain that learning.

Failing early and cheap is a virtue; failing expensive and late is a crime. Experiment as frequently and as cheaply possible. Fail fast.

History and Origins of the Practice

The slogan 'fail fast' has been around as long as Agile itself. Like so many Agile principles, frequent experimentation is rooted in entrepreneurship. Failing quick and cheap is natural to leaders of start-ups and entrepreneurial businesses.[65]

How This Helps

Experimentation is not a natural behavior for mid-sized and large businesses. This is certainly a factor in low learning levels. Mistakes are a source of raw material for group learning. Failed experiments create a rich new source of learning material. Getting playful about thinking in terms of low-cost experiments leads to all kinds of tests and develops an ***I don't know, let's see*** kind of attitude. The whole point of testing things out is to learn.

Rob Richman is the leader of Zappos Insights, the outreaching arm of Zappos that teaches organizations how to develop a strong company culture. He says that great experiments are all about learning. “We are very tolerant of experimentation at Zappos Insights, provided that

---

65 For an excellent article on this, take a look at: “Fail Fast, Fail Cheap: Get your idea into the marketplace, and learn from customers,” found at BusinessWeek: http://www.businessweek.com/magazine/content/07_26/b4040436.htm

somebody learns - that's the biggest thing that we want to make sure happens. If somebody doesn't learn, then it was a waste."

Experiments are the ultimate single-player game. You are opting in. You are defining a clear goal. You are establishing clear rules. And you are setting up in advance a way of receiving feedback on progress on status.

Costs

Experiments can be expensive when they fail. The key is: for any experiment, it is natural to take a shot at making a prediction about the result. Always calculate the cost of the experiment - *the cost of finding out* if your theory or prediction is *wrong*. Avoid expensive experiments in general.

Once you start thinking this way, the game gets interesting. For example, an experiment with a high absolute dollar cost that has a 50-50 chance of returning 100 times the investment is usually an experiment very much worth funding. The ***expected value*** of an experiment with a 50% chance of returning 100 times the cost is insanely positive.[66] The absolute dollar cost of the experiment and the size of the cash and non-cash payoffs relative to the cost both play essential roles in the decision to proceed.

Rob Richman of Zappos says that Zappos deliberately hires people who like to be adventurous, in part to develop a culture of curiosity. "We hire according to core values, and one that brings them in is {Be Adventurous, Creative, and Open-Minded}. That attracts a kind of entrepreneurial type of mindset into the company. People can then ask "what if we did this?" And our managers are trained to say, okay, how can we do this small? How can we test this out?"[67]

---

66 Think of expected value as the long-run average of the results of many independent repetitions of an experiment.

67 See APPENDIX B: Frequent Experiments at Zappos Insights

Rob Richman of Zappos Insights on Conducting Frequent Experiments

Rob Richman of Zappos Insights shares much more of his thinking on experimentation in his exclusive interview, located inside the Appendix. Flip to the back of the book to learn more about how Rob encourages and manages experimentation inside Zappos Insights. Is Zappos just one big experiment? Go and see.

In general, avoid high-dollar-cost experiments and seek to explore opportunities to conduct numerous, cheap experiments frequently. Always look for the potential to generate learning.

Results and Related Delays

Experiments that provide an immediate set of results (where you know up or down if the thing succeeds or fails) are attractive. Delays in results are generally zero for this type of test. In general, avoid experiments that do not provide an immediate way to measure results.

Details

In general, experimentation encourages a playful attitude, and a playful attitude encourages more experiments. Work is more like play when you are watching and waiting to see what happens. When you get results that do not match your idea of what ***should*** have happened, you will experience surprise. ***Surprise*** is when you get something you did not expect, and that is when you actually learn something. That is when you say ***WOW***.

Experiments that confirm our model of how things work are actually quite common. We ask questions to *confirm the model we currently hold, not to learn something new*. We want confirmation our model is still good. And we test for that. When is the last time you asked a question that, if answered in a surprising way, would challenge some of your most basic assumptions? Most people do not ask questions like this, because they are dangerous. The answer might require you to rethink *everything*. Instead, we usually ask questions that might affirm what we already know. Avoid this pattern and instead, ask questions, and conduct cheap experiments that might cause you to rethink everything.

Invitations Are Experimental Tests of Willingness

All experiments are tests. Sometimes, a good test is a test of willingness. We do not often refer to an invitation as a *willingness test*, yet that is exactly what it is. Open Space (see the Tribal Learning Practice {Open the Space} inside Part Two) features an invitation. It is a test of willingness. If people *must* go to the meeting, they may not be willing. If they are invited and attendance is truly optional, we know they really want to be there if they attend.

One might argue that frequent tests for willingness are manipulative. Nothing could be further from the truth. An invite is as respectful as it gets. If I want you there no matter what, I might attempt to manipulate, coerce, and control you. Ed Seykota calls this the *control-centric model*. But if I am respectful, I invite you and see what you signal next. Testing for willingness is very respectful precisely because it allows you to opt-in or opt-out. Either way, I am being respectful of you. Ed Seykota calls this the *intimacy-centric model*.[68]

In summary, we can think of an invitation as an experiment. It is a special kind of test, a test of the willingness of another person to respond positively to your invite.[69]

---

68 Ed Seykota is the creator of the Trading Tribe process, a set of tools for personal growth. Terms include the control-centric and intimacy-centric models. Learn more about the Trading Tribe at http://seykota.com/tribe/TT_Process/index.htm

69 Special thanks to Ed Seykota for teaching the willingness-test concept since 2003

Challenges

The main challenges to conducting frequent experiments are twofold and related. First, if your company culture says it is normal to point fingers and engage in blame, you can expect levels of experimentation to be very low. No one wants to commit career suicide, so why would they stick their neck out? A blame-game culture kills any kind of playful experimentation.

Second, you must be authorized to do the experiments that cost something. If the authority figures in your company are not doing experiments themselves, they are sending a signal that you probably do not want to be doing any either. As a manager, you must socialize the ***fail cheap, fail fast*** mentality by modeling the behavior.

The main challenge is one of safety. Leaders can encourage small tests and discourage blame. Rob Richman of Zappos says that failed experiments are an opportunity to model encouragement. "It is never coming from an accusing place of ***You failed. Why didn't you do this***?' It's always a ***we're in this together*** type of mindset, and that creates so much more safety and positivity in the group . . . we believe the upside of it is that people are free to innovate a lot more here than they otherwise would."[70]

Steps and Options

Implementing this practice involves the following steps:

1. **Discuss** the purpose of experiments.
2. **Teach** your people that you value cheap, quick experiments that deliver lots of learning, and that expensive, long experiments that yield little or no learning are evil. (Well, maybe not evil, but not good. Avoid.)
3. **Do experiments yourself,** and explain to your people exactly what you are doing. In other words, {Announce Your Intentions}.

---

70 See APPENDIX B: Frequent Experiments at Zappos Insights

4. **Model the opposite of blame when experiments fail**. Instead, harvest the learning.
5. **Socialize the Wins**. Tell others in other groups what you are doing, formally and informally. Celebrate the learning that comes from conducting frequent experiments.

Takeaways: Conduct Frequent Experiments

- Experimentation is a playful game to test your theory. Frame it that way.
- Be mindful of the cost to find out if your theory is wrong. Avoid experiments that come with a high price tag.
- Safety to fail (cheap) is something you have control over as an authorized manager. Create safe space by always valuing the learning that is generated from experimentation.

Chapter 15 - Manage Visually

Overview

Visual management is the management of attention using visual artifacts. Depicting essential work information on the walls of the workplace using posters and charts helps manage and focus attention. The use of visual artifacts radiates information and alters the atmosphere of physical spaces. These artifacts influence the thoughts, feelings, and perception of people occupying the space in which they appear.

Seeing is believing. Stop sending email and instead start displaying rich information on your workplace walls. Depict the work in charts and diagrams. Radiate information about the work visually to become collectively great.

History and Origins of the Practice

Visual management is nothing new. Kindergarten and elementary school teachers have been using the technique for over 50 years. By festooning walls with large and colorful pictures, diagrams, and posters, they draw attention to the information. You can manage focus more easily by depicting rich, colorful information on the walls of classrooms and workspaces.

Alistair Cockburn coined the now-standard Agile term ***information radiation*** as described in his book *Agile Software Development.*[71] Agile and XP development teams use large, visible charts, diagrams, and posters to depict essential information about the project and progress to date. Jeff Sutherland, a co-formulator of Scrum with Ken Schwaber, advocates the use of rows-and-columns task boards for depicting work and workflow in Scrum. More recently, software development teams have been using more sophisticated Kanban boards to manage work and

---

71 Cockburn, Alistair. Agile Software Development: The Cooperative Game, 2006.

Inattentional Blindness
The Inattentional Blindness (IB) concept is an important one. Because creative work on complex products like software is a cognitive act, understanding cognition is critical to designing and using practices that enhance the ability of the group to collectively recognize important facts and then learn, think, and act. The Tribal Learning Practices as a group tend to thwart IB effects and visual management is one of the more important practices in this respect.

work flow visually. Kanban boards take task boards to the next level, by defining work item types, classes of service, and work-in-process-limits.

Authors Arien Mack and Irvin Rock in their book *Inattentional Blindness* assert that there is no conscious perception without conscious attention. The book describes the phenomenon of *Inattentional blindness*, in which available visual information is ignored when you are explicitly focusing on and expecting something else. The research of these authors supports the notion that visual management using visual artifacts is an important aspect of managing cognition.

How This Helps

Visible charts and diagrams that depict and radiate information encourage focus and attention on the information. Focus on the work is more likely with the introduction of visual information about the work.

Cognitive Psychology research has identified Inattentional Blindness (IB)[72] as a real problem for people who want to learn. IB research indicates that people do not build any conscious perception of information to which they do not pay conscious attention. You need to pay attention in a conscious manner in order to obtain conscious perception and learning. What you pay attention to matters.

---

72 Mack, Arien, and Rock, Irvin. Inattentional Blindess. 1998.

Visual artifacts on the walls attract attention and get noticed; People in the room examine them, especially when periodic updating of artifacts that depict progress takes place. People learn according to what they pay attention to. By placing big, visual artifacts on workspace and meeting room walls, you leverage the power of IB dynamics. To pay attention is to build perception. Focus attention on the work with visual artifacts to guard against the phenomenon of Inattentional Blindness.

Visual depiction of work status helps to provide a ***sense of progress***, which is an essential ingredient in the basic recipe of human happiness (the four basic ingredients being a sense of control, a sense of progress, a sense of belonging, and a sense of higher purpose.)

Figure 16. Task Board

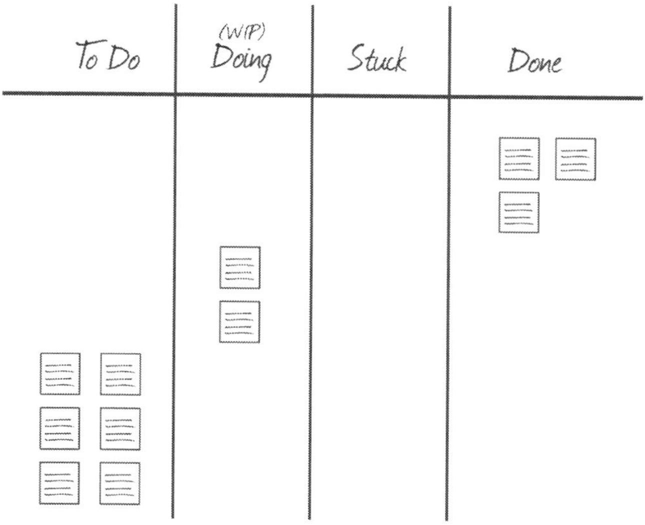

To Do	(WIP) Doing	Stuck	Done

Basic task boards and more elaborate Kanban boards are especially useful beyond their ability to generate a sense of progress. These rows-and-columns artifacts help develop a sense of a shared mental model about the work and work flow.

A ***shared mental model*** helps teams get agreement about the nature and structure of work. Shared mental models are an essential ingredient of group learning. Visual task boards and Kanban boards are in fact depictions of commonly held assumptions about the work and workflow. Inside Agile software development teams, it is common to stand in front of board to discuss the work and work flow, while pointing to specific cards on the board, moving them, annotating them, etc. as the discussion unfolds. As people update the board, they also update and elaborate on shared understandings.

Task and Kanban boards are the most powerful of the Visual Management tools precisely because they encourage and help develop shared mental models of the work and workflow.

Costs

Dollar costs are close to zero for acting on this step. Most offices have flip charts, stick notes, markers and so on. You can obtain these materials from current inventory in the supply closet. An excellent book on this subject that can provide you with many ideas is the book *Visual Meetings* by David Sibbet. I advise purchasing this book. Another excellent book with details the use of Kanban boards is the book *Kanban* by David J. Anderson. I advise purchasing this book as well.

Results and Related Delays

Results are nearly immediate when you implement Visual Management in the main workspace and in meetings. Visual Management helps maintain collective focus on the work. Discussions tend to drift away from non-work topic and towards work-related topics when large charts, diagrams, and task boards are visible in the space. As an experiment, I once took a position as a developer on a non-Agile software team for a short time. Everyone sat in cubicles and communication frequency was very low. The culture's unwritten rules include a rule that allowed a great deal of freedom to place information cube walls. I chose to radiate information about work and work progress by depicting the information on a rows-and-columns grid that illustrated the status of more than 30 work items. Each was a software module. Each item could be in one of about 10 positions in the workflow.

Because of radiating this information, several interesting patterns emerged:

- People I did not know stopped and looked as they walked by, often stopping to ask about the rich information depicted on the board.
- Authority figures on the project thanked me for depicting work status in this way. They told me they appreciated how I kept it current and that they came by to refer to it periodically. They told me that they had access to information about my work even when I was not in the cubicle.
- Casual visits to the cubicle workspace by team members often included conversations about non-work topics. But now with this large white board depicting a rich set of work-status information, a funny thing happened: discussion invariably drifted to a discussion about the work depicted inside the rows-and-columns on the white board.
- One team member, upon seeing the white board for the first time exclaimed, "Wow! This makes you look good." (The team member was a consultant).

You may find you get similar results when you begin leveraging visual management techniques in your work place.

Details

Seeing is believing. Visual artifacts on the wall change the space, like any decoration. The visual artifacts on the walls have a practical aspect and a symbolic aspect. There is a discussion of practical aspects above. The symbolic aspect works like this: what is on the walls is a *signal* of what is valued and what is important. When you enter someone's home, you notice the decorations including pictures in frames. Examining these pictures is useful for gaining an understanding of the people living there. By depicting specific work information on visual artifacts and placing these artifacts on the wall, the people occupying the space are receiving a signal of what is valued and what is important.

Possible visual artifacts you may choose to use may include:

- **Story Boards** - depictions of the flow of a process, a piece of work, or a related story.
- **User Story Maps** - depictions of the structure of a product, including features, how to use them, and in what order.
- **Personas** - Personas are depictions of typical or target users of the service or product being created. A persona is a depiction of a specific user, with a descriptive name. For a product like an internet-connected cell phone, related user persona types might include Matt, the music listener, Theresa the text messenger, etc.
- **Lists** - Lists of work, list of obstacles to the work, and lists of things to do are all candidates to display in a public way on the walls of work places.
- **Status Indicators** - Status indicators depict progress. ***Moving the needle*** visually can signal rich information about workflow or the lack of it. In a meeting, simply depicting the agenda and checking off the items are they are completed provide a sense of progress. Scrum Burn-Down charts (depicting the work that remains uncompleted in an iteration) also visualize the progress of the team.
- **Charts** - Charts such as Scrum Burn-down charts[73] depict work remaining and are status indicators. You can use other types of charts to depict complex concepts, to explain to outsiders what is going with the work, and provide a focal point for conversation about the work.
- **Task and Kanban boards** - These artifacts depict the flow of work and include a rich set of information on who is doing what, the status of that work, and information as to various status levels. These artifacts are useful for constructing a visual and shared mental model of the work and workflow.

---

73 The Burn-Down Chart is a Scrum artifact that depicts work remaining. The Scrum Guide from Scrum.Org is the definitive Scrum document. Get it here: http://www.scrum.org/scrumguides/

For visual items that depict status, be sure to keep information fresh and up-to-date. A stale depiction of status sends the wrong signal.

Challenges

The challenges here are almost nonexistent. It takes *time* to develop visual artifacts and a certain kind of *determination* to follow through and place them on the wall. As always, explaining the background story of the use of visual artifacts is useful for all participants during meetings. For workspaces, it is especially important to make sure everyone is on board with posters and other visual artifacts (like task). Agile teams often work in one large, shared space. A shared space makes it easy to use Visual Management tools like large, visible charts.

Steps and Options

Implementing this practice involves the following steps:

1. **Gather Supplies**. Get Sharpies, Post-It Notes, and Post-It Flip charts for conveying information visually.
2. **Socialize the Idea**. Incorporating visual artifacts in workspaces needs to be socialized. Scrum prescribes the use of a visible Burn-down chart, so opting-in to Scrum means displaying this chart in a visible way. Teams correctly expect to have authority over their workspace. Make sure everyone agrees to changes such as placing additional visual artifacts on workspace walls.
3. **Deploy Visual Management in Work Areas.** Develop a set of posters and deploy them, updating as needed.
4. **Utilize Visual Management in Meetings.** Visual Management is a critical success factor for successful meetings. Look at the book Visual Meetings from David Sibbet for guidance and ideas on using visual artifacts successfully in typical meetings.
5. **Inspect the Results.** Take note of results of incorporating the heavy use of visual artifacts in your meetings. Pay attention to levels of engagement, where attention is focused, and alignment

of the practice with your wider intentions to increase engagement and learning.

6. **Always Depict Progress Visually.** A visual artifact that depicts progress is an important artifact. It provides a sense of progress that is essential. In meetings, always depict the status of agenda items. When they are done, place a check mark next to them, to depict the visual status of the stated agenda items remaining.
7. **Be open to incorporating the most recent thinking**. Cognitive psychology is providing more and more details on the mechanics of cognition and perception. Pay attention to advances in the cognitive sciences.

Takeaways: Manage Visually

- Visual artifacts focus attention and thwart Inattentional Blindness dynamic
- Visual artifacts such as task boards and Kanban boards help build a shared mental model of the work.
- Visual artifacts that depict the status of work items contribute to a sense of progress
- Always make sure the people that work in the space authorize the use of visual artifacts.
- Placement of these artifacts by an authority figure in a team workspace sends the signal that what team wants does not matter. This reduces respect levels and thwarts the intention of encouraging more group learning. Always discuss changes, and provide the background rationale for any proposed changes.

Chapter 16 - Inspect Frequently

Overview

Inspection creates opportunity for observation, reflection, tuning, and adjustment. Frequent reflection and adjustment is essential for making sense of complicated and complex work. Iteration helps us make sense of complexity. Leverage the power of iteration to engage in sense making. Create opportunities to adapt by creating frequent points of inspection.

History and Origins of the Practice

Entrepreneurs have been engaging in iterative work for hundreds and hundreds of years. Working within small fixed intervals of experience and then inspecting them is an essential practice when starting a business. Especially when assumptions prove incorrect, iteration and frequent inspection can pull your fat out of the fire.

The iterative, incremental approach is an essential aspect of the Scrum framework. In Scrum, the iteration is known as a Sprint. A Sprint has a known starting point and a fixed duration. This creates a known end point.

Retrospectives provide an opportunity for inspection. Retrospectives are a core Agile practice and a core ceremony (meeting) prescribed in the Scrum framework.

How This Helps

Iterations are small experiments about which you have a good understanding of both the commitment size and cost to execute the experiment. Things we consider complex are usually new to us. Gaining some experience builds some understanding. Iteration creates a structure that contains the work in a ***time box*** or time-valued container. We know what the work is, when the work starts, when it stops. This approach of ***filling the iteration with work*** creates containment. This containment helps us make sense of complex work. The more complex the work is, the more the iteration is helpful.

An iteration is a time-based container. Name the container (iteration 1, iteration 2 and so on) and deal with it as a unit. This creates a convenient inspection point after each iteration.

Frequent iterations using fixed-length time intervals lead to the definition of known, predictable, scheduled inspection points. These inspection points provide the potential to engage in a rational, measured, explicit, group-level examination of the experience just past. (The retrospective is what we call this explicit examination in the Scrum framework.) Formal retrospectives provide an opportunity to reflect and discuss what is working, what is not working, and what we might want to change going forward in terms of approach and especially assumptions. Iterations of a fixed length of time create regular, predictable inspection points. These inspection points create a predictable opportunity to reflect on experience and adapt.

Costs

Dollar costs are zero for acting on this step. There are some non-dollar costs when you get the execution wrong. The details work like this: When you do work on an iterative basis, you create inspection points. When you work, others naturally want to see what you have created. The end of the iteration is the natural place to schedule this. Typically, there is a review (called a Sprint Review in Scrum) where the work is inspected. You may or may not schedule a meeting to inspect work.

People who are stakeholders come to enjoy the predictability and reliability of these periodic inspection points. Here is where it gets interesting: when you miss an inspection point, it costs you something. It costs you *trust*. The cost of not doing this practice right is the *trust* you lose when your previous predictability and reliability becomes suspect. You do not work in isolation; your group's work has implications for others. When you work iteratively, you create a cadence or tempo – a drumbeat. People start aligning their work and attention around your cadence, your drumbeat. When you miss a beat, it makes them unhappy.

Trust is a strong currency inside teams and work groups. You do not want to lose it. When you work iteratively, you need to remember two rules:

1. Always work from a fixed length of time
2. Never miss an inspection point

When you miss an inspection point, the people who previously relied on your timing and tempo feel unhappy. This is because your cadence and regular timing provides a sense of control and a sense of progress. The people doing the work and the people observing and inspecting the work gain a sense of control from the predictability. They also gain a sense of progress when you demonstrate completed work.

Now you can appreciate the high cost of missing an inspection point. The cost is a double-barrel cost: everyone involved loses the sense of control and sense of progress that was so satisfying and enjoyable. This makes everyone involved unhappy.

So, a cost of doing this practice is *doing it well.* If you do not stay sensitive to the dynamics of predictability, reliability, and trust, you may quickly find you are worse off, not better.

Results and Related Delays

Frequent inspection at first is difficult. It is painful. In theory, we are inspecting and adapting. In truth, inspection is hard...and adaptation is harder. We do not want to face the problems that are in our way. Often the organization has baked-in impediments to progress that are difficult to remove. The ability to remove them is beyond our authority or capacity to act. This realization is experienced as a loss of control and a loss of progress. The result is unhappiness.

Peter Senge calls this ***creative tension.***[74] It is the tension created in us when we know how good it can be, yet here we are in the here-and-

---

74 The Fifth Discipline, p. 132

now dealing with things as they are. Holding that tension- holding on to the vision- is an important discipline.

Frequent inspection has a way of growing on you when you experience it in groups. We examine what is holding us back, and we find some comfort in the fact that others are feeling what we are feeling. Little by little, it becomes OK to ***confront the brutal facts.*** And when that becomes the new normal, great thing happen.

One great thing that happens is the group starts aiming at things that they do have the authority and capacity to change. The group stops focusing about what it *can't* do, and start zooming in on what it *can* do. This is a big turning point.

The typical delay in getting there is about 3 to 5 iterations. It all depends on your context. Your context includes the organization's size, the ambient culture, and you willingness to act.

Details

Consider inspecting work every Friday afternoon. This is a good time because people are cycling down for the weekend and generally working at a lower intensity. This is a good time to inspect the work. You might choose iterations of 1 or 2 weeks, depending on your planning horizon, the nature of the work, your collective ability to focus and so on.

Inspecting frequently lends itself to a formal iterative approach and a related follow-up retrospective. During the retrospective, we ask three questions:

1. What's working well?
2. What is not working well? (these are pain points)
3. What can we change and what do we want to change now?

The retrospective is usually a facilitated meeting. When you {Inspect Frequently}, you end up {Paying Explicit Attention}, {Examining Your

Norms}, and {Managing Your Boundaries}. By inspecting frequently, you are engineering learning moments and opportunities.

Challenges

You might be used to ***unbounded work***. By this, I mean work that just keeps going. You might inspect its status frequently, but since it is not complete, there is not much to learning from it because there is nothing to show. What you are inspecting is not meaningful. Inspecting frequently requires iteration, if that inspection is going to be meaningful.

Say you set up one-week iterations. You pull your people together. You discuss the work, and discuss what your team believes it can accomplish in one week. Your team pulls some work into the iteration. Now, off they go. They execute on a commitment.

This is scary. You have bounded and contained the commitment. Some people do not like being accountable and so you get pushback. This is your first challenge. The way out of this one is to make sure everyone opts-in.

If you assign work, that means you have the authority and they have the responsibility. This is not a good idea. What you want instead is for the authority and responsibility for a piece of work to reside with the same people- *the people who do the work.* Don't assign the work; instead ask them to commit to as much as they can.

Another challenge is the inspection itself. How would I like it if you showed up and inspected my all of my work in one week? It depends, right? If we have a solid and agreed-upon definition of what done means, this definition can be very helpful to me. I know when I can declare victory on the work, because we have this shared definition of what constitutes done. Now I am OK with you inspecting my work. Always have a good and clear definition of done.

Steps and Options

Implementing this practice involves the following steps:

1. **Describe participation as optional.** Describe the whole thing as an experiment. Let everyone know we are trying something new to see how it works and how we like it.
2. **Define an iteration length**. Inspection follows. Choose an iteration length that makes sense for the kind of work you do. Do not define an iteration length longer than 4 weeks.
3. **Set up a list of work items you want to do in a spreadsheet**.
4. **Prioritize the list.**
5. **Discuss these things with your team.** Discuss what DONE means for each item.
6. **Ask your people to opt-in** to the iteration idea by asking them to select as much work as they think they can complete in one iteration. Ask them to select only high-priority items from the top of the spreadsheet.
7. **Set up some visual management**, like a task board that depicts flow of work.
8. **Complete a time-boxed iteration**. The work stops when the time is up.
9. **Inspect the results**. Convene a meeting to inspect the work. Keep in mind that you are going to be referring to the DONE definitions for each item as you inspect the results of the iteration.
10. **Do a formal retrospective.** Pull the people together to answer the three questions: What is working? What is not? What do we want to change?
11. **Repeat steps 3 through 10 at every iteration**.

Takeaways: Inspect Frequently

- Frequent inspection typically requires an iterative approach.
- Frequent inspection leads to more frequent discussion, about things that matter.
- Make sure you do not assign work to people. Make sure they are the ones that are specifying how much work can be done by when. If you mandate an iterative approach and you also assign

Iterative Work and Inspecting Frequently

This chapter is describing some of the core practices of Agile software teams. Iteration, frequent inspection, a formal retrospective discussion – these are all part of Agile. The predominantly used Agile framework is Scrum. Scrum is described in the Appendix. Go and look at it. Also, look at the Scrum Guide found at scrum.org. You do not need to know anything about software to understand Scrum and iterative work and frequent inspection. Knowing a little bit about Scrum is helpful for understanding the wider meaning of the Tribal Learning framework and practices. Go and learn a little bit about Scrum to get a good understanding of the practice of {Inspecting Frequently}.

the work and define a deadline, please do not be surprised when people feel resentful and ***check out*** on you.

- Iteration creates natural inspection opportunities. There is an opportunity to inspect the work at the end of each iteration. Iterations and frequent inspection go hand in hand.
- Formal retrospectives after inspecting work provide opportunities to learn.

Chapter 17 - Get Coached

NOTE: I am a coach to teams and organizations that are interested in the Agile-learning framework for software development. Increasingly, I coach executive teams on signaling and how to tune their organizations to respond to change rapidly. The Agile learning framework includes Scrum. Scrum has two influential roles that Agile coaches may choose to occupy, often to the detriment of the client. These roles are Product Owner and Scrum Master. (See the Appendix for an overview of Scrum.) This chapter refers to those roles in stories and illustrations. Please note this as you read along.

Overview

Coaching helps your organization by providing an external perspective concerning your organization. Engaging a coach implies that you are prepared to learn and receive guidance and advice. Organizations often go into a trance. Snap out of it with a coach, one who is there to serve your organization by literally staying out of it.

Get a coach – a watcher and an external observer – to help your organization cultivate more tribal learning. Actively solicit feedback and guidance from the coach, with the intent of achieving and sustaining collective greatness.

How This Helps

People in groups often daydream. For example, groups of people can quickly go into a kind of trance in meetings. Entire organizations can literally stop learning when this kind of thing becomes typical.

In my view, a coach can act as the active awareness of a team or group. There is a large body of research in the area of group psychology which strongly suggests that groups can start out very focused and quickly switch to a kind of unconscious state of being.[75] A coach can help your team or organization stay focused, and direct that focus towards behaviors and practices that can help you achieve collective greatness.

When you make a coach available to the people in your organization, you are helping them to become self-aware. They become aware of the specific tools and techniques for learning faster. Part mentor, part facilitator, part teacher, part problem-solver, part conflict-navigator, and part ***collaboration conductor***,[76] a coach can help your organization by facilitating your intentional journey towards a culture of continuous learning. A coach can help you become a genuine Learning Organization as described by Peter Senge in his book *The Fifth Discipline*.[77]

Costs

Coaching isn't cheap. The {Get Coached} and {Promote Specific Books} steps are the only activities listed in the Tribal Learning Practices which might cost you some money (the others do not cost a dime – all you need to do is commit to them).

The cost of NOT being coached is really the factor to consider when bringing in an Agile coach or executive coach. The best executives and their organizations consume a lot of coaching because they understand the very real value in avoiding wasteful organizational behavior that can have a huge cost. When viewed in this way, a highly skilled coaching

---

75 Group Relations theory of the group based on the work of Alfred Bion says that groups act in unconscious ways with some regularity. These unconscious group behaviors are often at odds with the stated aims of the organization. Paying explicit attention to boundaries on roles, task, and related authority can help. For more information on Group Relations theory, see: A.K. Rice Institute for the Study of Social Systems, found at: http://akriceinstitute.org/

76 Adkins, Lyssa. *Coaching Agile Teams*. 2010.

77 Senge, Peter. (1990). *The Fifth Discipline*. See page 175 for mention a mention of coaching.

professional can potentially save you millions in the course of just one year if your organization is large and relatively immature in terms of practicing organization-wide learning behaviors.

Coaching isn't cheap. However, mediocre results are much more expensive. Coaching has a very high return on investment if you structure the engagement to focus on specific areas of improvement for your organization.

How to Get Free Coaching

Free coaching is coaching that pays for itself. It is really quite simple to obtain free coaching. Here are the steps:

1. Measure your current results, before you find a coach. Use good metrics. Know what you measure, and how you are doing. For example, measure and collect the velocity of your teams.
2. Find a good coach for your teams.
3. Arrange the engagement to maximize learning.
4. Commit to the learning as a tribe.
5. Implement what you are learning, on the fly, with the help of your coach.
6. Measure your results after coaching, using the same metrics used to measure your results at the start.

Keep before-after metrics for group productivity, customer satisfaction, and employee turnover. Often you will find that the coaching provides a substantial return on investment if you find a good coach, if you actually do the things the coach advises, and if you engage in very deliberate before/after measurement.

Results and Related Delays

Coaching results can vary tremendously, and depend on what you intend to achieve from coaching, how you measure it, and the kind of ground rules you established for the coaching engagement. Some coaching outcomes are immediate, while others may have substantial delays. In the sections following, I discuss healthy ground rules for a coaching engagement. Your results and any related delays are a function of how you structure your relationship, how you select a coach, and what the coach is bringing to you in terms of experience, coaching education and skills.

Getting good results with coaching is largely a matter of organizational willingness. If your team is ready to receive coaching, the results may be nearly immediate. If, on the other hand, your organization is not open to coaching by an external consultant, the delay in results may be substantial. Coaching is a matter of fit. The organization is in a certain state of development, and the coach likewise is in a certain place in terms of skills, experience, and style. To get the right fit, discuss the right topics as described in this chapter.

Details

Coaching is a Profession

Coaching is an established profession with credentialing bodies. In the Agile community, the professional development of coaching is not as mature; the community is just now starting to formalize Agile coaching as a profession. Anyone can represent himself/herself as an Agile Coach, engage, and begin to interact with your leadership and teams. Meanwhile, organizations like the International Coaches Federation[78] and the Coaches Training Institute[79] have been actively promoting coaching as a genuine profession for years. These organizations offer training and credentialing for coaches.

Coaching is a Best Practice for Cultivating Personal Mastery

Having an Agile coach available for your teams also creates a new emphasis on personal mastery as described by Senge. A coach can coach the following people in your organization:

---

78 See http://coachfederation.org/

79 See http://www.thecoaches.com/

- Team members
- Teams
- Managers and Directors
- Executives

Having a coach to help your organization can also help individuals in your organization to become better at mastering personal challenges and developing new skills. To generate lots of tribal learning, a certain percentage of the people in the group must be life-long learners. A coach can help you to cultivate a higher level of personal mastery within your organization. This leads to more tribal learning.

Coaching Enables More Learning

As stated previously, coaches can help in many ways to bring learning to your organization. The main way that this happens is having the luxury of observation and a certain detachment. If the coach is careful to avoid any kind of authoritative role (formal or informal) in the organization, there is a much better chance of cultivating learning. The coach can bring difficult organizational and cultural issues to full attention, and challenge the individuals in the situation to step up and grow into new ways of working in psychologically safe space. The coach can also advise managers and executives in best practices, challenging them to send clear signals.[80]

The Coaching of Teams

Teams learn to generate much more team learning when coached. The coach can provide the following services:

1. **Introduction of games and role play** for teams to learn new skills

---

80 See "Announce Your Intentions" in Part Two

2. **Teaching interaction and meeting techniques** that get much better results, primarily by structuring interactions and meetings such that they are more enjoyable and generate more learning. As it turns out, all interactions and meetings are games. (See Part Two for more information on this)
3. **Observing interactions and team dynamics**, making specific recommendations on what to continue doing, what to avoid, and what to change.
4. **Challenging the team** to work at higher levels of intimacy and shared vision.
5. **Helping the team achieve shared vision** by teaching techniques such as Core Protocols, Nonviolent communication, and Grounded Visioning.[81]

Teams that receive coaching become more purposeful, as the coach helps them to incorporate all the Tribal Learning practices.

The Coaching of Executives

Coached executives are an essential piece of the tribal learning puzzle.

As discussed above, psychological safety can evaporate quickly. Everyone is aware of this below the level of conscious awareness. As a result people in a given tribe or group will continually ***poll*** or sample the space for levels of safety and respect. A typical pattern is to carefully observe the behavior of leaders and assign meaning to this behavior. People in organizations are very sensitive to *signaling* from executives in behavior, emails, and social interactions. People in organizations assign meaning to even small gestures and fleeting facial expressions of executive management. This creates a danger and an opportunity. The danger is that people assign meaning to random behavior and random signaling. The opportunity is that executives can leverage the constant

---

81 See "Structure Your Interactions" in Part Two

attention by being aware of this dynamic and then sending clear signals.[82]

Coaching of executives can help with the following tasks:

- Awareness of signaling
- Shaping culture via story dynamics and story generation
- Shaping culture via the use of highly interactive meeting formats

Executives literally hold culture in their hands and have more potential influence than any other group of people in terms of shaping culture. A skilled coach can assist executives in cultivating a culture of continuous improvement. This can have an immediate effect on the bottom-line results after a very brief delay.

The Coaching Deliverables- the Memo

One of the best things a coach can do for your organization is to draft a memo approximately every two weeks or every few visits. In the memo, the coach can list the following:

1. Observations on follow-through with respect to guidance from the last memo
2. Observations on the period just past, mapped to the goals and objectives of the organization with respect to tribal learning cultivation
3. Guidance on observed impediments to the learning and how to remove them in the near term
4. Recommendations of a longer-term nature, which anticipate learning development and increase its velocity

---

82 See "Psychological Safety" in Part One and the "Announce Your Intentions" practice in Part Two.

Challenges
The Role of Service in Coaching

In her excellent book, *Coaching Agile Teams*, Agile coach, and author Lyssa Adkins says, "Perhaps this book will set the aspiring Agile coach on a journey of enlightenment, where their motivation and intention is for the team, rather than for themselves." [83]

Coaches who genuinely serve the organizations they work for are the kinds of coaches who help these organizations learn much faster than their competition. To be this kind of coach, I believe it is important to establish two ground rules:

1. The coach is leaving after a reasonable period of time defined in advance of the engagement, and
2. The coach has no intention of assuming any formal or informal, *highly authorized* role(s) in the organization.

Coaching is a calling! Coaching is not cheap, and the income that can be derived from coaching attracts many people into it. Some of these people are not called to coaching. This can be the cause of many sorrows. While one can derive a good living from coaching, the primary motivation needs to be something more. The vast majority of coaches are sincere and well intentioned.

The Role of Authority in the Coaching Relationship

For Agile coaching, the typical engagement scenario includes a client that seeks specific advice and guidance on implementing Agile practices in their IT (information systems) organization. Typical organizations often want the coach to act as an ***authority figure*** in the coaching role. These organizations often want to be told what they ***should*** do. They are, after all, paying for expertise and want specific guidance. This is reasonable and advised. Or is it?

---

83 Adkins, Lyssa, *Coaching Agile Teams*, 2010, page xxii.

The coach's mission is to increase levels of learning and understanding. The coach typically receives compensation by the day or hour. The coach, as a consultant with creditors to pay, rationally seeks the greatest amount of billing possible. The difference in goals sets up a nearly automatic co-dependent relationship: The client organization wants to be ***told what to do*** by an authority, and the coach, essentially a highly paid consultant, seeks to generate billing. This is a huge problem for client and coach. The client wants to be dependent on an authority to come in and tell the client what to do. The coach is often very happy take up an authoritative role, perhaps within the organization itself. The aim is to become a more permanent fixture and thus generate a predictable stream of billing.

The way out of this problem is for the engagement to have clear ground rules and a fixed length, after which the engagement is over and the client and coach examine the experience.

Healthy Ground Rules

Here are some healthy ground rules for a coaching engagement:

1. The coaching role is a transitional one; the coach is not to take up authoritative roles inside the client organization.
2. During the engagement the coach is required to teach, mentor, guide, and transfer as much of his or her knowledge and skills as possible to everyone, at every opportunity.
3. The client organization is required to focus on learning as much as possible whenever the coach is present or otherwise interacting with the client organization. The client organization commits to actively receiving and integrating the teaching.
4. The engagement is of a fixed length that is long enough to get results yet short enough to create a sense of urgency in both the coach and the client concerning knowledge transfer and learning.

In my coaching, I always have this conversation with the client up front and describe the purpose of these ground rules. What is happening here is the introduction of a specific structure on the relationship in service to the client and in service to cultivating higher levels of group-level learning.

The structure above is designed to manifest the following outcomes:

1. Client independence from the coach
2. Free-standing, sustained, and continued learning inside the client organization, after the coach leaves
3. The cultivation of high levels of group-level learning in the organization through coaching, leading to more adaptation to changing business conditions
4. A taking up of the responsibility for learning on the part of the client organization
5. A fixed and known engagement length for the coach, specifically to keep the relationship at ***arm's length.*** A arms-length relationship is one where both parties are on an equal footing.

Without these ground rules in place, the outcomes may include:

1. Total dependency on the ***do it all*** coach – a coach does everything while occupying various roles and does not teach anyone how to operate in these roles effectively
2. Evaporation of any learning obtained after the coach leaves.
3. The taking up of authoritative roles in the organization by the coach, designed to induce and maintain more dependency
4. Abandoning of responsibility for learning on the part of the client organization
5. Extended-stay for the coach with higher revenues for the coach

Intentionally choosing to develop more tribal learning in your organization is a big decision. Bringing in a coach is a big part of your strategy. During the interview phase, be sure to discuss a fixed engagement length. More importantly, be sure to explore how the coach feels about taking up authoritative roles in your organization. You do not want an Agile coach in your organization that takes up (or creates) authoritative roles and holds them for a long time. The coach is supposed to *teach* these roles, not *occupy them indefinitely*. If the coach occupies important roles, no one is learning how to occupy them. Instead, the coach is increasing dependency and reducing learning. To increase tribal learning in your organization, get agreement to the ground rules listed above.

Often the client organization prefers the Agile coach to take up the influential Scrum roles of Product Owner and Scrum Master. The Agile coach is supposed to decline this offer, occupying these roles only briefly. The idea is to *model* how these roles work, rather than becoming a fixture in the organization.

The main thing about an arms-length agreement is the way the coach is encouraged to function as a teacher, provide an experience, and not hold anything back. Since the engagement is understood to end on a specific near-term date, the coach is encouraged to deliver a strong learning experience.

Clients often attempt to draft the coach into a position of directing, commanding, and controlling instead of steering, influencing, and guiding. If boundaries are fuzzy, the coach might allow himself to be drafted into this unproductive stance. When boundaries are clear, the coach has no incentive to take up this stance, since the engagement has a definite end and there is no possibility of extension in the current coaching role. This also favors the cultivation of tribal learning, by challenging the client to stretch and grow in various ways, rather than the coach occupying a position that might slow the learning. Keeping engagements short places the responsibility for learning directly on the client and the responsibility to teaching on the coach. This is healthy.

Coaches for teams, managers, and executives cost you something in time and money. What are you getting for your investment? That depends on how your structure the ground rules. If you do not engineer the rules to encourage lots of learning, your coach might actually cost you a great deal of money and produce absolutely no learning! Once the ***do it all*** coach leaves, your organization can (and will) quickly revert to the old way of being. This is because the ***coach*** took up various authoritative roles and held them. (In Agile coaching, the typical dysfunctional pattern is for the 'coach' to take up the Scrum Master and/or the Product Owner role for a very long time).

Structure the engagement to encourage the coach to impart as much knowledge as possible and for the organization to receive and integrate it as rapidly as possible.

Steps and Options

Implementing this practice involves the following steps:

1. **Educate yourself**. Learn about coaching and set your expectations.

2. **Know what you want**; know your metrics for the results you desire
3. **Interview several coaches** for fit and chemistry
4. **Be explicit** about ground rules
5. **Use a fixed engagement length with clear objectives**
6. **Inspect results** carefully

Takeaways: Get Coached

- The coach can see and hear things you cannot. The best organizations purchase a lot of coaching for this reason.
- Be careful to avoid drafting your coach into a position of authority. The coach is there to help you and your organization, not to tell you exactly what to do. Be responsible for your own learning.
- Coaches bill for their time, and like any other person who earns money this way, they must continue to bill for time to pay creditors. Acknowledge this by fixing the length of the engagement and establishing what is expected when the engagement ends.

- As part of what is delivered, ask for and receive written report that memorializes the observations and insights of your coach with respect to your organizational habits and culture.
- Use an iterative process to engage a coach. After each iteration, inspect the results and proceed accordingly.

Chapter 18 - Manage Your Boundaries

Overview

Be mindful of boundaries and use them to create structure and containment. Focus on boundaries expressed in time, as tasks and as physical territory. When facilitating work (including meetings) learn to loosen boundaries for inquiry and dialogue and to tighten boundaries when deciding and executing. Manage boundaries actively to create the kind of space your tribe needs to do every kind of work.

History and Origins of the Practice

The Agile practice of Scrum includes clear boundary management. A Sprint is bounded by time and is typically two weeks long. The Daily Scrum meeting is also bounded by time and is fifteen minutes maximum. Likewise, each the three Scrum roles are responsible for specific tasks. One and only one Scrum role is responsible for any specific task.

Each meeting in Scrum is facilitated. The Facilitator helps manage boundaries such as the start time, stop time, breaks, and agreed-upon agenda. Roles in all Scrum meetings are clearly defined. Scrum has a short set of clear rules, and it's the task of the Scrum Master role to make sure these rules are followed by everyone playing the Scrum game.

The three Scrum roles are also clearly bounded. Each role has a specific set of tasks it is both authorized to do and responsible for. This minimal but essential set of boundaries in Scrum create containment. Containment helps people ***become situated*** and ***know where they are***.

How This Helps

Fuzzy boundaries require constant negotiation. Clear boundaries do not. Agreed-upon boundaries create containment. Fuzzy boundaries tend to favor people who have negotiation skills. This can create an imbalance where those with less-developed negotiating skills are not as effective on the job.

Boundary rules are part of the clear rule set that is part of any good game. Boundaries create containment. Containment increases

Authorization

We often talk of permission or empowerment, but what we are really talking about is authorization, which is defined as ***the right to do work*** when used in this chapter. The authorization might come as a perquisite of occupying a role, or it might be granted by an individual. Either way, authorization has a source. It comes from somewhere, something, or someone. Formal authority comes with a role. Personal authority comes from inside you and informs how you take up a role. Some people overstep. Others actually ***under step*** and create problems when they cede or abandon the authority granted to them. Informal authority is the authority others grant you because of your education, reputation, or perceived presence.

For an excellent discussion of how to manage boundary, authority, role, and task, see The BART System of Group and Organizational Analysis, found at: akri.affiniscape.com/associations/8689/files/BART_Green_Molenkamp.pdf

predictability and reliability as people test and verify the boundaries and see that the containment is real. The lessons of Agile are clear. Iterations use time to create containment. The containment creates a sense of control and increases learning.

Costs

Boundary management does cost something. It is costly in terms of paying attention, examining what is a normal and structuring interactions. If you examine your meetings, for example, you may find that boundaries around these meetings are very fuzzy. People arrive late. Cell phones and laptops are out. People are talking over each other, and there are side conversations going on. In the absence of any boundary management, every behavior is normal. More importantly and to the point, without clear boundary management everything is a negotiation. When good boundary management is in play, all the energy consumed by negotiating is freed up and can be focused on the work.

Example:
Boundaries at Zappos

Zappos actively encourages all employees to demonstrate alignment with ten specific core values. These core values constitute a boundary set. Employees are encouraged to refer to these values for guidance when executing on day-to-day tasks. The values make it easier for employees to make decisions and to act on them when the situation is unusual. The classic example is found in *Delivering Happiness*, from Zappos CEO Tony Hsieh. In the book, he describes a story, where hungry friends are encouraged to call Zappos late one night to order a pizza (Zappos does not sell pizza.) The Zappos representative picking up the phone listens to the comical request and then responds in alignment with the Zappos Core Values. Be sure to check page 146 of *Delivering Happiness* to find out what happened.

Results and Related Delays

There may be one or two people who do not like or comply with clearly described boundaries on time, task, etc. When this happens, there is a delay is getting good results. These one or two people keep ignoring the stated boundaries, leading to the need to remind them of the new limits. Consider the case of punctuality. By valuing punctuality, it makes it easier to start meetings on time. This raises levels of engagement. Even so, one or two people may continue to be late and perhaps not even apologize for being late. In this case, others notice, and soon you are back to where you were before with lateness being normal. Expect delays in getting good results unless and until everyone honors the new agreements around being on time.

Details

Boundaries include time, task, territory, and access to resources. Task boundary is a function of *authorization.* You either are authorized to perform a task in your role, or you are not. A territory boundary defines space that you work in, such as your desk or the space within your office. Time boundaries include deadlines, start and stop times for meetings, appointment times, and so on.

Challenges

Managing boundaries can introduce conflict. Once we establish boundaries, we must manage them. This can lead to conflict as we remind people of these limits. Since conflict can be stressful, most of us avoid it by avoiding good boundary management. This leads to all kinds problems. If we value respect, it is important to make sure everyone is displaying respect to others. To do so, we must call out interactions that are not respectful. If we are encouraging a culture of mutual respect, we must honor the value of respect by displaying it in day-to-day interactions.

A complete absence of clear boundary descriptions creates stress and worry because it requires a constant need to examine the limits and see where they are. Clear and explicit boundary descriptions help people know where they are. When you are defining good boundary definitions, you can go too far and prescribe too much structure. Unnecessary structure can cause people to disengage. Install the bare minimum boundary definitions and then commit to them.

Steps and Options

Implementing this practice involves the following steps:

1. **Socialize these ideas**. Be sure to communicate boundaries on roles, tasks, and meetings. Make sure everyone understands the reasoning for any new boundary definitions.
2. **Target specific problems**. Your teamwork problems are often associated with fuzzy boundaries around who has authority to do what, when.
3. **Pay attention to tasks inside roles**. Link specific tasks to specific roles. Increase clarity by listing the tasks a role is authorized to perform.

4. **Pay attention to time boundaries for group work.** Learn to loosen time boundaries somewhat when encouraging inquiry and dialogue and to tighten boundaries when deciding and executing.
5. **Expect to have to remind people of boundary definitions.** Rather than avoid conflict, make a statement about what is valued. Engage in active boundary management. This leads to and supports the practices of {Pay Explicit Attention}, and {Examine Your Norms}.
6. **Don't overdo it.** Use boundaries for containment, but keep that list very short. Have a bias towards a short, tight list of very well defined boundaries. Then actively manage each of them.

Takeaways: Manage Your Boundaries

- <u>Use explicit boundary management to create containment</u>. Simple working agreements, for example, define what is normal in a meeting. When we have good working understandings, we can focus on work instead of guessing about where lines are drawn.
- <u>Boundary definition is part of the clear rule set that is an essential of any good game</u>. Make the game clear by clarifying essential boundaries. These definitions help create the social space people are working in.
- <u>Be mindful of task boundaries.</u> Actively look for places where people have responsibility and lack authority. This is a classic problem. Link responsibility for doing a task with clearly authorized access to the resources needed to achieve that task. Never assign responsibility without related authority to access resources.
- <u>Pay attention to role definitions.</u> Role definitions are often not well defined. This means people occupying roles must interpret the role. This creates worry and a need to test and negotiate. It also favors people who are good at negotiation, in effect punishing good people who are not. Examine roles carefully and try to list all the tasks a role is authorized to perform. It is often a difficult exercise to create this list. Pay explicit attention to authorized tasks by role.

- Be mindful of time boundaries. Loose time boundaries are OK for tasks like inquiring into or exploring a topic and related dialogue. Tighten time boundaries when moving away from dialogue and into a decision-making mode. In all cases, pay attention to simple things like defining break times and durations in meetings. Participants will actively pace their focus and attention in alignment with time-related boundaries.
- Keep boundary descriptions small and the list short. Too many rules kill creativity and engagement. Less is more. Define and actively manage key boundaries that create containment for people. Be mindful to keep the list short.

Chapter 19 - Socialize Books

Overview

Shape, confirm, and validate your culture by making books widely available. By doing this for your tribe, you make a high-impact, values-loaded statement about culture and collective learning.

Use the audio, video, and writing of others as resources to advance the learning of your organization. Gift and share these learning resources to develop communities of practice, mix ideas, leverage the learning to be more adaptive, and develop more operational excellence. Use the active socialization of books to signal both what you value and what you intend.

How This Helps

Explicit knowledge is the knowledge found in books, videos, podcast, audio, and other forms of documentation. The media type does not matter. The point is that explicit knowledge is documented. It exists in media such as a book or video.

Tacit knowledge is knowledge that is not easily obtained from books or documentation. You get it from proximity to others. It is obtained by doing, watching, and interacting with others. A good example is learning to ride a bike. You can read about riding a bike and get the general idea, but you still need to do it to get it. And you still need someone around who has done it to help and encourage you. The knowledge needed to ride a bike is tacit knowledge.

Making books available, and encouraging your tribe to read and discuss them is a powerful exercise in developing knowledge. The {Socialize Books} practice represents explicit knowledge about the topic under discussion. The tribal discussion and awareness of what is said constitute tacit knowledge about the tribe and its level of understanding, positions, and opinions of the topic. {Socialize Books} is a simple, cheap, and effective way of developing and sustaining a culture that values learning.

Costs

Cost varies depending in implementation. Implementing a lending library might cost about $60 per title, assuming two copies in the library. The bare minimum for making {Socialize Books} possible is probably in the range of $600-$900 depending on the number of titles you are making available. You can have a cost of zero if you get participants to opt-in with their own book purchases, but be careful – this also sends out signals about cheapness, actual commitment to the book idea, the wider idea of tribal learning, and the space created to do that. So be careful and deliberate in how you design and roll out the {Socialize Books} step.

Results and Related Delays

You can expect varied results depending on the features of any {Socialize Books} practice you choose to implement. The one constant is a small delay. You can expect a small delay between the implementation of the practice and the results. The typical delay is from about one month to about three months, depending on the features of your {Socialize Books} practice implementation.

Details

Socializing books works in several dimensions to increase learning. There is the content and, more importantly, the cultural signal that making books available represents.

Make a Statement

Making books available states that your organization values learning. Such a statement underscores your other efforts in the development of a tribal learning culture.

Develop Community and Alignment

Books can be used as a focal point for socializing. You can develop opportunities for face-to-face meetings, reading circles, and discussion groups around the books. By developing these opportunities to socialize, you are socializing the ideas in the books themselves. Some of these meetings may be on paid time during work hours or during lunch.

Socializing the ideas of books in small groups is a way to develop community inside your company. For example, a {Socialize Books} practice that includes an opportunity to meet with others is a perfect entry point for new employees to connect with others inside your company. New hires can become members of existing and new reading circles.

See Who's In and Who's Out

The design of your {Socialize Books} practice must include opting in. By making participation optional, you can see who is really interested in your programs, to improve culture and collaboration. This is important and valuable information when you are iteratively evolving your culture. The people that actively participate are signaling strong willingness to locate themselves in the new story, the one that now includes tribal learning. Those who do not participate may be signaling something else. Either way the data on participation is useful as you proceed.

For those who opt-in, the books chosen can also be useful for getting to know the people in your organization; specific titles that people select from those available provide useful information about interests and expertise levels in the subject matter that these books socialize in your group.

Inspect and Adapt

By developing a {Socialize Books} practice, you can periodically inspect the learning results and adapt the practice in light of those results. Depending on your goals and objectives, you can tailor the practice to match. Details on participation provide valuable information you can use to gauge your progress and proceed in an iterative, adaptive fashion.

Shape Your Culture

Over time, you can expect the {Socialize Books} practice to play a role in the shape of your culture. The books you choose to include in the available list contain specific content. You make a statement by making the content available. When people actually do examine these books and discuss them, you will have shaped a discussion. What they discuss is the content in these books. By making titles available, you perform a ***steering*** function, directing organizational attention in an intentional direction. This helps shape a culture that values organization-wide tribal learning.

Here are some of the design details to consider as you design you {Socialize Books} practice:

Lending library

You might choose to build a library and lend books to the people interested in them. This has the advantage of being cheaper but also requires some admin overhead to keep track of the books. It also limits how many people can be reading these books at any given time.

Making Books a Gift

You might choose to make the books available as ***free for the asking*** up to a certain limit, bounded by expenditure and time.

In the 1990s, I operated a staff augmentation company. We provided technical consultants to client companies. I created a practice where any technical employee could purchase up to $400 in books per year. The book had to be ***related to work*** (a loose constraint), and the cost was 100% reimbursable via the submission of hard-copy receipts. The receipts contained information on the cost of the book, the purchase date, and the book title.

That was the basic practice. We intended the practice design to support the following objectives:

1. Support ongoing professional growth and development of skills
2. Be adaptive to changing conditions during a period of substantial change in the technologies the consultants were working in for clients

3. Provide some data on which employees were ordering books, the actual titles of interest, etc.
4. Provide a context for discussions with employees about what they were interested in

You can institute a similar practice if you have similar goals. Zappos handles books differently. Zappos currently provides books to all employees, maintaining a library with multiple copies of multiple titles and restocking as necessary. Each book has sticker inside that indicates that Zappos made the book available. The books are also available to literally anyone who takes a tour of the Zappos facilities. Zappos does not track activity on the part of employees or those who tour Zappos facilities. Zappos simply makes these books (about 35 titles in all) available to employees and anyone in the world who tours Zappos.

Creating Reading Circles

A reading circle is a book discussion group. Encouraging a discussion around books can take many forms. At one extreme, you might choose to schedule periodic meetings and/or create groups for this purpose. At the other extreme, you may not schedule anything but rather encourage discussions and see what develops. Making time and space available during work hours is also a very definite way to signal support for tribal learning via {Socialize Books} and reading circles.

One idea is to hold a periodic Open Space meeting around tribal learning. Open Space is a meeting format that encourages community. You might choose to schedule time for a company-wide Open Space that addresses the topics found in the books you make available. Such a meeting amounts to a company-wide reading circle held in one space at one time for anyone that chooses to attend. Such a meeting socializes both the books and an opt-in culture of collaboration.

Organizational Memory

Most organizations these days have people all over the world. Small companies use people from everywhere.

The problem of how to maintain a cohesive, coherent, and commonly held culture of learning is an interesting problem, that the {Socialize Books} practice can help solve.

Creating opt-in online groups for discussion is one way to implement a {Socialize Books} practice across time and space. The online group becomes an epicenter for thoughts, comments, and thinking about the books in your organization. In addition, the group forms a written history of ideas and people around the books in your organization.

Having an online group on Yahoo or Google, for example, can be either a central feature of your practice or simply a feature that augments your wider practice design. Either way, this is an option worth considering.

Referring to the {Socialized Books} in executive communications

Executives and leaders set the tone in an organization, and what we say and do signals what is valued. By referring to specific books in communications, leaders are signaling that the book and the ideas in them are important. Quoting a passage or a key point found in a title serves to energize the idea of the book as it applies to your organization. On the other hand, implementing a {Socialize Books} practice without any reference to them in the day-to-day work signals only that you promote the latest ***management trend,*** that is hollow, empty, and without meaning. Leaders who implement a {Socialize Books} practice need to be mindful of this ***before*** embarking on implementing the practice.

Challenges

Depending in your practice design, you can choose to gather various data on the activity around your {Socialize Books} practice. You can track which books are of interest to which people, when they gained access to the book, and so on. You can look at which titles are most interesting to your people and have conversations around that. If you encourage discussion by and between the readers of the books, you can inspect the data around that and see how your practice is working. You can take the hands-off approach of Zappos and make the books free to everyone without any data collection, or you can use the {Socialize Books} practice as a source of data about usage, interests, and so on.

Encouraging more learning in your organization and developing a learning culture takes time. You may choose to measure your progress by instituting some data collection around your {Socialize Books} practice.

Steps and Options

Implementing this practice involved the following steps:

1. **Select the books.** Pick books that have content that aligns with what you want your organization to value. This assumes you have socialized a set of values that everyone is opting-in to (in terms of participating).
2. **Design the rules of the game**. Your implementation of this practice might be strict or loose. You may implement reading circles during work time and track results. Or, you might simply make books available via a lending library or free to anyone that wants one. How you design this depends on your goals for implementing the practice.
3. **Execute**. Deploy your books into the wild.
4. **Inspect**. See what happens

Takeaways: Socialize Books

- <u>Books have an individual and a group learning aspect</u>. When individuals read, they start to integrate the cultural values you are promoting. When multiple individuals do this, the effects spread socially and you can build community around book-related activities.
- <u>Making books available as a practice has a wide range of design features</u>. You can develop a library or present the books to the participants. You can also make the titles freely available or impose some constraints to help collect data on usage. The data can be useful for measuring your return on the investment in the practice.

- You make a statement when you make books available. You are choosing the titles and, in some sense, framing a potential conversation around the titles. When you make books available, you signal that learning is valued. You also signal what kinds of topics are important to learn.

Chapter 20 - Pay Explicit Attention

Overview

Attention is valuable and scarce. It is a both a medium of exchange and a store of value. That is why we call it ***paying*** attention. By paying attention to obstacles, your people can start to make sense of how and why things are or are not working well. When paying attention is genuinely valued, the other related practices such as {Examine Your Norms}, {Manage Your Boundaries}, {Structure Your Interactions}, and {Conduct Frequent Experiments} become easier to implement. By valuing the focus of attention, you *signal* that the game has changed and that continuous improvement is the new normal.

History and Origins of the Practice

Inside Agile teams using Scrum, teams pay explicit attention to any impediments that stand in the way of the team. The Scrum Master identifies impediments with the help of the team. The Scrum Master then takes action to remove the impediment that stands in the way. This process of identification and removal is often painful.

During Scrum retrospective meetings, explicit attention is paid to three big questions:

1. What worked well during the last iteration?
2. What did not work well during the last iteration?
3. What do we want to change going forward?

Once again, the explicit examination may be painful. Paying explicit attention means measuring progress and managing processes and procedures. What is measured tends to be managed, and what is managed tends to improve. Scrum provides an opportunity for reflection, inspection, and adaptation.

In the book, *Good to Great*, author Jim Collins devotes an entire chapter to 'Confronting the Brutal Facts'. This is paying explicit attention.

The Toyota Way is a set of Fourteen Principles that encourage continuous improvement and respect for people. Continuous improvement is impossible, if we do not pay explicit attention to removable obstacles and impediments.

In the book *Inattentional Blindness*, the authors make the radical claim that there is no conscious perception without conscious attention. What you choose to pay attention to creates your reality. One of the implications of this is that you do not build perception on what you do not pay attention to. Another implication is that we can elevate attention (and perception) by starting a task instead of delaying it. By starting the task of deliberate observation, you literally notice things that were "not there" previously. By starting, you pay attention. Attention builds perception and learning.

How This Helps

Confronting the brutal facts and focusing on the removal of impediments to greatness creates an environment of continuous improvement. This continuous improvement is actually the result of team learning and team adaptation. Formal teams, informal tribes and entire organizations become more adaptive when it is normal to confront the facts, no matter how painful they may be. We cannot change what we do not acknowledge. Paying explicit attention helps accomplish both.

Costs

Any manager can create an environment of inquiry and continuous improvement. There is no dollar cost associated with this. However, to set this up, the space must be safe for everyone to tell the truth. Participants in the space need to feel safe about naming obstacles and impediments that stand in the way of the work. Safe space is space where it is safe to tell the truth, as you understand it. As a manager with authority to convene meetings, the cost to create and hold a safe space (to take interpersonal risk) requires that you model the behavior yourself. This is a very real cost of implementing this practice. Modeling the behavior of paying explicit attention means that you may ultimately be allowing others to identify some of *your* behavior as a problem. Creating a place where it is safe to call out problems (regardless of the problem source) is a hallmark of great teams and organizations.

Results and Related Delays

There are delays that vary when implementing this practice.

Paying attention to impediments to the group's work and then paying attention to related details is really the first step in a 2-step process. Identifying problems is one thing, removing them is quite another. Often the impediments in the way of group greatness are created by authority figures- people with *positional authority* who exercise it to the detriment of the people doing the work. Often these impediments are experienced as reductions in perceived safety. For example, when an authority arrives late for meetings and uses cell phones or laptops when people are speaking, people assign meaning to that behavior and experience the feeling of being disrespected. This associates with a drop in safety levels in the space. Any delay in addressing the problem is a function of the safety to call out this kind of behavior. This chicken-and-egg problem can prolong the delay between noticing a problem and addressing it.

Details

This practice is really more of a pattern or principle and can manifest in several ways. If you intend to create the safety to call out problems and suggest solutions, you must learn to value paying explicit attention. Valuing it means you reward observation… and refrain from incenting selective ignorance of the brutal facts. The whole point of paying attention is to improve continuously. If this is your aim, model the behavior of identifying problems and suggesting solutions. In the previous example, an authority figure attended a meeting late and then signaled disrespect by interacting with a hand-held device while others with less authorization were talking. As the convener of that meeting, discussing the situation with some of the participants shows that you are willing to identify problems and are paying attention.

Challenges

The space has to be safe for you to be able to make the most of this practice. For your people, this means you have to be mindful of the signals you are sending.

Encouraging your group to pay explicit attention to problems implies you collectively intend to do something about it. If you do not do something about it, you send signals that the space is not safe for calling out problems. This can create a drop in morale as people see the differences between the stated and actual values being played out.

Problems that are blocking group greatness generally fall into three categories. These categories are:

- Immediately addressable problems
- Moderately difficult problems that require the help of others to address
- Very difficult problems generated by the current culture and context of the enterprise
-

The more difficult problems need to be socialized as such, so that people do not get frustrated with the pace of progress.

To continue valuing paying explicit attention, immediately addressable problems must be removed immediately. If easy-to-remove problems are not addressed in a timely fashion, you send the signal that no one cares.

Steps and Options

Implementing this practice involves the following steps:

1. **Consider a facilitated meeting** for the purpose of identifying and discussing obstacles that are in the way of your group's work.

2. **Discuss attention to detail**, especially the details of impediments to the greatness of the group. Discuss things that are blocking the group's purpose and aims.
3. **Develop a list of things that can be improved**. Categorize them into three groups: easy to fix, not so easy to fix, and very difficult.
4. **Dialogue on solutions**. Discuss potential solutions with your group.
5. **Meet periodically**. Have this meeting and discussion.

Takeaways: Pay Explicit Attention

- {Pay Explicit Attention} is more of a principle than a practice. The implementation of the principle can take many forms.
- Discussing the identification of obstacles and roadblocks to the group's work sends a signal that explicit examination of the situation is OK. The discussion opens the space for dialogue
- Paying explicit attention means taking feedback well. As an authority figure, be prepared to receive uncomfortable feedback.
- In practice {Pay Explicit Attention} means examining everything, including what is normal, the behavior of leaders in your group, and the wider culture.
- Encourage everyone to work to remove the easy-to-remove obstacles. Also, encourage everyone to recognize what can be easily changed and what cannot. The ambient culture tends to reinforce certain unproductive norms, and this culture is not easily changed. Aim instead to create a subculture inside your group that promotes healthy habits like respect for people, continuous improvement, and values like courage, commitment, focus, and openness.

Chapter 21 - Open The Space

Overview

> **Hold The Space**
> Opening space means taking steps to help self and others address a range of what might be uncomfortable or even taboo topics. ***Holding the space*** means maintaining that space made safe for exploring the issue. One can hold the space inside various social structures: pair-wise dyads, three-person triads, small groups, and tribes. The earliest reference I know to the term ***hold the space*** dates back to Harrison Owen's books (circa 1990 or so) on formulating Open Space Technology. If you know of an earlier reference, please let me know.

Let's not go there.

When you say this, you signal that that you are unavailable to others to discuss a certain topic. That space is *closed.* Opening the space means being available, usually with many others, to explore what might be difficult yet essential issues. A particular meeting format called Open Space Technology is designed to *open* and *maintain* a space for dialogue, inquiry, and debate about issues people are passionate about.

An Open Space meeting creates and holds *safe space*. Open Space is different from most other meeting formats. These meetings generate opportunities for group expression, inquiry, dialogue, and learning. With these meetings, you can evolve your tribe in the direction of more safety, learning, and adaptation to changing conditions.

{Holding the space} means that you intend to maintain a safe-space atmosphere. This is the job of the Open Space facilitator.

Liberating Structures

There are many different meeting formats designed to open space for dialogue and inquiry. The concept of *dialogue* is to defer decisions, invite a range of ideas, is "divergent on purpose", shares authority broadly, and requires a more open meeting format. *Deciding* is a more focused activity that is "convergent on purpose", seeks to narrow choices, and requires a tighter meeting structure with rules to help focus attention on making a decision. ***Liberating Structures*** is a term coined by William Torbert, a professor now retired from Boston College. The term has come to represent meeting formats that allow groups of people to change how they interact and work together to address issues, solve problems, and develop opportunities in a radical manner. Open Space is one such structure of many. Other structures in this group include World Cafe and 31 other group activities and meeting formats. Many of these formats are actively employed by Agile software teams throughout the world.

History and Origins of the Practice

Open Space meetings are always facilitated. In Agile practice, Scrum supports this facilitate-your-meetings idea. In Scrum, all the meetings are facilitated. Open Space meetings began to get traction in Agile circles around 2005.

Open Space meetings in Agile work well for Retrospectives that create spaces where it is OK to explore the answers to the questions:

1. What is working?
2. What is not working?
3. What do we want to change?

Open Space is simply a larger elaboration of this ***OK to explore*** signal. The Open Space meeting format creates space for exploring otherwise difficult issues a group of people is facing. Open Space is a safe space to do some of the Tribal Learning Practices, including {Pay Explicit Attention}, {Examine What's Normal}, {Be Playful}, {Manage Visually}, and {Facilitate Your Meetings}.

> Liberating Structures are aligned with the Tribal Learning Practices found in this book and compliment them. Open Space is one of (if not *the* most) popular Liberating Structure meeting format.

How This Helps

Open Space creates Tribal Learning via the mechanisms of High Play and High Learning. According to Harrison Owen, author of several definitive books on Open Space, High Learning is a function of High Play. He says, "One of the more curious aspects of an {Open Space Technology} gathering is the presence of play. Even in the most serious of situations where major conflict and complex issues dominate, there is a playful atmosphere."[84]

Concerning High Learning, he writes:

> In {Open Space Technology} it is a common experience that previously unthought-of, and perhaps unthinkable, ideas show up with regularity, allowing impossible situations to find resolution when apparently conflicting ideas coalesce to form novel approaches. In retrospect, the ideas and solutions may seem obvious and natural, but in prospect, they are so far out of the box as to be off the table and out of mind.[85]

Open Space encourages so many aspects of Tribal Learning as to be indispensable for any coach or manager who is seeking to create higher

---

84 Owen, H. (2008). Wave Rider: Leadership for High Performance in a Self-Organizing World, p. 74

85 Ibid

levels of engagement inside affiliated groups of people. I recommend the reader purchase all of Harrison Owen's books for this reason.

Costs

Costs for Open Space meetings include the cost of a facilitator, the supplies, space, and food needed for running the meeting. An Open Space meeting has all the costs associated with a large meeting. The food is really a requirement, since the meetings flows without any formal breaks.

Results and Related Delays

The very act of convening an Open Space meeting in an organization is a signal from authority in that organization. The signal is clear: ***We welcome your disclosure of what you want, what you think, and what you feel***. Sending this signal kicks off a chain reaction of curiosity and engagement. It also generates momentum to act on the issues identified and discussed during the meeting. Open Space creates a safe space for playful learning and richly detailed interactions in small groups. ***Be prepared to be surprised*** is a slogan of Open Space. One of the results you are sure to obtain is a willingness to collaborate and interest in more aspects of self-organization by and between the people in your group.

Details

Rich and detailed explanations of Open Space execution and dynamics are plentiful in books and on the web. The following is a brief summary of what is involved in convening and executing on an Open Space meeting.

Planning- Developing the Theme and Invitation

The meeting has a theme and a related invitation. The theme provides a definition of the territory to be explored. For example, the Agile Boston user group convened an Open Space meeting with the theme "What Do We Know About Agile in Boston?" This theme helps to define the space to be explored during the meeting. The written invitation further refines this definition by providing just enough detail to explain the theme more fully, while at the same time being welcoming and inviting. The purpose of the invite is to attract people with energy, a sense of responsibility, and passion about the theme.

Meeting Logistics

Where, when, and for how long are all addressed by logistics. Space needs to be secured and the start and end times need to be suggested. I say ***suggested*** because, as you will see, Open Space maintains a welcoming and inviting tone and tempo by striking a delicate balance between prescription and self-organization. Food is always a good idea for every Open Space meeting you convene. The meeting also requires enough chairs, flip charts, and markers to handle the number of people and the issues that they wish to explore in the meeting.

The Five Principles and One Law; The Visual Artifacts

Open Space works from five principles, one law, a few roles, some artifacts, and some slogans. These are as follows:

- **The Five Principles**: These principles set up the basic rules of the game. Open Space is very much a game, and these five principles make up the rules.
  Whoever comes are the right people.
  Whenever it starts is the right time.
  Whatever happens is the only thing that could have.
  Wherever it happens is the right place.
  When it is over, it's over.
- **The Law of Two Feet**: You are responsible for your learning. If a session you are attending is not delivering what you want or need, go elsewhere to find what you are looking for.
- **The Roles**: Roles include the Host, the Announcer, the Facilitator, Participants, Conveners of sessions (aka "Initiators"), Bumblebees, and Butterflies. ***The Host*** arranges the meeting and may speak briefly at the start to introduce the Facilitator in the absence of an

Announcer. The Announcer, if present, thanks the Host, introduces the Facilitator, and makes other announcements.

Participants may act as Initiators of sessions, and as a Bumblebee, or Butterfly. Conveners offer sessions and take responsibility to see to that the session is documented and makes it into proceeding.

Bumblebees go from session to session, cross-pollinating ideas they hear and learn about.

Butterflies are part of the space, alternately observing sessions, eating food, drinking beverages and conversing with others in the physical space.

- **Visual Artifacts and One Slogan**: The one law and five principles are placed on posters and arranged throughout the meeting space. The one slogan is ***Be Prepared to Be Surprised***. This is also placed on a poster and displayed. You may be noticing (as you read this) that these posters are actually an object example of the {Manage Visually} Tribal Learning practice.

Additional visual artifacts include the session descriptions posted to the marketplace. This is explained below.

The Facilitated Meeting: The Open, the Sessions, and the Close

The Open: Arrange chairs in a circle. An Open Space meeting has a tribal feeling, tone, and tempo. The Facilitator opens by walking inside the circle and explaining the structure of the meeting. Next, s/he invites attendees to become participants by convening sessions.

The Sessions: In the center of the circle are pads and pens. Attendees come forward, write their session name on the paper, sign it, and announce both the session name and their name. They then post the session on the wall and it becomes part of the agenda. The agenda for the meeting is a dynamic and creative act. Anyone with passion about a topic who is willing to take responsibility for convening a session may come forward in this way.

When everyone who wants to convene a session has described their session and placed it on the wall, the sessions begin. Arrange groups of chairs in designated parts of the room to convene small-group sessions. Several sessions in several time-slots occur over at least several hours.

The Proceedings: Conveners are responsible for seeing to it that someone takes notes and provides an opportunity for all Participants to inspect the notes. Convening a session means taking responsibility that notes from that proceeding are captured and produced.

The Close: When the sessions are over, arrange all the chairs in a circle, and the group reconvenes to share thoughts on the meeting experience. When the last person has spoken, the meeting is over.

The After-Meeting: What happens after an Open Space event dictates the success of the meeting. Proceedings are distributed. The act of convening the meeting is an implicit signal that the organization (a team, unit, department, or division) was ready to move on issues of genuine concern. What happens after the meeting is a function of the passion and willingness to take responsibility of the people present. Authority figures play instrumental roles in continuing to hold the space opened during the meeting.

As stated in Part One of this book, work is game and meetings are games. Open Space is clearly a game with opt-in participation, a clear goal, clear rules, and a way to receive feedback. The clear goal is the exploration of the Theme. The clear rules include the one law, the five principles, the roles, and the guidance on use of related artifacts such as session descriptions, proceedings, and the like. We can easily track progress over time, in terms of the proceedings that document what happens and from what discussions take place during the meeting. Open Space is a good game.

Harrison Owen, the chief formulator of Open Space, says:

"**High Play** is the antidote to dogmatic thinking and therefore an essential companion to High Learning. It is also fun. In [some organizations], **play** is strictly prohibited, for after all there is work to be done, and it is always very serious. Even worse, **Play**, almost by definition, is out of control – which is what makes it **fun**. Can you imagine anything worse than **playing a game** where the results are always known in advance? Boring!"[86]

Challenges

Composing the theme and invitation are essential for a successful Open Space event. Make sure you do this very deliberately.

Planning takes time and so does getting the meeting socialized. You need at least one month to socialize an Open Space event in your organization properly.

The choice of Facilitator is important. The less entangled this person is with your organization, the better. Never choose an authority figure for this role. Facilitators of Open Space need to take a hand-off approach and encourage the group to be who they are without interference.

What happens after the meeting is key. Always distribute proceedings and follow-through on the inspected results of the meeting. Do not convene an Open Space if you are not ready to engage in the after-care, follow-up, and follow-through after the meeting. Often a new collectively created and shared vision emerges. At a minimum, do not do anything that might oppose the emerging vision. Instead, encourage the people with passion and responsibility to step forward. These people have already identified themselves. They are the people who displayed leadership during the meeting.

Good Grief

You need to understand that the true aim of Open Space is to facilitate transitions. Open Space according to Harrison Owen is actually about processing ***grief***. He argues that grief is a natural consequence of change – the old way is dying away, and with that comes the realization that it will soon be gone. On the other hand, as is more commonly the case, the old way is already gone, perhaps for some time, but we just noticed.

---

86 Owen, H. (2008). Wave Rider: Leadership for High Performance in a Self-Organizing World, p. 132, (emphasis added by the author)

We usually call this a crisis or a ***forced awareness***.[87] This plays out for individuals and groups as grief. People seldom realize it as such. After a while, people realize that the future is something to deal with creatively, and from that, a new and possible vision can emerge. It is at this point that Open Space can do its work: Helping a group of people move from grieving about losing the old familiar way, towards a more hopeful tempo in which a new vision can emerge and be shared.

This definitely plays out in Agile adoptions. Specifically, the technique of convening an Open Space at the beginning in an Agile adoption is one I have used very successfully with many client organizations. The safe space created in the meeting provides a venue to legitimately express concerns, and give voice to worries and issues around the move to Agile. The very act of being heard has a certain calming effect. You create a natural bias toward movement when you provide a time and place to voice genuine and passionately held concerns. Open Space helps with this.

Expounding on this coaching technique and the dynamics that make it work are beyond the scope of this book. For those who are intrigued by this concept, I recommend the following manuscript, available around the web as a freely downloadable PDF file: "SPIRIT: Transformation and Development in Organizations" by Harrison Owen[88].

Steps and Options

Implementing this practice involves the following steps:

---

87 Mark Douglas wrote a book on the dynamics of belief change called *The Disciplined Trader: Developing Winning Attitudes*. This is an interesting book about belief dynamics. Douglas coined the term *forced awareness* in this book.

88 At the time of this writing, the SPIRIT manuscript from Harrison Owen (1987) is available in PDF form at the following link: http://openspaceworld.com/Spirit.pdf

1. **Realize what this is**. Open Space is safe space. The meeting creates a safe space for expressing whatever it is that people have on their mind.
2. **Plan carefully.** A successful Open Space meeting requires careful planning. People need time to process the Theme and Invitation. Plan carefully and allow at least one month for proper socialization of the event.
3. **Be mindful of signaling.** Convening the Open Space event broadcasts a clear signal. The clear signal is that openness is valued. Keep this in mind and make sure this is true, before you begin the effort to convene an Open Space meeting.
4. **Do your homework.** Read the available literature and get familiar with Open Space. The web site openspaceworld.com is a good place to start.
5. **Execute well.** Hire or otherwise obtain the help of an experienced facilitator. Do a complete job and do not cut corners. For example, do not skimp on food and make sure you create tangible proceedings.
6. **Be sure to take action after the meeting.** The Open Space meeting generates energy and movement. Keep that alive by inspecting the results after the meeting and encouraging movement in the direction the meeting indicates.
7. **Convene periodically.** Convene an Open Space periodically and repeat the process. Change happens slowly at times, and effects are cumulative. We often miss important details because we are still working from the old way of thinking, and thus miss important changes. Lower the pain-to-change ratio by leveraging Open Space to hear what people are experiencing in your organization.

You may want to re-examine this chapter after you have explored Part Three: Triads and Tribes. Open Space can be used by a triad of managers to effect change more broadly in the organization. Doing so requires some planning and a little bit of authorization. That being said, a larger Open Space that is socialized through the entire organization could generate a substantial amount of movement towards more and better Tribal Learning. The trick is to execute with others at the right time and the right place. This and other topics are explored in more detail in Part Three.

Takeaways: Open The Space

- Meetings are games. Open Space is a game. Play it.
- People who are not invited cannot opt-in to your game. People required to attend by a supervisor cannot opt out. An essential of Open Space is the invitation. DO NOT attempt to mandate people to attend Open Space events. Send the clear signal that opting-out is OK.
- Open Space is ideal for keeping ideas fresh and spirits up. Convene Open Space meeting periodically to check in with your tribe. Retrospective meetings (after an iteration of work) are ideal opportunities for the periodic use of the Open Space format.

Chapter 22 - Be Playful

Overview

Eliminate the distinction between work and play. Leverage formally defined group-participation games to increase learning and do work.

To enhance learning, engage in simulations to learn new and complex concepts related to the work, in a safe space. Gain experience and practice before setting out on real work around the concept learned.

To enhance work, play formally defined games designed to get specific kinds of work done, such as gathering ideas, gathering market research, or developing consensus. Play these games as early and as often as possible when exploring new possibilities and ideas.

Play games to raise levels of engagement, connectedness, and safety.

History and Origins of the Practice

The Agile community employs many games to do work. These games include Planning Poker, a game used to develop work estimates.[89] Scrum itself is a game that encourages teamwork in pursuit of great results. You can think of both the Scrum retrospective and the Daily Scrum as well-designed games with the key essentials: opt-in participation, clear goals, clear rules, and ways to receive feedback on progress.

Recently, other specialized games have emerged to perform specific work, such as the Innovation Games®.[90] Games of this type typically use a metaphor for engaging people around the development of ideas, options, and plans.

---

89 You can get familiar with Planning Poker and examine a tool for playing it, here: http://planningpoker.com/

90 Learn more about Innovation Games® at: http://innovationgames.com/

How This Helps

Playing games to learn something is engaging in a simulation of actual work. Simulations are useful for learning and practicing. The military uses this technique to train pilots and soldiers. Simulations offer a low-impact way to learn quickly by trying things out, making mistakes, and learning from them.

Games for doing work create an activity that focuses on answering questions, exploring an issue, or developing a plan. For example, the Innovation Game called Speed Boat depicts a boat held back by anchors. The use of these unlabeled anchors is a metaphor for encouraging a discussion of obstacles and impediments that are holding back a specific product or service from being great. This type of game provides a simple and well-understood framework for discussing an otherwise complex topic.

Games raise levels of engagement, connectedness, and safety. By convening a meeting around a game activity, the signaling is clear: ***Work is Play***.

Games also break down barriers created by limited beliefs. People might be resistant to an idea simply because they have no beliefs that support the notion that a particular idea might actually be a good one. By immersing people in a group activity where they must interact with each other, you create a space where people may ***get lost*** in the activity. Participants often report later that a 45-minute period felt more like 10 minutes total. This is especially true when they play a game with others who they do not know that well.

Costs

Books that catalog and explain interactive activities (games) have a nominal cost. Branded games such as Innovation Games® have costs associated with the materials needed to execute the games.

Results and Related Delays

Results with games for learning and working tend to be immediate. Delays are minimal and participants often report a surprisingly deep learning experience. Playing games tends to speed up integration of new knowledge.

Details

As discussed in Part One and in the chapter "Game Your Meetings" in Part Two, games create group engagement and experience. Since a good game is opt-in, you are choosing to play. Games usually involve many different activities. These activities engage the whole person. Games can engage all your people in learning because they have sounds, sights, and action. These correspond to the three major learning styles: auditory, visual, and kinesthetic.

Games and Simulations for Learning

People learn complex work-related subjects best by engaging in games. There are readily available games and simulations on the web. You can find games to learn and practice communication, management, and product/service development, to name just a few.

Games for Doing Work

The idea of playing a game to get some work actually *done* is a radical idea for some people. But this idea is not that radical; we do this all the time at work by creating games to get some work done. We call these games ***meetings***. We implicitly play games through the way we run meetings, the way we structure our teams and how we structure our interactions.

Games to do work turn that idea on its head by defining a formal game activity for getting work done. The big difference is the use of ***visual artifacts***.[91]

---

91 See the chapter "Manage Visually" in Part Two for more detail on this.

The method to tie into this concept is to use a metaphorical device, such as a picture of a speed boat held back by anchors, to focus attention, and get some work done. These games often make strong use of visual artifacts to engage participants. Games to do work are often optimized on ***sense making*** at the level of group. We make sense of a topic and exit the game, retaining the sense making we have created. This enables us to convert abstract concepts into shared understandings and actionable plans quickly.

These games differ from a social system design like Scrum, which defines roles, tasks, and rules to optimize effort toward a specific direction. Games to do work are more like a formalization of what we already try to do when we are engaging in dialogue and inquiry. With a formally defined game, we formalize the structure of dialogue, by focusing it on a combination of visual artifacts and activities.

Games to do work also differ from practices such as {Game Your Meetings}. Games that do work are explicit in the use of visual management and other techniques to get some serious work done through the game approach. Using games to do work involves convening a meeting in which the focus of the meeting as a game activity whose output is a specific deliverable, such as market research data, or a set of agreements about plans.

Good Resources

The following books and websites are very useful for exploring game ideas you might want to try at work:

Moving Beyond Icebreakers: An Innovative Approach to Group Facilitation, Learning, and Action by Stanley Pollack and Mary Fusoni, 2005: This is a great resource for anyone looking to increase the quality and frequency of high-quality communication in organizations. Highly recommended.

Innovation Games: Creating Breakthrough Products Through Collaborative Play by Luke Hohmann, 2006.

Luke Hohmann: Gaming Work

Dan's book is exploring a critically important topic: The nature of learning, at work, in groups. This complex, multi-dimensional subject requires us to consider such things as engagement, trust, motivation, purpose, and our core values. *Serious games* can help. Serious games are games that are played to accomplish a business goal, instead of games that played for purely entertainment purposes.

TastyCupCakes.com: This web site contains a repository of all kinds of games for learning and working. Included are games around communication, management, product/service development, and so on. Most of the games are available free of charge.

Common examples of serious games include:

- Simulations, which help workers do everything from learning how to fly a plane, drive a truck, or act like a product manager;
- Market research games, which provide insights into customer and market preferences and desires;
- Do-work games, which use the ***act*** of play to ***solve*** a business problem;
- Adver-games, which motivate the purchase of physical goods through game play.

Innovation Games® are a class of market research and do-work games that are used by thousands of companies to have used to:

- Uncover unspoken needs and breakthrough opportunities
- Discover what customers don't like about their offerings
- Understand where their offerings fit into their customers' operations
- Clarify exactly how and when customers will use their product or service

Game Challenges

A good game is opt-in. Therefore, never try to force people to play games. Instead, invite them, and give them some very good reasons to believe the game might actually be fun. Do not expect everyone to play.

- Deliver the right new features, and make better strategy decisions
- Increase empathy for the customers' experience within their organizations
- Improve the effectiveness of their sales and service organizations
- Identify their most effective marketing messages and sellable features

The Innovation Game called Speed Boat, is included in the Appendix of this book. I invite you to consider how playing serious games at work can promote much more active learning in your organization and culture.[92]

Steps and Options

Implementing this practice involves the following steps:

1. **Do your homework**. The idea of playing formal games to learn new things and actually deliver some work takes some getting used to. Do some research.
2. **Experiment**. This book describes meetings and interactions as games. This chapter says that you can go one step further and formalize gaming as a practice in your organization for learning and working. Try out some games and see how they work.
3. **Consider some specific games** to do actual work. Pick one out.
4. **Socialize the idea**. Discuss games, and make sure your people are opting-in to try this with you. If you plan to play a game at a

---

92 See Appendix D: "Games to Do Work: *The Speed Boat Game* from Innovation Games" for the details on setting up and playing the Speed Boat game.

meeting, say so. Allow people to opt-out of participating if they so choose.

5. **Execute**. Play some games at meetings.
6. **Consider using a coach or facilitator to get started**. Agile coaches are in the business of teaching you how to learn rapidly. Consider getting a coach engaged to begin leveraging formal games for learning and working.

Takeaways: Be Playful

- Games can be used for learning and to do work.
- Games raise the level of engagement and connectedness with others.
- By playing games, you address all the people and all of their learning styles: auditory, visual, and kinesthetic.
- By introducing games, you raise safety levels and send the signal that work is play.

Part Three: Tribes and Triads

Chapter 23 - Develop Your Triad

Overview

The Tribal Learning Practices described in Part Two are a set of resources you can use to encourage team learning inside any group. Great teams engage in many (if not most) of these practices. If you have used some of them, you know how following these practices tends to expose faulty assumptions and manifests positive change by elevating the learning levels of the team.

Once your group is stable in executing at least four of the practices consistently and well, you can consider socializing the practices inside the wider organization. This chapter shows you how to do this by leveraging *triads*. Triads are social structures in which three people aligned on values execute a small strategy in pursuit of specific and intended results.

The use of triads to socialize and spread Tribal Learning Practices throughout the organization is the third essential part of the three-part Tribal Learning framework. (See Figure 6 on page 39.)

Tribal Leadership Overview: Triads

The book *Tribal Leadership* describes five stages of culture in organizations. This book is arguably one of the best management books on leadership ever written. The authors, Dave Logan, John King, and Halee Fischer-Wright, expose five levels of culture, and identify *tribes* and *triads,* as fundamental structures for manifesting change in organizations. The authors offer very specific guidance on how to identify the stages, function as a leader in any of the stages, and encourage movement from lower stages to higher stages.

The five stages show up as stories that people tell themselves and others. The Tribal Leadership Stages, ranked from lowest to highest, are as follows:

"Life Sucks": This is the stage of criminals and gang members. The basic story is that life is bad and will never get better. Individuals at

Stage One seek organizations (such as gangs) that reinforce Stage One ***Life Sucks*** language and related story telling.

"My Life Sucks": This is the stage of people with a victim mentality. The basic story of a Stage Two person is that other people can, and do, have good lives, so there is evidence that life can be good. However, right now, there is little that s/he can do to improve things. Individuals at Stage Two are attracted to organizations where workers are told what to do and have little or no autonomy to make decisions on the job.

"I'm Great (You're Not)": This is the stage where ego and competition take the spotlight. The basic story a Stage Three person tells himself/herself is this: ***For me to win, someone else must lose***. Individuals at Stage Three tend to be attracted to organizations that provide an opportunity for them to stand out from the crowd.

"We're Great": This is the stage where belonging to a great team, group, department, or organization becomes a source of identity and pride. The basic story is similar to Stage Three, and has evolved from ***I'm great*** to ***We're great***. I also believe there is follow-on to ***We're Great***, which is, ***They're Not***. Stage Four people operate in teams and tribes. They look for tools and techniques to build up the collective knowledge and the overall learning of the group. Triads are a tool that Stage Four tribes use to build and maintain a strong culture based on ***we*** language. Individuals at Stage Four tend to be attracted to mature Stage Four organizations.

"Life is Great": This is the stage of world building. The tribe has a noble cause and acts on it without regard to competition per se. Instead, the tribe focuses all of its attention and cultural strength on achieving the world-changing vision they collectively hold. Tribes that achieve the world-changing objective may become unstable for a period, unless they develop a new and collectively held world-changing vision. People at Stage Five tend to be attracted to organizations that have a legitimate chance to change the world.

Triads and Stage Four

According to the *Tribal Leadership* authors, most people and organizations are at Stage Three. Moving to Stage Four is difficult. For leaders who actively want to move the culture from Stage Three (***I'm Great***) to Stage Four (***We're Great***), triads are very useful tools. Triads socialize ***we*** language and tend to encourage goals, objectives, and projects that require a team to accomplish. The key behavior in moving from Stage Three to Stage Four is the behavior of leaders. Leaders move away from pair-wise relationships (known as dyads) and toward working relationships that involve three people who are focused and highly functional.

> NOTE: A completely detailed deconstruction of ***Tribal Leadership*** is beyond the scope of this book. In this book, we provide the basics and then build on them. Understanding the strength of triads as a tool for socializing ideas is of particular importance and is the focus of this section of the book and all of Part Three. See the Bibliography in this book to discover other sources.
>
> The reader is invited to purchase and read ***Tribal Leadership***, to learn more about the five stages, triads, and how language frames reality for individuals and organizations.

Socializing the Tribal Learning Practices Using Triads

According to Dave Logan, "A triad is a three-person structure where all three people are aligned on values, and where each person is responsible for the quality of the relationship between the other two."[93] This focus on values alignment is key; if we hold values in common, we have a basis for taking action together.

Being responsible for the quality of two other peoples' relationships may seem counter-intuitive: How can I be responsible for the quality of others peoples interactions? The answer lies in shared values. People who form triads do so with a bias

93 Personal Interview, October 2011

and intent towards action on a ***we*** basis. The language is inclusive ***we*** language, not exclusive ***I*** language. Triads are ***we*** structures that generate ***we*** language by and between the triad members. This means taking responsibility for the quality of the relationship between the other two people is actually very simple, because in so doing you are taking care of the triad as a whole, in ***we*** terms. Larger and more dynamic than a pair, smaller than a team, the triad, when properly designed, is a very strong interpersonal structure.

A well-designed triad has these characteristics:

1. The people in the triad align on values. They enjoy being together precisely because they hold values that they all share.
2. They embrace we-language. Embracing we-language encourages inclusive thinking and makes it easy for each member to be responsible for the quality of the relationship between the other two. This we-language orientation literally gives life to the triad.
3. The members clearly define objectives supported by shared values. The clearly defined objective is expressible in we-language and is achievable by the triad. The objective focuses attention. The members have a goal and a way to get there. Executing a clearly defined ***micro-strategy*** is the focus of a well-designed triad. (Micro-strategies are discussed in the sections that follow.)

Triads get things done by leveraging the power of ***we*** and the power of three. Two is company; three is a crowd. Three aligned individuals who focus and have a plan can accomplish much.

Micro-Strategy

Dave Logan has written extensively on organizations and getting results with them. According to Dave, the focus of a triad is executing a micro-strategy:

> A micro-strategy is the design and execution of plans that focus on very specific outcomes, with very narrow time horizons, while

> leveraging available assets and employing specific behaviors to achieve the intended results. . . Triads form around designing and executing on a micro-strategy. Forming triads and experimenting with them is something almost any manager can do immediately.[94]

Key to the design is a careful analysis of outcomes, assets, and actions. ***Outcomes*** are the desired end-state and manifest as results. ***Assets*** are available resources including but not limited to relationships, talent, and money. ***Actions*** are behaviors that combine with assets to achieve outcomes.

When designing a micro-strategy, the designers answer three questions: What do we want? (resulting in *outcomes*), what do we have? (resulting in *assets*), and what will we do? (resulting in *actions*).

These ***micro-strategies*** work well because they are:

1. Easily managed
2. Less overwhelming
3. Provide feeling of frequent accomplishment
4. Easily stacked together to achieve longer term strategies
5. Easily modified when strategic direction shifts

The key step in developing and executing a micro-strategy is confronting objective reality by asking some very hard questions. These questions include:

1. What do we value?

Answering this question can be difficult if you have never examined the subject explicitly. Examining this question with others can be even

---

[94] Dave Logan and Halee Fischer-Wright, "Micro Strategies: Planning in uncertain times," http://onlinelibrary.wiley.com/doi/10.1002/ltl.364/abstract. Readers may want to visit the following web pages found on the CultureSync web site for more information on micro strategies: http://www.culturesync.net/blog/90-day-strategy-for-2011. The CultureSync site contains many free resources distributed under an open license.

more difficult. This is the first and most important question when working with others.

2. What do we want?

Any actionable answer to this question includes a specific set of measurable results with a due date. It is important that the desired results are an extension of the stated values. Discussing what we want leads to a clear definition of outcomes.

3. What do we have?

This question results in an inventory of assets. Everyone involved makes a long list of what assets are available. Assets include skills, expertise, relationships, access to resources, access to funding, location and proximity, and more. Use your imagination. It is a good habit to update the asset list periodically, because it will change as you execute small projects.

4. Do we have enough assets for the outcomes?

If the answer is no, adjust the expected outcomes. Scale down the ambition, or develop a near-term strategy to build the assets needed to achieve the larger desired outcome, or both. If the answer is yes, then ask:

5. What will we do?

The result is a list of actions that you need to take.

6. Will the actions accomplish the outcomes?

If the answer is no, then define smaller and more detailed actions to ***move the needle***, either by producing supporting outcomes, developing new assets, or both. When adding highly detailed actions, it is important to focus on opportunities to convert assets into actions.

The stepwise micro-strategy approach is aligned with the Agile approach developed by the software development community. The micro-strategy approach has good game dynamics: it is an opt-in game (what do we value?), it describes a clear goal (what do we want?), it provides a clear set of rules (through the questioning sequence), and provides a clear way to keep score (will the actions accomplish the outcomes?).

Executing a micro-strategy with others is a good game.

Micro-strategy and Triads

Triads and micro-strategies go together naturally. "Triads are especially useful for executing a deliberate micro-strategy," says *Tribal Leadership* co-author Dave Logan. "The practices described in this book can be used as tools in a micro-strategy to elevate levels of thinking and learning in organizations. You can use them yourself, and then form a triad to extend the work."[95] Micro-strategies focus triads on measurable work that focuses on very specific outcomes within short time frames.

In the next section, we look at how triads embody many of the principles and practices of the Tribal Learning framework.

How Triads Embody Most of the Tribal Learning Practices

Triads are three-person relationship structures where all three people share aligned values and where each person is responsible for the quality of the relationship between the other two. The triad members use values as a foundation for discussing, defining, and executing on work, typically using a micro-strategy approach. Like all the effective Tribal Learning Practices, the structure encourages respect for people and continuous improvement. These principles associate with greatness in teams and organizations.

The following table depicts the substantial alignment of the Tribal Learning Practices and the use of triads:

Figure 16: Triads Manifest and Align with Tribal Learning Practices

Practice	Values-Aligned Triads Executing Micro-Strategies
1. Be Purposeful	Micro-strategy executed in triads always focuses on an objective.
2. Be Playful	Triads executing micro-strategies have good-

[95] Personal Interview, October 2011

	game attributes (opt-in, clear goal, clear rules, accessible feedback on ***the score***)
3. Announce Your Intentions	Triads form around values-aligned, clearly articulated intent that is expressed and shared by all three members.
4. Manage Visually	Not applicable
5. Structure Your Interactions	Triads are three-person relationship *structures* where all three people share aligned values, and where each person is responsible for the quality of the relationship between the other two.
6. Game Your Meetings	Meetings between members of a genuine triad are sure to be opt-in, and have a clear goal, clear rules, and accessible feedback on meeting progress.
7. Get Coached	Triad members coach each other, especially when being responsible for the quality of the relationship between the other two members.
8. Facilitate Your Meetings	Triad members take turns facilitating and coaching, typically using we-language.
9. Examine What's Normal	Triads change what is normal. Forming triads deliberately is a move from pair-wise dyads and "I-language", towards group-level relationships and "We-language".
10. Pay Explicit Attention	The series of questions in the micro-strategy framework call explicit attention to the essentials of assets, outcomes, and actions.
11. Socialize Books	Not applicable.
12. Inspect Frequently	Micro-strategies have a specific due-date, typically 90 days or less, followed by inspection

	of the outcome and related assets and actions.
13. Manage Your Boundaries	A triad executing a values-aligned micro-strategy is engaging in boundary management. Boundaries include the due date, the goal, and the limits on available assets.
14. Be Punctual	Focus, commitment, and respect associate with greatness in teams and organizations. Genuine and authentic triads with an aim must hold these values to achieve the aim. Punctuality supports these values. Triads are punctual for appointments and meetings.
15. Open The Space	Triads aligned on values are unlikely to maintain closed space. The micro-strategy framework asks questions that open the space for dialogue and inquiry. Triad space is values-aligned open space and safe space for learning, thinking, and doing.
16. Conduct Frequent Experiments	Triads executing a micro-strategy with a near-term due date for outcomes are by definition conducting frequent experiments.

How to Socialize Tribal Learning with Triads

Now we can begin to explore the mechanics involving triads to socialize the Tribal Learning Practices in your organization. With this step, you move Tribal Learning Practices beyond your team and into your informal and internal network. "Most organizations have some dysfunction that tends to influence teams and weaken team learning," says Dave Logan. "Managers forming strong triads can help develop a strong local subculture."[96]

96 Personal Interview, October 2011

Taking the lead in socializing the practices using triads assumes the following:

1. You know the Tribal Learning Practices intimately.
2. You have experience socializing the practices within your group and know how to use opt-in invitations and good-game dynamics before proceeding with implementing a practice.
3. Your group is happy and stable using at *least four of the Tribal Learning Practices for at least six weeks.* ***Stable*** means the people in your group do at least four of the practices with regularity when working, genuinely enjoy using them, and value the results obtained.

If the people in your group are telling positive stories about the meetings they are now attending, that is a good sign that you are ready to proceed with socializing the Tribal Learning Practices out from your teams and into your wider informal network. Do not rush it. Make sure the stories your people are telling about the practices are positive and upbeat before proceeding with socializing the Tribal Learning Practices further.

Dave Logan says that once you are there, "the next step is to form more triads. When your first triad is successfully executing the micro-strategy, the three people committed to it can repeat the process."[97]

Overview

Socializing the Tribal Learning Practices involves executing the following steps:

- Confirm Your Values
- Identify Candidates Who Already Align
- Name a Theme and Invite Them

---

97 Personal Interview, October 2011

- Test Each for Willingness to Proceed
- Develop a Micro-Strategy
- Execute
- Iterate, then Inspect and Adapt
- Stabilize
- Coach and Facilitate
- Form New Triads

It is important at each step to consider what you are trying to achieve (outcomes), what resources you require to make it happens (assets), and what behaviors you must execute (actions) to reach your goal of socializing the Tribal Learning Practices. The ten steps listed above form a micro-strategy to reach the goal. This strategy leverages triads as the fundamental relationship structure for interactions with others around achieving this goal.

Let's look at each of these ten steps in turn.

Step One: Confirm Your Values

Before you begin, take time to articulate to yourself exactly what you value. One way to do this is to engage in some exercises that help you discover these values.[98] These exercises can help you identify and further clarify your own core values. This is an essential step before working intimately with others in a triad. A genuine triad is a set of three people with substantial values alignment. This alignment takes on certain explicitness when working closely in triads. Be sure of what you value. Once you do this, you can more easily align with others. This is essential.

---

98 Dave Logan's company CultureSync developed a set of resources for doing exactly this. These resources are available for free download at http://www.triballeadership.net/happiness. In the event the named link is not working, you can go to http://www.culturesync.net/ and enter the search string ***"Mountains and Valleys"*** to locate this resource.

"Values alignment is powerful," says Tribal Leadership co-author Dave Logan. "When you speak to someone who shares your values, you find that you are both speaking the same language."[99]

Step Two: Identify Candidates Who Align

Your informal network of contacts contains a set of people. Their names are in your phone contacts and email address book. From this list, try to identify at least ten who you believe share common values with you in a substantial way. Since your phone contacts is a more intimate list of people, start there. According to Dave Logan, "your current informal network is populated with people who share many of your values. If this were not the case, these people would not be in your network."[100]

Another thing to do is to observe people during your meeting, specifically those attending from outside your group. If you use the Tribal Learning Practices, your meetings are different from other meetings in the organization. Your meetings have good game dynamics, start on time, and you might be facilitating them. Your meetings might make heavy use of visual artifacts on the wall and have other distinguishing characteristics. People attending your meetings from other groups will notice this, and some may comment positively. Pay attention to this signal. It is another source of candidates for socializing the practices more broadly.

Remember, you do not need permission from anyone to form triads at work. You are already empowered and authorized. "The beauty of forming triads is that you do not need to ask permission," says Dave Logan.[101] "Triads require relationship based on values, not permission based on formal authorization. You just do it. You act alone at first, in effect modeling the idea. From there, seek to form triads to create real

---

99 Personal Interview, October 2011

100 Personal Interview, October 2011

101 Personal Interview, October 2011

movement. By teaming up with two other people, at your level and aligned on values, you can accomplish much more."

In summary: Find candidates that have substantial alignment with you around core values. Narrow the final list of candidates down to ten people.

Step Three: Name a Theme and Invite Them

In the Tribal Learning practice {Open the Space}, the Open Space meeting format is discussed. This meeting format features an opt-in invitation that names a theme for the meeting that is clear and definitive, while also being big enough to hold many different points of view. The theme's design is both attractive and repulsive. It repulses people lacking enthusiasm around the theme, while it attracts those who have strong feelings about it. Here you want to do that same thing: name a theme, issue an invite, schedule the meeting, and see who shows up. You want to socialize the themes of ***Respect for People*** and ***Continuous Improvement***. You want to explain how you are using these ideas and Tribal Learning Practices to help your group learn, respond to change, and become more adaptive. For example, if you are using {Facilitate Your Meetings} and {Be Punctual} inside your team, be sure to tell a brief story about these experiences.

Inviting people in your organization to experiment with the practices is an informal, two-step process. The first step is to invite each of them to discuss the themes of teamwork, learning, and adapting to change as it applies to their work. The next step is to test further for willingness to proceed to form a triad.

Socialize This Book

One way to socialize a theme of teamwork and more active learning (and fun at work) is to invite people to read this book. Make it available. Leave it on your desk. Create a Reading Guide that lists what consider to be the essential reading. Pass the book around. Doing so is an indirect statement of intent, and signals that you are open to discussing the book content with others. Consider obtaining several copies of the book and initiating a collective reading of it, perhaps with an occasional meeting and as described in the {Socialize Books} chapter in Part Two. The managers who express interest in the book are good candidates for forming triads around implementing the practices.

Discuss It Casually

Use informal discussions as tests of willingness to discuss and implement the Tribal Learning Practices. Move through your day looking for opportunities to socialize the ideas with other managers. Locate people with pain points looking to relieve their pain. Create opportunities to discuss the practices at lunch and during ad-hoc interactions. Focus on good candidates and see if they send you a positive signal when you open the topic.

If they do not, move on for the time being. As Dave Logan says, "You cannot force people to triad. They must be willing. Triading is an opt-in game."[102]

You are trying to find willing people who send strong positive signals of interest in what you are doing.

Invite Observers to Your Meetings

Once you have located a manager in your network who signals strong interest, a good next step is to invite them to observe a meeting.

One good technique for gaming meetings is to define roles. Most meetings can have an Observer role defined. (The chapter "Game Your Meetings" has more information on defining an Observer role). Set this up, and invite those who signal strong interest to attend one of your meetings as an Observer.

According to Dave Logan, "Creating a list of people with which you align on values is easy. The next step is to find the people in that group who are most willing and most able to execute on a specific micro-

---

102 Personal Interview, October 2011

strategy with you now." Inviting a friend to a meeting that is using some of the Tribal Learning Practices is a great place to start.

Step Four: Test for Willingness to Proceed

Figure 17. A Triad

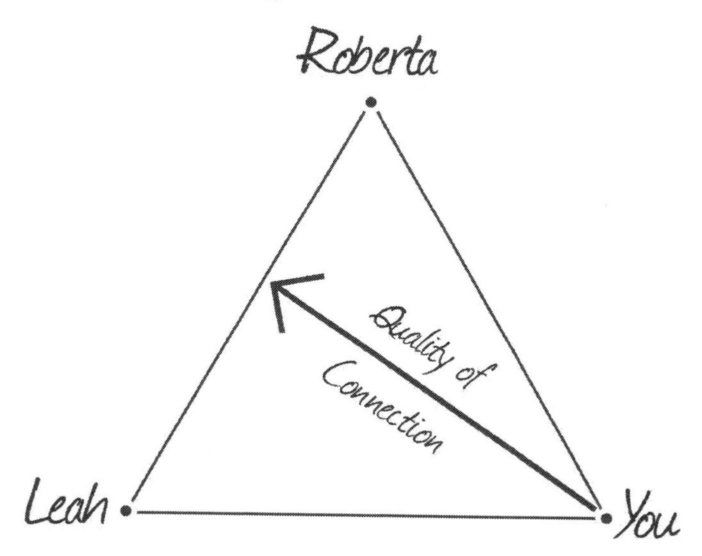

By this point, you have identified a short list of managers who are signaling positively. They are familiar with you, and familiar with how you are using the Tribal Learning Practices. You have socialized the theme of using Tribal Learning Practices to help your group learn, respond to change, and become more adaptive. You might have four or five people signaling strong interest. Strong signals might include reading this book and attending some of your meetings on an invited opt-in basis.

Once you have identified these managers, it makes sense to form one or more triads.

The first time through, you may choose to form more than one triad (perhaps because of strong interest from more than two solid candidates). My guidance to you is to form one solid triad at first and really focus on it to get some traction. Then move to create more.

Use Your Judgment

As the person initiating a triad, you are in a position to choose form a range of options, as you decide with whom to connect around work in your triad. Consider the following:

- Your purpose, aim, and desired outcomes in forming this triad
- The chemistry by and between the members
- The level of authority of each member. Try to connect managers who are at the same level of authority, and at roughly the same Tribal Leadership stage (Stage 3 or higher, as described in the Tribal Leadership book.)
- Specific skills each member brings
- The ability of each member to form triads later as you do now
- The working groups. If the members come from different groups, consider how those groups relate, and how this to leverage that relationship to achieve the micro-strategy for this triad.

After deciding to form a triad, select your triad members. Explain the triad concept. By this point, you have provided them with access to this book. Now introduce them to the *Tribal Leadership* book and the related materials (including the free audio book) found on the CultureSync web site (CultureSync.net). Explain the triad definition as described in the *Tribal Leadership* book. Review the micro-strategy concept. Refer to Chapter 11 of *Tribal Leadership: A Tribal Leader's Guide to Strategy*. This section provides a great and actionable working description of the micro-strategy framework in detail in terms of assets, actions, and outcomes. It provides everything you need to take action.

Step Five: Develop a Micro-Strategy (Context is King)

Now you have your first triad. This is the time for you to move into a coaching and collaboration position. Keep in mind that everyone knows the direction, and that you have provided the tools. Now is the time to listen and take responsibility for encouraging a high-quality relationship between the other two members of your triad.

This will play out in the development of your micro-strategy. Context is king here. The particular context of your triad will include what everyone will work on, real constraints around the work, each person's skills, and the wider organizational context (in terms of culture). Now you can begin the discussion of specifics, by describing the situation in clear terms. Recall that you personally implemented some of the practices, and are consistent and stable in using them. You formed this triad.

Listen to your triad carefully. Collaborate with the other two members, taking care to avoid dominating the discussion. Instead, take a coaching stance. Ask powerful

Take a Step Back

You designed this triad. You created it. The other two members now automatically look to you for signals on how to proceed. If you have cast the triad carefully, everyone is at or around the same level of authority (as managers), and at the same basic stage of Tribal Leadership (probably late Stage Three) as you. This is essential.

When they look to you for signals on how to proceed, they are attempting to ***draft*** you into a potentially ineffective role as the authority in the room. Avoid taking up this authoritative role, because doing so would stunt the growth of the other two members. Instead, work to facilitate the development of a clear, immediate, and shared objective.

Presumably, the desired outcome is more Tribal Learning, using the practices in service to the greatness of the wider organization. The form and specifics to reach questions[103] and pay careful attention to the needs and concerns of the other two members. Work at increasing the quality of the relationship by and between the other two triad members. Work to help them develop and set a near-term goal for the entire triad that is achievable in terms of readily available assets, and actions that you can take now.

> this goal will vary greatly depending on context and situational variables as discussed in this section.
>
> Your goal is to help the triad achieve a clear short-term goal by taking responsibility for the quality of the relationship between the other two members. Take up a facilitative coaching stance and see what emerges from the unique chemistry of your triad.

Now is the time to *serve* the other two members. Avoid even an appearance of dominating discussions. Instead, play a facilitation role and see what emerges from the triad.

In forming a micro-strategy, allow the consensus of ***what's possible now*** to emerge. Do not try to steer anything. You already engaged in steering when you formed the triad. Now let it go and do your job maintaining the quality of the connection between the other people. Simply open up some space to answer this question and then hold it. Once you have obtained the collective answer, reduce it to a clear statement of the desired outcome, and inventory assets and actions of the triad as described in Chapter 11 of *Tribal Leadership: A Tribal Leader's Guide to Strategy*. This is the chapter of Tribal Leadership which details the steps needed to finalize your micro-strategic plans.

In your triad, the possible variables for spreading the Tribal Learning Practices include:

---

103 For guidance on powerful questions, search for the phrase ***coaching powerful questions*** or see the following link, which provides a good overview: http://coachingforchange.com/pub08.html

- ***Timing*** - When should you introduce them to people in the groups managed by the other members of the triad?
- ***Selection*** - Which practices should you introduce?
- ***Support*** - How you intend to support the others, (and then yourself) to spread these practices?
- ***Social dynamics*** - Which people in which groups are supporting, merely tolerating, or being outright resistant to using these practices? In addition, what do people with higher authorization (***higher-ups***) think and feel about using these practices?
- ***Opportunities*** - Which upcoming events, such as meetings, represent opportunities to either socialize or implement some Tribal Learning Practices?

Resistance to Change

Resistance to change takes many forms. Some folks might not like the Tribal Learning Practices. In this case, you need to socialize them more completely. In micro-strategy terminology, we need to develop the asset of ***willingness to proceed*** within the group. One way to do this is to socialize the practices through others that are supportive and in the group. This works especially well. Identify two or three strong supporters and ask them to help you socialize the practices. Socialize it through others.

Step Six: Execute

Now it is time to execute. This is the easy part! You have formed your triad and defined your micro-strategy. Now the triad executes it. Focus on the defined outcomes using your assets and taking action. Try to keep the execution interval as short as possible. Use frequent, short iterations to create frequent inspection points. Use uniformly sized iterations, for example, one week or two weeks (avoid varying the iteration period). Having a consistent iteration length builds predictability and reliability. These feelings in turn create a sense of control, progress, and trust in the triad.

At the conclusion of each iteration, conduct a review (a *retrospective,* to use Agile terminology), to inspect the near-term outcomes and adapt.

Step Seven: Iterate, then Inspect-and-Adapt

At each inspection point, answer three questions:

1. What is working?
2. What is NOT working?
3. What do we want to change?

Pick One Thing

Often, retrospectives yield a great many possible adjustments. In coaching teams and organizations, I often encounter what I call weak organizational memory. This is where a retrospective yields good workable actions and then these actions are not executed. One remedy that I find works well is to focus on ONE change of the highest-impact, and execute that. Pick one thing you want to change and do it in the next iteration.

Throughout this process, continually focus on the quality of the relationships with and between the other two members of your triad. By focusing on the relationships, you ensure that the actions you take will produce outcomes. This cannot be overstated.

Continue to iterate over your micro-strategy until you achieve your outcome or you regroup and aim at a sub-objective that builds any assets you are missing.

Step Eight: Stabilize

When your triad achieves the intended outcomes, declare victory! Doing this is associated with happiness because it creates a sense of progress. When your triad is successfully socializing some of the Tribal Learning Practices in the groups under the authority of your triad partners, the next step is to develop consistency and stabilize around the practices.

To stabilize means that you allow ***no backsliding***. A common pattern is that an organization begins to use some practices and then, over time, these practices become conveniently ignored. Change is difficult, and lasting change in groups is even more difficult.

Prime measures of consistency and stability include:

1. You actually use the practices you have chosen (at least four) as a matter of policy in the target group. If one of your triad members is using {Be Punctual} and {Manage Visually}, these practices are in strong use in that member's group for at least six weeks. People in the group see the value and enjoy using these practices.
2. You experiment with other Tribal Learning Practices. (The practices tend to support each other, so adding a practice is easier than getting started).
3. There is little, if any, resistance to using the practices. The whole group enjoys using the Tribal Learning Practices and understands the value they provide.

Step Nine: Coach and Facilitate

Reaching this step is a great achievement. You are now almost ready to fan out. Now is the time to perform the following steps with your triad:

1. Review your successes. Pay careful attention to lessons learned, as they typically are informed by both your context and the ambient culture. Pay attention to what works and how it works.
2. Review how you formed this triad, paying careful attention to selection criteria.
3. Focus on establishing two new triads. A good approach is for you to form one more, and for one other member to form one as well.
4. Coach the others on your selection criteria and advise them to use the same or similar criteria and techniques.

Your objective is to form one or two new triads. Adding two new triads to your current setup looks like this:

Figure 18. Core Triad with Two New Triads Attached

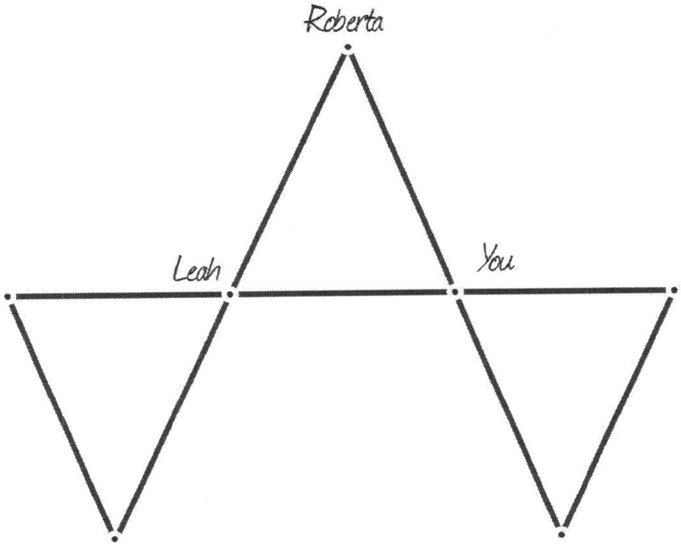

Roberta

Leah

You

Step Ten: Form New, Related Triads

When you finally move to form more triads, you are literally creating a tribe, and you are participating in the engineering of intentional culture. You are in fact *culture hacking*. Dave Logan says that, "tribes are formal and informal groups of about 20 to about 150 people. Your informal network is a tribe."[104]

Tribes can be less than 150 people and usually are.

When you leverage multiple triads, you are constructing a tribe. This is significant, because it can tip the culture in the direction you intend. Dave Logan says that you can bring definition to your tribes by leveraging triads. "Because triads are based on shared values, they have the potential for a strong bond," explains Dave, "extending that strength to the tribe is possible by expanding the number of triads executing on

[104] Personal Interview, October 2011

the same or similar micro-strategies."[105] This is exactly what you are doing. You are expanding the number of triads executing on socializing Tribal Learning Practices across the organization.

This is especially powerful because your triad members are managers who have direct reports and the authority to convene meetings. The number of people directly influenced by your triads is all of your triad members *plus all of their direct reports*. This is a significant amount of leverage. When all those people start telling stories, the real game begins.

Tribal leadership co-author Dave Logan is a big believer in language. Dave explains, "Language is the code we use to express our stories. Stories spread language and terminology. The culture can tip when the stories contain 'we're great' language."[106] There is a huge amount of cultural leverage in this. It means that, using triads with other managers, you can actually move the culture by moving the language. It's all in the stories people are telling and in the language they are using. Employing triads with other managers allows you to build tribes of people speaking the same language rapidly.

People tend to code stories into their language. Stories contain memes, which are units of culture and contain values and other information. Stories, slogans, saying, even jokes are all cultural memes. When people start telling stories, and you are influencing the stories they are telling, you are directly influencing culture.

Do not underestimate the power of stories. According to Dave Logan, "Tribes have the potential to tip an entire culture towards greatness, through the use of language."[107]

Triads encourage ***we-language***, and the people with whom you interact through triads each have direct influence on their direct reports. The Tribal Learning Practices also encourage we-language, a lot of

---

[105] Personal Interview, October 2011

[106] Personal Interview, October 2011

[107] Personal Interview, October 2011

collaboration, a lot of inquiry, and a lot of adaptation. The potential is there to move the culture further. That's the good news.

The bad news is that moving to form more triads is a step with real risk that you will want to manage. You will be building on successful outcomes with one triad, and you want that momentum to continue.

The main thing now is to use the micro-strategy framework of assets, action, and outcomes. Clearly describe your goals and objectives, and make sure your assets and available actions can support your goals and objectives. Here is a clearly described goal: ***To implement Tribal Learning Practices in a consistent, stable, and measurable way across three total triads with at least fifty people directly affected by these changes by June 1.***

Before you begin, perform the following steps:

1. Make note of ripple effects. You can be certain that others in the organization notice what is happening. Responses include resistance, tolerance, and outright support and enthusiasm. Start mapping the terrain. Realize that people can and do change. Resisters can become tolerant, and merely tolerant people do become supporters of what you are doing, over time. Notice what is happening.
2. Rate the maturity of your triad members and your own maturity in leveraging triads to achieve your intended outcomes.
3. Focus on establishing two new triads. A good approach is for you to form one more, and for one other member to form one more as well.
4. Avoid creating more than two new triads, and definitely do not be responsible for all of these. Creating more than two new triads introduces the risk of diluting focus and attending to much too much work-in-process.
5. Use the micro-strategy framework to clearly define what you intend to do and by when with one or two new triads.

When you are done, you three triads might look like this:

Triad One: Roberta, Leah, You (Your first triad)
You 01+07 direct or indirect reports
Leah 01+05 direct or indirect reports
Roberta 01+09 direct or indirect reports
Total for Triad One: 8+6+10 = 24

In this illustration, Triad One is affecting 21 additional people.

You take the lead in developing Triad Two, with two new players. Leah takes the lead in developing Triad Three, with two new players.

Here is what Triad Two looks like: Candidate Triad Two:
You 01+07 direct/indirect reports (member of Triad One)
Erik 01+11 direct/indirect reports (new member of Triad Two)
Kayla 01+08 direct/indirect reports (new member of Triad Two)
Net Increase: 12+9 = 21 new people (from Erik and Kayla) affected by Tribal Learning Practices

Here is what Triad Three looks like: Candidate Triad Three:
Leah 01+05 direct/indirect reports (member of Triad One)
Kevin 01+06 direct/indirect reports (new member of Triad Three)
Brian 01+08 direct/indirect reports (new member of Triad Three)
Net Increase: 7+9 = 16 new people (from Kevin and Brian) affected by Tribal Learning Practices

Summary Counts of People Affected:
Triad One: 24 (Roberta, Leah, you, all of your direct reports)
Triad Two: 21 (net of you and your seven people included in the Triad One counts)
Triad Three: 16 (net of Leah and Leah's 5 people included in the Triad One counts)

TOTAL people now using Tribal Learning Practices: 61

Your tribe now looks like this:

Figure 19. Core Triad and Two new Triads with Counts

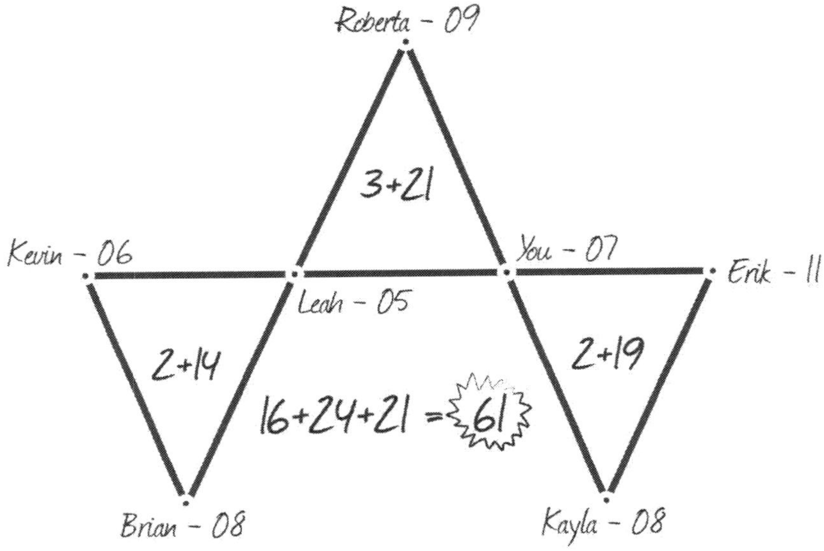

Tribes and Triads

You now have a *learning tribe*. They are using the advanced, double-loop learning practices described in this book.[108] The Tribal Learning Practices encourage a habit of questioning assumptions. This adaptive habit associates with evolution towards greatness in individuals, teams, tribes, and entire enterprises.

You are now effecting positive change in the working lives of dozens of people. The people affected are enjoying higher levels of satisfaction

---

108 Double-loop learning always questions the goal, and often modifies the goal in light of experience, dialogue, and inquiry. See: http://en.wikipedia.org/wiki/Double_loop_learning.

and meaning at work because they are more engaged in the work, with others.

You have created space to call out problems, ask for help, and offer solutions. People now hold space open to accept the current best idea, regardless of its source. The people using the Tribal Learning Practices feel safe to disclose what they want, what they think, and what they feel about the work. As a result, your organization is enjoying higher levels of communication frequency and adaptively responding to change with surprising regularity.

And this is a good thing, because the velocity of change has doubled in recent years and is set to double again, driven by technology. Working groups that do not adapt will become obsolete in a few short years. There is no turning back. We have seen amazing changes in the world of work recently, and the capability to respond to it is the ultimate new team sport.

Those who ***learn how to learn*** as a tribe and as an organization are the winners in the new game of change.

The Next Chapter is Yours to Write. Go Write It!

- In 1978, Chris Argyris & Donald Schön published *Organizational Learning.*
- In 1990, Peter Senge published *The Fifth Discipline.*
- In 2001, a tribe of pioneering people in software published *The Agile Manifesto.*
- In 2008, Dave Logan, John King, and Halee Fischer-Wright published *Tribal Leadership.*
- In 2011, Jane McGonigal published *Reality is Broken.*
- In 2011, I wrote this book for you, a how-to manual of sixteen learning practices you can use to change your world of work.
- What's next is up to you. Good luck!

Part Four: Resources and Tools for Further Study

Appendix A - The Game of Scrum.

An Overview

By Dan Mezick

Scrum is a teamwork framework that defines three roles, three meetings, three artifacts, and a few rules that bind these elements together. Recent changes have changed a few of these definitions (there is now a fourth artifact called the Release Backlog) yet the essentials of Scrum have not changed very much in 10 years. Scrum emerged as a solution to the problem of how to develop and ship working software on time. The task of creating software in teams is notoriously difficult.

This overview is a quick summary of Scrum and is not intended to be comprehensive. The definitive guide may be found at the following link:

scrum.org/storage/scrumguides/Scrum%20Guide.pdf

This Appendix is sufficient for those new to Scrum to get familiar enough with it so you can enjoy this book, as it makes many references to Scrum; the Appendix is designed to orient readers who are new to the framework.

Scrum leaves out many details. The idea is not to be too prescriptive with people and teams. Instead, Scrum defines essential elements of a social (team) structure that encourages focus, commitment, courage, respect, and openness. These values are associated with greatness in teams and organizations. The description that follows explains how Scrum manifests greatness in teams.

Introduction

Scrum employs iterations. Iterations are spaces bounded by time during which teams perform work. It is important to recognize this time-bounded container. In Scrum, each iteration is called a ***Sprint***. A Sprint is usually 2 weeks, but it can range from one to four weeks long. At the end of each iteration, the team inspects their results. They will continue to do things that went well. The team discards things that did not go so well, in favor of trying something new that might work better. This process continues, iteration by iteration. Frequent iterations lead to frequent and explicit inspections, which help teams improve. Questioning everything is part of what happens inside teams that do Genuine & Authentic Scrum. This inspect-and-adapt mechanism encourages dialogue, respect for people, and continuous improvement.

Scrum is a learning framework. Teams using Scrum learn and use the learning to improve results. This is an example of double-loop learning, using the feedback to make changes in your assumptions.

One of the great strengths of Scrum is the very clear goals, clear structure for rules, and clear way to track progress as a team. Scrum has the potential to make working with others become a very satisfying and enjoyable experience. It is important to notice that Scrum is a game played as a group. The object of the game is produce great results as a group.

Three Roles

Scrum has three roles:

- Product Owner
- Team
- Scrum Master

The Product Owner (PO) serves the business. The Product Owner creates a list of features to deliver. This is a to-do list, called the Product Backlog. The PO prioritizes items in this list by moving items of highest value to the top. The team uses this as a starting point to plan an iteration of work. You may think of the Product Backlog as an announcement of intention for the Product's characteristics. The Product Backlog is a kind of vision statement expressed as a list of features to develop and build into the Product (or Service, if you are a service organization).

The Team serves the Product Owner and each other in pursuit of great results. The Team considers the work described in the Product Backlog. The Team then selects as many items from the top of the Product Backlog as the Team believes it can complete in one Sprint.

The Scrum Master (SM) serves the Team by helping them. The Scrum Master facilitates Team meetings, and reminds everyone about their agreement to follow Scrum rules. (People often need to be reminded about their commitments.) The Scrum Master protects the Team from distractions and if the Team needs anything, the Scrum Master goes and gets it. Finally, the Scrum Master identifies and removes obstacles that are in between the Team and greatness.

It is important not to tamper with these three roles. Everyone in the situation needs to find a place as a PO, and SM or a Team member.

Three Meetings

Scrum has three meetings:

- Sprint Planning
- Daily Scrum
- Sprint Review

The PO is the authority in the Sprint Planning meeting. Sprint Planning is where the PO presents the Product Backlog to the Team. The Team looks at it, and selects as much of the work from the top as it thinks it can complete in one Sprint. If your Sprint length is two weeks, the Team loads the two-week Sprint with work during this selection. Once they select the work, the Sprint begins. Ideally, during this meeting the Product Owner is not hatching anything on the Team, but rather has socialized the contents of the Product Backlog well in advance of the Sprint Planning meeting.

After the Team selects the work, the Sprint begins. They take the work items, carve them up into tasks, and begin doing these tasks.

The Team is the authority in the Daily Scrum. The SM facilitates this meeting. The Daily Scrum is a daily ritual. It is a meeting where the Team meets each day and discusses the work. Each Team member answers three questions: What did you do yesterday? What are you doing today? What obstacles are you facing? The Daily Scrum provides a way for everyone to know what everyone else is working on and what issues they are facing.

The Sprint Review has two parts:

- Product Demo
- Retrospective

Both occur at the end of the Sprint.

The PO is the authority in the Product Demo. The SM facilitates this meeting. During the Demo, the Team displays the work completed. An important aspect of this is the definition of Done. For each items of work in the Product Backlog, a description is inserted as well as a definition of Done. This definition of Done describes the acceptance criteria. If the Team completes the work so that the acceptance criterion is satisfied, the work is declared Done. (The PO defines the definition of Done for each work item, sometimes collaborating with the Team to describe the Done definition.) When things go well, the Team gets to declare victory on the Sprint just passed. When things do not go as planned, we inspect why during the Retrospective.

The entire group consisting of the Product Owner, Team, and Scrum Master attend the Retrospective. The Team is the authority during this meeting. It is the Team's meeting. This meeting occurs after the Product Demo.

The SM facilitates this meeting. During this meeting, three questions are considered by everyone attending: What went well? What did not go so well? What do we want to change going forward?

The Retrospective is where substantial group learning takes place.

Three Artifacts

Scrum has three artifacts:

- Product Backlog
- Sprint Backlog

- Burndown Chart

The Product Backlog contains the work descriptions, prioritized by business value. The topmost items are the highest priority. These are sized small enough to be digested by the team. The PO populates the Product Backlog with work items, and prioritizes and edits the Product Backlog. This is called Product Backlog grooming.

The Sprint Backlog is the list of work the team selects from the top of the Product Backlog during the Sprint Planning meeting. This is the list of items the Team expects to complete during the Sprint. The team often carves the work items into tasks, and people on the Team sign up to do the tasks.

The Burndown Chart depicts work remaining. The chart has a vertical axis and a horizontal axis. The horizontal axis represents time in days. The vertical axis represents work remaining. Each day, the work remaining is plotted a point on the graph. The Team is responsible for updating this artifact daily and making it visible to anyone that might want to see it.

Some Rules

Scrum has some rules:

1. The Product Owner is always a person, never a committee. Others may help the PO but the PO is always a single person. The Team interacts with this person around the work.
2. Only the PO is authorized to edit the Product Backlog.
3. The Product Owner may never be the Scrum Master
4. Tasks are clearly defined and authorized by role.

The tasks per role are as follows:

Product Owner:

- Define acceptance criteria and ***definition of done*** as part of work requirements

- Gather estimates and place into Product Backlog
- Prioritize and properly size Product Backlog items
- Present PB at Sprint Planning meeting
- Preside in authority at the Sprint Planning meeting
- Behave in conformance with Scrum rules at all Scrum ceremonies
- Optionally abort the Sprint
- Accept or reject the increment per definition of DONE
- Develop Plans
- Preside in authority at the Sprint Demo
- Participate in the iteration retro
- Abort the Sprint

Team:

- Supply estimates to PO for PB items
- Pull work (the ***what***) from PB to SB during SP meeting
- Carve SB into tasks (the ***how***) during Sprint
- Execute Daily Scrum meeting per Scrum rules
- Update the Burndown Chart daily
- Deliver per-Sprint increments
- Demo increments at Sprint Review
- Participate in iteration Retro

Scrum Master:

- Facilitate Sprint Planning meeting for PO
- Facilitate Sprint Review (demo) meeting for PO
- Facilitate Sprint Review (retro) for Scrum Team
- Facilitate Daily Scrum (each day) for Team
- Protect Team from distractions and threats during the Sprint
- Referee the rules of Scrum (keep the process)
- Identify and remove impediments for Team
- Arrange for Daily Scrum (location and time)
- Help identify a Product Owner

Summary

Scrum's elegant set of roles, meetings, documents and rules allow considerable latitude in how Scrum is implemented. Sprint by Sprint, the Scrum framework encourages the PO, the SM, and Team to engage in respectful interactions and continuous improvement.

Appendix B - Frequent Experiments at Zappos Insights

By Rob Richman

Zappos is one of the most progressive and adaptive service organizations on the planet. Rob Richman is the Director of Zappos Insights. What follows is an interview with Rob on the Tribal Learning practice known as {Conduct Frequent Experiments}. [109]

Here, you will learn how Zappos itself was initially based on a cheap and quick experiment, how Zappos Insights encourages experimentation, and more. . .

Interviewer (Dan): All right. So we're ready to get into this?

Rob: Sure let's do it.

Interviewer (Dan): All right. So first question: What is the mission of Zappos Insights and what's your role in this organization, Rob?

Rob: The mission of Zappos Insights is to create workplaces all over the world that are dedicated to happiness; creating workplaces where people love to work and thus deliver great service to the world.

It all started at when so many organizations had an interest in Zappos because they found out that the service was so great, and we knew that's because the culture is so great.

People at Zappos really loved coming to work to the point that they actually look forward to Monday mornings. We don't get what others had referred to as the Sunday blues because you're thinking about work on Monday, and we really want to share that happiness with the world.

My role in the organization is to manage this as a business. We started off just as a web site sharing information about what we do, and we received so much interest from people that we structured a whole set of course offerings from brief meetings all the way to two-day immersive boot camps and a membership site that allows people to ask questions and learn specifically about what we do.

---

109 The interview took place in March of 2012 in Las Vegas, NV

Now we've created a whole company around it with a 15-person team dedicated to sharing how to create a strong culture.

Interviewer (Dan): I examined the book *Delivering Happiness*_and in that book the Zappos CEO Tony Hsieh mentions Zappos Insights several times (specifically around page 209). He writes about how many of his efforts were dismissed by some board of director members as ***Tony's social experiments***.

Rob: Yeah.

Interviewer (Dan): Is experimentation part of the overall Zappos culture and, if so, how does it show up from day to day?

Rob: Yeah it's definitely part of the Zappos culture. As teams we do off sites at least once a month to bond to the team. We often times take time as individuals to get to know each other beyond work. We shut down the entire office four times a year to get together and celebrate and talk about our successes, and we do all kinds of crazy events.

Everything from doughnut eating contests to balloon throwing outside, and it's really created a fun environment where people love to be every day. We challenge the notion that you get to have fun on the weekends and work is just work.

We believe that they can be integrated together and where a lot of the experimentation started happening is really on the social side, but actually the history of Zappos itself starts as one big experiment because it was started in a time where a lot of money was being infused into .coms.

You'd see tens of millions of dollars being put into websites that weren't even proven – just based on their business plans, and Zappos was entering a very untested market in terms of selling shoes online in the 90's when people were skeptical to really buy anything online, let alone something that required such a tactile experience.

So rather than doing a whole huge business plan and then investing in a big site just to see if it even works, the founder originally took pictures of shoes at a shoe store, put them on a website, and then would go down and buy those shoes when somebody purchased them and sent them out by mail himself.

Interviewer (Dan): Beautiful.

Rob: So yeah. He wanted to prove a concept immediately with an experiment. That's the entire story of how Zappos started. It was only after that that he really started getting the financial backing and then came in touch with Tony and Tony's venture capital group. Then they started to really invest money into it.

So we used that as an ethos throughout the business to say, okay, how can we find low-cost, quick ways to determine if something is going to be successful, because we can easily cut it if it isn't working . . . or if it is then we know to throw fuel in that fire and keep going.

Interviewer (Dan): When a company is small, especially a startup, it's easy to experiment because not learning and not adjusting means you get stale you get to die financially.

As you grow up as a company (Zappos is now probably over 2,500 people) how does Zappos maintain a culture of playful experimentation after reaching a successful critical mass, and going public, and being a big huge company?

Rob: Yeah. It's really keeping that entrepreneurial spirit in terms of just testing things out. So we hire according to core values and one that brings them in is {Be Adventurous, Creative and Open-Minded}, and that attracts that kind of entrepreneurial type of mindset in the company.

People can then say what if we did this? Then the managers are trained to say, okay how can we do this small? How can we test this out?

Especially with anything internal. Somebody says they want to have a certain kind of class, or learn about something, or do a parade, or start an event. Rather than that going through management, they might say, okay what would you do if you want to start that out, and how can we use minimal money or resources to do it?

It's really put back on the employees who want to do it because it's easy for anybody to have a good idea. It's hard actually to implement it and make it happen.

So rather than just talking ideas and having a leadership make it happen we all usually put it back on the person and say, everybody's really responsible for the culture so how can you make this happen yourself? How would you do it?

We reverse that workload on to the people who had the idea and challenge them to think in a way that it can be done small, quick, and fast.

Interviewer (Dan): That's really interesting. Now, what Zappos Insights is doing with culture and values education for business people has never been done.

There are *some* companies that are teaching some aspects of culture but over all, this is a new deal. So what's the role of experimentation specifically inside Zappos Insights? Can you give a few specific examples?

Rob: Yeah Zappos Insights itself has been one big experiment and it's been paying off very well in terms of both as a revenue stream as well as delivering great service.

We thankfully have had very high scores from our tours and classes, and people love learning about the culture. We continue the experimentation through different things that we do. For example, we tried out a group-coaching platform and were able to just roll it out to a small number of members and roll out a 90-day coaching program.

We got to see what work and what didn't about that; certain things we expected and certain things we didn't. We only limited it to a small number of our customers; did it as a small bonus rather than charging a lot, which set high expectations, and we got to see what worked and what didn't within Zappos Insights.

We also do it with tours for example. We've got a set of hand held microphones and earphones to try it and see what happens . . . we said, okay, would this make the tour better? We experiment with the kind of gifts that we give out to people, the kind of cards that we write.

We're constantly just seeing, just throwing things out there to see what feels good for us and what feels good for the customers.

For example, we just decided to take the tour and break it up into two tours and do two separate buildings. We decided to do a video for the intro history of the tour rather than doing it with one person saying it live every time and found that saves us a lot of time while pretty much delivering the same results.

Now we're experimenting in terms of the membership site where we're creating a core curriculum and culture of really creating the foundation by first starting with articulating your values, then making sure you get the right people in the door with the recruiting.

And then training them and then making sure they're delivering great service and then once they are all trained and really delivering great service how do you keep them engaged and once they're engaged how do you develop them into leaders?

That whole cycle we're developing as a program from scratch entirely with the new membership site rolling out. So it's definitely constant experimentation within Zappos Insights.

Interviewer (Dan): Excellent. Now I am wondering: Does Zappos Insights do more experimentation than Zappos as a whole? I'm guessing probably yes, as Zappos Insights is a smaller business and probably has more of a startup feel.

Rob: Yeah. Zappos Insights is definitely more so than the main business. We have our own customer service. We have our own web servers, our own contractors, everything that we need to be agile, to be able to try different things. We have a much smaller footprint.

So the risk is certainly much lower. Whereas Zappos can sometimes do up to $12 million dollars a day, we certainly don't have that level of exposure. With Zappos, something that can bring a server down for half hour can be a huge impact on revenue. If we do something that takes us down for a half hour it's not going to really make a big difference.

Interviewer (Dan): I heard about an experiment you're doing at Zappos called zFrogs.

Rob: Yes.

Interviewer (Dan): Tell me a little bit about that.

Rob: Tony realized that as the company was getting a lot bigger and that it took a lot longer to create change and experiment with new things and he would take a look at the tech development pipeline for example, the backlog, and would see that there's two years' worth of projects on there.

And he said, okay. Well, what if we had the great idea that we need to move quickly on? How do I as a leader know that we can really green light those?

So what he did was create essentially an internal venture capital board made up of the top four senior executives in the company and they get together four times a year on a Saturday. So any employee can sign up for that and do an eighteen minute pitch of what their idea is.

It can be an internal. It can be an external. It can be a new customer service offering, a lot of different things...and they essentially give up their Saturday four times a year to hear those ideas and I've been actually to two of them now.

It's amazing – no matter what idea they provide. Something, even if it has nothing to do with Zappos, they'll give some feedback or some connections, some networking to help them get the idea accomplished and the ones that are related to Zappos they tend to move forward in one way or another.

Certain ones get more of the green light than others in terms of resources and really fast tracking it to make it happen but the leadership is so encouraging of the people who have really devoted a lot of time in preparing their 18-minute presentation.

The people pitching don't just come in and say, hey, this is my idea. What do you think? They do a lot of research. They put a lot of time into it, a lot of passion, because they care about the company, and they care about what we're doing and their role in it.

So four times a year we get to hear about new ideas and experiments that employees want to do and then Tony has the chance to really fast track those so they don't get caught up potentially in the bureaucracy of the company.

Interviewer (Dan): Wow. So that's kind of a back to the future thing, because Venture Frogs was his original investment entity right, the one that initially became aware of the shoe business online.

Rob: Yeah.

Interviewer (Dan): And in the book he talked a little bit about how that wasn't that much fun because he wasn't really engaged in the execution of these businesses; he was ***just an investor*** in them and how that was not really fun for him.

Rob: Yeah.

Interviewer (Dan): And now he and the other leaders help keep the entrepreneurial spirit alive with zFrogs as a place to pitch ideas that can make Zappos and the world better.

Rob: That's right!

Interviewer (Dan): A core value at Zappos is ***Do More With Less***. We talked a little bit about this before, Rob, and you talked about the cost of doing experiments. I'd like to zoom in on that a little bit. How does this value influence your work when you're considering experiments for Zappos Insights?

Rob: It really guides it because it challenges us to think how we can solve this with fewer resources. So it's a great mindset to be in that will challenge us to think what if I had no money. Who's a partner that I can utilize or can we do this in house or do we really need to contract? Do we really to hire some service?

Interviewer (Dan): Rob, experiments usually fail and then the experiment's often considered as a mistake, or a failure, or wrong. So my next question is how tolerant are you, as the leader of Zappos Insights, of ***failed experiments*** and why or why not are you tolerant of these things?

Rob: We are very tolerant, provided that somebody learns - that's the biggest thing that we want to make sure happens. If somebody doesn't learn then it was a waste. If they learn then we could have prevented a much bigger mistake in that sense.

But we've found too is that people who are really great employees and are all-stars tend to beat up themselves a whole lot more than their bosses would. So somebody who makes a mistake, a real all-star, you have to talk them off the ledge and say, look it's not that bad.

When you have a great team and then it becomes a question of okay, is this a valuable lesson that we can learn here? How can we prevent that from happening again? It really generates new behaviors.

It generates new fail-safe checks in some situations. Somebody actually made literally a million-dollar mistake in the company and Tony considered that a million-dollar investment in learning. The lesson was learned. If that mistake escaped us, then it could have been much, much worse in the future.

It was a situation where prices were put down to a much lower level than they should be, and a lot of customers took advantage of it. In our terms of service, we could have not honored the agreement because the price was wrong, and we could have not sent them those products for all those extremely inexpensive prices.

Whenever I've gone in with my leaders and managers and something is screwed up, or we didn't have as much revenue as we thought this week or this month they said, "okay, what can we do here? How can we work together? What did we learn?"

It is never coming from an accusing place of ***you failed. Why didn't you do this?*** It's always ***we're in this together*** type of mindset, and that creates so much more safety and positivity in the group . . . we believe the upside of it is that people are free to innovate a lot more than they otherwise would.

Interviewer (Dan): Interesting. Okay, so we spoke about this a little bit already . . . what specific thing do you do to encourage the people in your organization to conduct frequent experiments and test them out? For example, what specific techniques do you use to encourage your staff to be playful with experiments that are frequent, cheap, and quick?

Rob: I really put it back on them in terms of somebody brings up okay we're getting a low score on this. I say, okay, great what are you going to do differently? Rather than me solving it for them, I just put it back on them to come back to me and say what they want to do that can improve the experience.

That's what I challenge them to do, and it tends to happen more with the newer people on my team. The people who have been there already know that I operate that way.

In some ways it's training them how to manage management, because I train them to come to me with all the factors considered with a solution in mind with a very short summary of what's going on and then what they need from me because I just don't have time to really, as a leader of this company, to get into the weeds about solving all of the issues going on.

I need them to really decompose it for me. And so they come at it with their own ideas and say, okay here's the problem, this is what we've researched looking into it, here's how I think can solve it, here's what I need from you. And it makes my job really easy and it empowers them to come up with solutions and experiments.

Interviewer (Dan): In this book, I argue that conducting lots of experiments and the other 15 practices found here encourage and generate lots of group learning. It's things like managing your boundaries, getting coached, being punctual, managing visually, you know the items.

How many of these Tribal Learning Practices did you find yourself using at Zappos Insights before learning about this list?

Rob: I think all these principles are ones that we like to use, and I think bringing them into awareness makes it so much more powerful, especially in terms of Zappos Insights, because we want to share exactly how this is done with the world. I think that these 16 practices really make explicit what's already implicit.

Interviewer (Dan): One last question Rob: If you could suggest one cultural experiment to a leader of a company who wants to have a strong and well defined culture – what would that experiment be?

Rob: That experiment would be to do something where they share what it is that they're looking to create in a culture. I found that culture is really created in language because all business is communications.

So what if what you want to create in the culture is not in the language? Ask yourself – whatever value it is that you want to create more of, how can it be shared explicitly with the team? How can the team share it back with each other? How can it be shared external to the organization? You share it in language.

So for example, we do a whole printed culture book and we share that culture to the world through the book about how we do what we do. You can take whatever you love about the business and put that in some kind of format or context that it can be easily shared both internally and externally that tends to be what really fuels the fire.

Interviewer (Dan): Thanks Rob!

Rob: You are very welcome Dan.

Appendix C - Stories and Culture

By Michael Margolis

Subject: Stories and Culture: An Interview with Michael Margolis

Background: As a business storyteller, Michael Margolis has consulted to dozens of leading institutions and world-changing initiatives. With a background in entrepreneurship and cultural anthropology, Michael has been featured in *Fast Company*, *Brandweek*, and *Storytelling Magazine*. As Chief Instigator of Get Storied, Michael develops curriculum, online learning events, and training workshops around the globe. He teaches Brand Storytelling at the business school level and is the author of the book *Believe Me: A Storytelling Manifesto for Change-Makers and Innovators*.[110]

Dan: Alright Michael, so why don't tell us a little bit about yourself and Story University and Get Storied so we can have some context for the interview?

Michael: Yeah, sure. So I'm the chief instigator of Get Storied, which is a leading destination online for the business of storytelling. My passion is teaching entrepreneurs how to tell their story.

Dan: So, that would be like quite a few millions of people who are probably looking at needing to do that.

Michael: Well, you know, story is relevant to anybody who's an entrepreneur, anybody who's a change maker, a leader. The essence of what any of us is trying to do is to get others to see what we see, and in the process communicate a story that people want to be a part of.

Dan: What do you mean by see what we see? You mean, they don't see it before the story is told?

---

110 This telephone interview took place by telephone September 15, 2011. You can receive a free PDF version of Michael's storytelling manifesto. See: believemethebook.com

Michael: I've been thinking about this a lot lately Dan, this notion of . . . *what do you see*?

We all see the world differently. And in many ways, that's what makes us special or unique. It's sort of, like that classic old question when you look at a piece of art and you could be like, oh, what do you see? And the answer is, oh, I don't know, I see a naked woman, and the other guy says, well, I see the history of mankind. We each have a different way that we can see the symbolism or derive meaning out of something. Art is a classic example. The same applies to business.

The quintessential challenge or struggle that we face in our life is this issue of getting others to see what we see. That's essence of entrepreneurship, getting others to see, care, and believe in the value of what you're offering.

Dan: What is your fascination with narrative and storytelling all about?

Michael: Simple: For most of my life, I felt lost in translation. My father is from Zimbabwe, and I have lived all over the place. As a kid, I grew up in many unusual places from Switzerland to Los Angeles. When I arrived at each of these places, explaining myself to others was difficult. So, that is the fascination . . . how to construct the story, and how to deliver it so it is received 100% and people receiving it are not confused. Instead, they are receiving your story 100% and they get you.

Here is an example Dan. Consider the entrepreneur, or, even better, the change-maker type in an organization. Same thing: This person sees something that's broken or not working and needs improvement. They're like, "I could do this better." They say "I can improve this", and then they do. They make it better. That's the easy part! Now, they have to go through this whole process of getting others to care about it the same way that they do. The change has to get its story across.

Dan: Yeah, especially when it's a whole new thing. People want to hook new concepts to things they already know.

Michael: Yes.

Dan: For example when TV came out, the producer people, the people making the broadcasts, they didn't know what the heck to do with it, right? So they used it like an extension of radio. They were not inventive. Radio was well understood, TV was a question mark. There were 40 million radios in the U.S. In 1947, and there were about 44,000 television sets (with probably 30,000 in the New York area). Everyone producing shows were scratching their heads.

Michael: Exactly.

Dan: But some people figured it out.

Michael: Correct. And again, that's the easier task. Once you figure it out, you have to convey it. This is the hard part. So, if you think about it this way, in many ways all that we're ever doing is basically taking a vision, communicating a vision and trying to turn it into reality. The way that you turn vision into reality is to get others to see what you see. Then they can locate themselves in that story you are telling. And when you develop a shared common picture and a shared common understanding, people will follow you to the ends of the earth.

Dan: So is that what's happening with stories collectively? They help us develop shared models?

Michael: Exactly. Yes. I call it *discovering the invisible lines of connection*. Most of us think we're really separate and different and distinct and that there are just a few people who get us. And this happens not only in our own personal lives but it happens in organizations. Think about it – we each have our own teams, our work groups. We are organized in departments, our ***divisions***, and there are lots of politics. There are all these different barriers that reinforce and remind us how different we are from each other. Storytelling helps to basically remind us of our connection and shared humanity.

Dan: The typical organization has the typical problems. Low communication frequency. Low-fidelity communication via totally unbounded and excessive use of email. Too much noise, not enough signal. Way too much specialization of skills, leading to isolation and little of any mixing of skills and ideas. So what's the remedy in the workplace? How does story become part of the solution towards more work place health and wellness?

Michael: Well I think it begins with the notion of truth. It's having the courage and the conviction to talk about what's missing from the conversation, to have the courage to actually speak about what you see, to speak the story line, as you know it. There's always competing story lines – some cultural friction – inside whatever issue you are facing in your group, or whatever organization you're in. And I say: Have the willingness to embrace that.

Here is a good example. Avis rent cars. Once day they decided to make the story line ***We are proud of being #2. We are Avis. We try harder.*** Someone in that company spoke that story line and it worked.[111] It resonated, and it made it easy for people in that company to locate themselves inside that story. They called attention to the fact they were in a dogfight with Hertz and were out the kick some ass. The story about being #2 was true, it mobilized the Avis people. It took guts to speak the truth of that out in a public way.

Dan: So, it is essential to confront the truth – ***the brutal facts***, as author Jim Collins *Good to Great* says?

Michael: Part of this is about re-framing things and understanding: where are the objections here? And having the courage to call these objections out and to plainly talk about them. And very few leaders are willing to do this. To be truth-tellers. And that's a huge way of building trust and credibility, by (1); speaking truth, (2); showing that you really care about what people are going through, demonstrating some empathy and then (3); being vulnerable.

---

111 The person responsible for the Avis story was Robert Townsend. His story and the Avis are interesting. Learn more at http://en.wikipedia.org/wiki/Robert_Townsend_(author)and http://en.wikipedia.org/wiki/Avis_Rent_a_Car_System

Dan: It sounds like what you are saying is that signaling in these three ways is the secret sauce for leaders to create and hold safe space.

Michael: That is exactly what I am saying. And more than that: for example, consider vulnerability. Here's what vulnerability does, and you'll appreciate this. Vulnerability redistributes power. In your language, it distributes authority.

Dan: Yes, but authority to do what?

Michael: The authority to get things done, the authority to do work. People with lots of positional authority often posture a stance of invincibility. By signaling vulnerability, authority isn't concentrated in such an imbalanced fashion. It's being shared because signaling vulnerability is an indirect way of asking for help.

Dan: Ok, so for all you leaders out there: tell the truth about the place, demonstrate that you understand what people are experiencing here, and let them know you do not have all the answers. Is that it?

Michael: Yes. Be real and avoid posturing every chance you get.

Dan: So this 3-part framework you are describing (truth, empathy, vulnerability) maps to specific practices described in this book. Some of these include Open The Space, Be Purposeful, Structure Your Interactions, Examine What's Normal, Pay Explicit Attention, Inspect Frequently, and Manage Your Boundaries, in this relaxing or loosening them. {Open the Space} seems to be the big one here.

Michael: Yes. These are actual behaviors that lead to truth telling, and empathizing with those you are leading, and disclosing what you are facing.

Dan: OK. We talked earlier about how Open Space is really open. We talked about how as an organization, you need to be ready for it, because it sends a strong signal of openness and the organization has to live up to that signal. So what about a less ambitious goal, like socializing a specific story that you want to spread? What if you want to develop a new collective story around a set of values for example?

Michael: Yes. For example, say you have a new set of values you want to socialize. Now you are facilitating the session and the session is underway. What you want to do is you want to present those values. One simple thing that you can do is you can list them – let's say there are 7 or 10 values you want people discussing.

Dan: OK.

Michael: At this session, you print each one individually on an index card and you put it up on the wall.

Dan: Alright.

Michael: And you have multiple people in the room. They all opted in to being there.

So let's say you have 30 people in the room and you only have seven values or so, so you print the same seven values 3 or 4 times, so people have ready access to these cards with the values on them. Multiple cards for each value are all on the wall.

Dan: Okay.

Michael: Next, you introduce these values and then you ask everybody in the room, to go and pick just one value off that wall that really resonates with them personally, the one value that they really have a connection to.

Dan: Okay, so far so good.

Michael: So everybody who wants goes and does that. They self-select themselves in. And then you go around and you ask people to tell a story – about what this value looks like in action for them, something that they've seen happen inside the company, or if not there, then something that's happened in their own life that makes them want to champion this value. That action has them basically opting in to say yes, this matters to me personally, and I think it matters to us as a company.

Dan: Okay.

Michael: And in that process, you start to reinforce the collective mind and socializing those values into the new collective truth.

Dan: So you put them up on the wall, you ask them to pick one and then you ask them to tell a story.

Michael: That's it.

Dan: Okay, so I see several Tribal Learning Practices in here. This is interesting. I see: Facilitate Your Meetings, Be Purposeful, Be Playful, Announce Your Intentions, Structure Your Interactions, Pay Explicit Attention, Game Your Meetings, and even Conduct Frequent Experiments since there is some opting in going on here, and we are going to inspect this carefully afterwards right?

Michael: That's it. They all opted in. Now the participants are all engaging in this exercise.

Dan: Like in a small group setting?

Michael: Yes. And then the interesting part: you're going to have a conversation about what do we need to do as an organization to further or better embody these values into our culture.

Two things are being articulated here collectively: where are we doing these things already, and where could we be doing these things even better.

Dan: I see it.

Michael: And then it allows you to have this conversation that this is a living process and one that everybody can contribute to.

Dan: This type of session has a lot in common with Open Space: you are inviting the folks, there is a themed structure, there are activities that are optional, there are conversations, and there is story telling in these conversations.

Michael: Yes. And here we have all of that and a more focused space. The conversation space is more clearly defined. You invite them and explain what the goal is. You define a clear purpose for the meeting and they opt-in, just like Open Space. Same concept. The set of people who have the passion have a sense of responsibility to do something about it show up.

Dan: That's good. That's really good. So alright, what about a typical manager in a typical company who wants to make things more engaged at work? This person wants to create more genuine and authentic engagement. For this person, assume they have 6 to 10 people reporting to them, you know, not so many people. What's the one thing they can do with story and narrative that will move the needle in this spot?

Michael: Well, so embody those three principles I mentioned earlier: truth, empathy, and vulnerability. You know all the statistics that says something like, 70% of people leave their jobs because they had a bad manager?

Dan: Yes.

Michael: Think about it, if you work for somebody who values truth, empathy, and vulnerability – and practices that, this is somebody you're willing to go to battle for because that's somebody you respect. Because they're going to tell you like it is, right? You're excited to tell stories about working on a team that's led by this person.

Dan: Yeah, they're going to feel your pain.

Michael: Exactly, right? And you know that regardless of the wider culture in the organization, they're going to fight for you, they're going to defend you, right? Because you know that, they've already invested in you and that they're a genuine human-being first and your ***boss*** second.

Dan: Right. They're disclosing about what their challenges are.

Michael: Yup.

Dan: Okay, that's some good advice. And that doesn't require a budget or any kind of authorization; you can just choose to do it.

Michael: You can create your own little sort of cultural pod containing a high performance team.

Dan: Right.

Michael: Based on embodying those three principles, you can socialize those principles across your team.

Dan: Now, how do these principles play out in – and how do I leverage story dynamics in getting this going? I mean, obviously if I am a manager, and I tell the truth and say it like it is, and if I genuinely feel your pain and I'm disclosing of my own challenges, that's going to generate some stories – people are going to tell stories about that.

Michael: Yup. Now, apply those same principles to the business agenda of the organization or the business agenda of that team or department, same thing applies. Whatever line of business that you're in, you have to speak truth to it. And the opportunities come along. There is not usually a long wait. Usually there's sort of an onset or trigger event. If you're on a path of innovation, there's always a new problem to solve. So truth is being willing to actually name that ugly problem and commit to cleaning it up, right? Empathy is showing that you care about your customer or whoever the stakeholder is that you serve. And then the vulnerability is being able to talk about the obstacles you have or what are the challenges that you need to overcome. Going back to the truth, the truth is also giving people something to live for. The truth is, hey, there's a bigger game to play, there's more out there for us. Let's open some space to have these explicit conversations.

The truth elevates. Empathy connects. And vulnerability is the great equalizer.

Dan: And what that does is it tends to attract the helpers right? Because when you disclose your obstacles – the helpers show up.

Michael: Yeah. See, if you're somebody with formal, positional authority and you're able to signal some vulnerability, the act of signaling some vulnerability is distributing your authority. You're sharing it out instead of holding it, does that make sense?

Dan: Yes, that's really good, that's a really great three-part answer to that question.

Michael, thank you for explaining your relationship with narrative and how we can leverage the power of narrative in our own organizations. Thanks for the tips on generating stories and how to create open, focused, and fun meetings formats that get people talking and telling their stories.

Michael: My pleasure Dan. Thanks for your book!

NOTE: You can learn more about the power of narrative to transform your life and organization at Michael's home on the web, GetStoried.com. You'll find videos, blogs posts, papers, and other resources that can help you leverage the power of story for yourself, your tribe, and your organization. To receive a free copy of Michael's storytelling manifesto, go to believemethebook.com.

Appendix D - Games to Do Work: The Speed boat Game

By Luke Hohmann

Luke Hohmann published the book_*Innovation Games: Creating Breakthrough Products Through Collaborative Play*, in 2006. That was really early, in terms of what has transpired with games and business. Luke has a software background and is an original thinker and energetic entrepreneur. This is yet another example of teamwork innovation emerging from the software community as discussed in Part One.

This Appendix contains the chapter "Speed boat: Identify What Customers Don't Like About Your Product or Service," from the *Innovation Games* book. You can get a good sense of how games can help you gather market research data from customers (and in fact, any group of people focused on a goal) by examining the game details in pages that follow:

Speed boat: The Game

Customers have complaints. And if you simply ask them to complain, they will. This may be okay, but be careful; the seemingly harmless snowflakes of a few minor problems can quickly become an avalanche of grievances from which you can never recover. I've sat through a few of these ***let it all hang out and complain about anything sessions***, and just about everyone leaves the room tired and frustrated. Think ***angry mob*** and make certain you know where the exits are located.

It doesn't have to be this way. You can ask your customers what's bothering them if you do it in a way that lets you stay in control of how complaints are stated and discussed. In the process, you'll find fresh new ideas for the changes you can make to address your customers' most important concerns.

The Game

Draw a boat on a whiteboard or sheet of butcher paper. You'd like the boat to move really fast. Unfortunately, the boat has a few anchors holding it back. The boat is your system, and the features that your customers don't like are its anchors.

Customers write what they don't like on an index card and place it under the boat as an anchor. They can also estimate how much faster the boat would go if that anchor were cut and add that to the card. Estimates of speed are really estimates of pain. Customers can also annotate the anchors created by other customers, indicating agreement on substantial topics. When customers are finished posting their anchors, review each one, carefully confirming your understanding of what they want to see changed in the system.

Why It Works

Although most customers have complaints, few customers are genuinely ***against*** you or your product. Even if they express extreme frustration, the reality is that they want to succeed when using your product. Giving them a way to express their frustration *without* letting a group mentality or a single person dominate the discussion is what most customers want. *Speed Boat* creates this relatively safe environment where customers can tell you what's wrong.

Another significant reason that *Speed Boat* works is that many people don't feel comfortable expressing their frustrations verbally. Giving them a chance to write things down gives them a way to provide feedback. It also gives them an opportunity to reflect on what is genuinely most important. The opportunity to reflect is especially important for those customers who just seem to be somewhat unhappy people (you know, the ones who complain a lot about the little details). Asking them to verbalize their issues, especially in writing, motivates them to *think* about these issues. Many of them will identify trivial issues as just that—trivial issues—and, in the process, focus on the truly big issues. Thus, they end up voicing their complaints, but they're put into perspective. When they get used to *thinking* about their complaints, especially quantifying what the impact is, they are more reasonable and will contribute more to success—theirs and yours.

However, there are products for which the sheer number of seemingly trivial complaints adds up to one truly large complaint—the product or service offering might have been good enough to purchase, but not good enough to continue using or to recommend to others. In this case, *Speed Boat* helps you identify the set of problems that you need to address before your product fails. Although we don't require that customers use different sized or shaped anchors, the game does not prevent customers from changing the size, shape, weight, or number of anchors that they add to the boat.

Figure 20. ACM's Simple Speed Boat Design

Preparing for the Game

Use the best possible imagery that you can to keep the mood playful. Buy pictures of boats and stickers of fish at stores that stock school or craft supplies and post them on a whiteboard. Print anchors on your index cards. Keeping the mood playful helps everyone deal with the potentially stressful content of the feedback. Aladdin Knowledge Systems, Inc., the world's leading provider of hardware-based software antipiracy solutions, went so far as to merge a fast boat with a USB dongle to create vivid imagery that helped set the proper tone for their session (see Figure 22). You can also go ***low tech*** for your boat, which the Greater Boston Chapter of the ACM did when they played *Speed Boat*. In this game, Tobias Mayer simply drew a Speed boat on a chalkboard.

Steve Peacock of Air Transport IT described a variant of this game he played with customers at an annual users' conference. Instead of using anchors, they referred to complaints as barnacles. Barnacles were of three sizes—small, medium, and large—where the size represented the strength of the complaint.

Although you want customers who can, and will, contribute, avoid including any customers who are likely to be overly dominant or negative. If you must invite such customers, consider running two *Speed Boat* sessions: one for the unruly crowd and another for the quieter, more thoughtful crowd.

It helps to review your service and support systems to identify any specific items that may exist for customers coming to the event, because they use this opportunity to ask pointed questions about the status of reported problems. It also helps to make certain you're aware of any plans to address known problems. Although it is important to try to avoid addressing issues during the game, there are times that you will have to do this, so be prepared.

Materials

1. Pictures of a speed boat
2. Anchor cards - cards that customers can use as simulated anchors to capture their concerns

Speed Boat for Expensive Products

Few customers hope or expect that a product will fail. Instead, after a product has been purchased, customers will often work hard to ensure that the product succeeds. This is most easily observed in Business-to-Business (B2B) and Business to Professional (B2P) product and service offerings, where the commitment to success is proportional to the price of the product. Someone who just spent hundreds of thousands or millions of dollars on a product is facing considerable pressure to make certain that they made the right choice—pressure such as their next raise, promotion, or even their own job! These people tend to be great candidates for *Speed Boat*, providing direct, candid, and honest assessments of the anchors that are slowing down their use of your product. They want you to succeed. Let them show you how.

Playing the Game

After the facilitator introduces the game, give customers a few minutes to gather their thoughts before you expect them to create anchors. Then, to help get the process of posting the anchors to the wall started, the facilitator should gently ask a few customers for completed anchor cards and tape these to the wall on behalf of the customer. After this, other customers will spontaneously join in and add anchors. There is no requirement that customers take turns posting anchors. In fact, the game works better if several customers and the facilitator are posting anchors at the same time because there is a formal review process.

Participants walk up to the wall, add their anchors, and return to their seats.

When customers have finished posting anchors, the facilitator begins the review process. Try to review *every single anchor*. This lets your customers know that their feedback is important. The approach that works best is to let customers finish adding anchors, and then ask them to be seated. Walk up to the anchors and review each one. Although only one customer created the anchor, invite the whole group to comment on what was written. As you review the anchor, it is *critically important* that you refrain from trying to solve the problem, respond to the feedback, or justify why a certain choice is made. Doing this will dramatically change the game dynamic. Instead of encouraging forthright and sincere discussions of perceived problems, customers will interpret your response as a defense mechanism and will quickly become guarded in their communication and cynical of the process. Seek to understand the underlying reason why this anchor is holding them back from success, not in responding to or justifying the status quo.

Facilitator reviews each card with the customers. Observers keep track of what was said.

Figure 21. Reviewing the Anchor Cards

There are practical reasons why you should not attempt to address or respond to anchors during the game. You probably don't have all the data needed to make a thorough response. You probably don't have all the necessary decision makers in the same room. You are almost certainly violating your product development and product management practices by making decisions in this manner. Perhaps most seriously, you're probably not in the right frame of mind to address these concerns, and you don't want to let the stress you may feel during this game result in short-sighted decisions.

Note that reviewing every single anchor doesn't necessarily mean reading or sharing each anchor. Sometimes it is better to quickly group anchors with similar content and/or themes and talk about these anchors as a group. This means that you need to scan the anchors that are being added during the game continually, to see if there are obvious trends. In rare cases, you can move anchors that customers have added to start the process of group formation during the exercise.

The spatial arrangement of the anchors usually has important meanings to the participants. One example has already been mentioned—grouping similar cards. Sometimes customers will naturally put ***heavier*** or ***larger*** anchors near the bottom, or designate that there is more than one boat, where different boats have different meanings. To preserve the spatial memory of the exercise, take many photos during the game. Always take photos of the final card arrangement.

No Defensive Response—Even if They Are Wrong!

One of the hardest things about *Speed Boat* is not responding to customers during the game—especially when they write an anchor that is just wrong! This is where good facilitation skills are critical. In these situations, the facilitator must keep the focus on understanding the issue presented by the customer. There will be plenty of time to address the customer after the event. And chances are you'll want to communicate this to all of your customers because chances are good that more than one will share this misunderstanding.

Consider asking customers to vote on the top three or five anchors whose removal would have the most positive impact on the boat's speed.

One variant that can be useful is to ask customers to add ***engines*** to the boats after they've finished. The engines represent features that can ***overpower*** the anchors and enable the boat to move faster. Do this carefully, because it changes the focus and dynamics of the game. If you really think that you need to focus on adding features, consider *Product Box, Buy a Feature,* or *Prune the Product Tree*. Sometimes, however, the energy of the room changes and the participants naturally start talking about adding features. When this happens, go with the flow and add some horsepower to your boats.

Processing the Results

The goal of processing this feedback is to classify each anchor (or common grouping of anchors) according to three key attributes:

1. The specific area of the product associated with the problem
2. The severity of the problem
3. The priority or urgency of fixing it

Begin this process by transcribing the anchors into a spreadsheet or other system that you use to track product requirements. When there is more than one anchor around a common complaint, record the number of anchors that related to this complaint. Determine the root cause or area of the product associated with the problem. Here are some common root causes:

1. Poor documentation — Incorrect, improper, misleading, outdated, incomprehensible, and so on.
2. User inexperience—Users didn't know that something could be done with your product.

3. Defect—An error or bug in your product. It is best if you explore this just enough to confirm that you understand the problem, so that you can correlate it with your defect-tracking system.
4. Technology incompatibility—A previously unknown or improperly communicated incompatibility with your product.
5. Mismatched expectations—For example, a customer expected the fountain pen to work while on a plane and expressed frustration when it didn't.

As you're processing the cards, be certain to include photos of the original cards written by your customers, because there is both meaning in the spatial arrangement of the cards and a certain empathy and intimacy that comes from working directly with your customers' feedback. In some cases, you can even get a sense for the passion a customer has about a given topic by looking at the card they've created. I've seen cards with lightning bolts, frowns,*!#@&!#*, phrases like ***grrrr*** or statements punctuated with several exclamation points. All of these are reflective of a customer who cares pretty deeply about the topic. Retaining this information is important to motivating your team to action.

Characterize the perceived severity of the problem. A common approach used in managing bugs associated with software systems is to assign each bug a numeric ranking from 1 to 5.[9] Even if you're not working on a software system, you might find that this list provides you with a useful way of characterizing customer feedback.

1. Crash with no workaround. Often associated with unavoidable data loss, and typically considered the worst kind of bug. For non-software-based products, this kind of problem could be considered equivalent to a serious safety issue that motivates a product recall. Using this as a baseline, you can adjust the rest of the rankings in a way that makes sense for your product.
2. Crash with workaround.

3. Serious problem.
4. Minor problem.
1. Not a bug (something the customer reported as a problem, but isn't).

Characterize the priority of fixing the problem, again using a numerical ranking from 1 to 5:

- Immediate — the problem must be fixed immediately, with the updated product delivered to customers as quickly as possible.
- Urgent — the problem must be fixed before the next major product milestone.
- Before next release — the problem must be fixed before the next version of the product is released to customers.
- As time allows—although it would be nice to fix this problem before the next release, customers can live with the problem.
- Defer—we understand that at least one customer perceives this as a problem, but we're explicitly going to defer addressing the issue.

It is relatively easy to create consistency within your organization for severities, because they can be objectively verified. Priorities, on the other hand, are subjective. A misspelling in your documentation may get a "4" for severity, but different cultures will ascribe different priorities to fixing such a problem. I've found that Americans and Europeans are more tolerant and are happy to give these kinds of problems correspondingly low priorities. Japanese customers tend not to be as tolerant and give documentation bugs high priorities. Because of the subjective nature of bug priorities, use a cross-functional team approach to establish priorities. As you can guess, high severity problems correlate with high-priority fixes.

Even this level of analysis may be insufficient when making a good choice on how to handle a problem. Consider that sometimes trying to fix a Severity One problem (crash with no work-around) could cause other problems. This situation often happens in older software systems, and makes deciding what to fix extremely challenging.

Review the results, organized by priority, to define how you will address each priority. It is especially important to communicate your choices to your customers so that they can understand how you're addressing their feedback.

Index

P

R

S

Acknowledgements

Where do I start?

There are many people who helped shape this book. My Agile coaching clients are the first people to thank. Without them I would have never conceived of this book. Special thanks to my coaching clients, who teach me something new every single day.

My close friends, those most fascinated with culture, need to be thanked as well. Without them, there is no book. Being able to discuss ideas with these great thinking partners is something I cannot do without. Special thanks to Michael Margolis from GetStoried.com for turning me on to the power of storytelling, and for being a whole and great friend.

Special thanks to Dave Logan for always being completely irreverent, for encouraging the writing of this book, and for always coming through with the essential help I needed to write Part 3.

Very special thanks to Robert Richman of Zappos Insights, who encouraged me to document our many conversations and make them the content in this book. Thank you Rob for your tremendous support of my work around culture hacking, culture tools and cultural design.

Thanks to Jim and Michele McCarthy, for encouraging me always to do great work, and for encouraging the development of the body knowledge coming to be known as: Culture Hacks. Thanks for inspiring me with your amazing *Software For Your Head* book, especially pages 290-293.

Many folks in and around the Agile Boston user group community helped with proofing, edits, and formatting. In no particular order, I acknowledge the help of friends and fellow travelers Karen Spencer, Dan LeFebvre, Frank Saucier, and Ralph Fink.

Special thanks to David Resnik for his formatting and editing of the manuscript. His encyclopedic knowledge of organizational development proved invaluable as the book took shape.

Special thanks to these thought leaders and book authors, for influencing my thinking: Jane McGonigal, Tony Hsieh, Dave

Logan (again!), and Jay Forrester. All are great creative geniuses who have influenced my thinking at the intersection of games, business, culture, and learning.

Lastly, thanks to my good friend, traveling companion and loving wife Roberta, for taking good care of me, and making sure I took good care of myself as I wrote this book.

Dan Mezick

In North Haven CT

May 2012

Bibliography

I have cited most of these titles in the body of the book. All have influenced the creation of this title.

Adkins, L. (2010). *Coaching Agile Teams a Companion for ScrumMasters, Agile Coaches, and Project Managers in Transition*. Upper Saddle River, NJ: Addison-Wesley. [Print].

Anderson, D. J. (2010). *Kanban: Successful Evolutionary Change in Your Software Business*. Sequim, WA: Blue Hole. [Print].

Appelo, J. (2011). *Management 3.0: Leading Agile Developers, Developing Agile Leaders*. Upper Saddle River, NJ: Addison-Wesley. [Print].

Bion, W. R. (1961). *Experiences in Groups: and Other Papers*. London, UK: Tavistock Publications. [Print].

Blank, S. (2006). *The Four Steps to the Epiphany: Successful Strategies for Products That Win*. (2nd ed.). Foster City, CA: Cafepress.com. [Print].

Booth, S. L., & Meadows, D. L. (2010). *The Systems Thinking Playbook: Exercises to Stretch and Build Learning and Systems Thinking Capabilities*. White River Junction, VT: Chelsea Green Publications. [Print].

Cockburn, A. (2007). *Agile Software Development: The Cooperative Game*. (2nd ed.). Upper Saddle River, NJ: Addison-Wesley. [Print].

Collins, J. C. (2001). *Good to Great: Why Some Companies Make the Leap – and Others Don't*. New York, NY: HarperBusiness. [Print].

Coplien, J. O., & Harrison, N. (2005). *Organizational Patterns of Agile Software Development*. Upper Saddle River, NJ: Pearson Prentice Hall. [Print].

Csikszentmihalyi, M. (1990). *Flow: The Psychology of Optimal Experience*. New York, NY, USA: Harper & Row. [Print].

Derby, E., & Larsen, D. (2006). *Agile Retrospective: Making Good Teams Great*. Dallas: Pragmatic Bookshelf. [Print].

Douglas, M. (1990). *The Disciplined Trader: Developing Winning Attitudes*. NY: New York Institute of Finance. [Print].

Fried, J., & Hansson, D. H. (2010). *Rework*. New York: Crown Business, 2010. [Print].

Gharajedaghi, J. (2006). *Systems Thinking: Managing Chaos and Complexity: a Platform for Designing Business Architecture*. (2nd ed.). Amsterdam, NL: Elsevier. [Print].

Godin, S. (2010). *Linchpin: Are you indispensable?* New York: Portfolio. [Print].

Godin, S. (2011). *Poke the Box: When Was the Last Time You Did Something for the First Time?* The Domino Project.

Godin, S. (2008). *Tribes: We need you to lead us*. New York: Portfolio. [Print].

Gray, D., Brown, S., & Macanufo, J. (2010) *Gamestorming: a Playbook for Innovators, Rulebreakers, and Changemakers*. Beijing: O'Reilly. [Print].

Heath, C., & Heath. D. (2010). *Switch: How to Change Things When Change Is Hard*. New York: Broadway. [Print].

Hohmann, Luke. (2006). *Innovation Games: Creating Breakthrough Products Through Collaborative Play*. Boston, MA: Addison-Wesley. [Print].

Hsieh, T. (2010). *Delivering Happiness: a Path to Profits, Passion, and Purpose*. New York: Business Plus. [Print].

Joiner, B., & Josephs, S. (2007). *Leadership Agility: Five Levels of Mastery for Anticipating and Initiating Change*. San Francisco: Jossey-Bass. [Print].

Kline, P., & Saunders, B. (1998). *Ten Steps to a Learning Organization*. (2nd ed.). Arlington, VA: Great Ocean. [Print].

Le Bon, G. (1995). *The Crowd*. New Brunswick, NJ: Transaction Publications. [Print].

Lencioni, P. (2002). *The five dysfunctions of a team: A leadership fable*. San Francisco: Jossey-Bass. [Print].

Logan, D., King, J. P., & Fischer-Wright, H. (2008). *Tribal Leadership: Leveraging Natural Groups to Build a Thriving Organization*. New York: Collins. [Print].

Mack, A., & Rock, I. (2000). *Inattentional Blindness.* Cambridge, MA: MIT Press. [Print].

Margolis, M. (2009). *Believe Me: Why Your Vision, Brand, and Leadership Need a Bigger Story.* New York: Get Storied. [Print].

May, Matthew E. (2009). *In Pursuit of Elegance: Why the Best Ideas Have Something Missing.* New York: Broadway. [Print].

May, M. E. (2011). *The Shibumi Strategy: a Powerful Way to Create Meaningful Change.* San Francisco, CA: Jossey-Bass. [Print].

McCarthy, J, & McCarthy, M. (2002). *Software for Your Head: Core Protocols for Creating and Maintaining Shared Vision.* Boston, MA: Addison-Wesley. [Print].

McGonigal, J. (2011). *Reality Is Broken: Why Games Make Us Better and How They Can Change the World.* New York: Penguin. [Print].

Owen, H. (2008). *Open Space Technology: a User's Guide.* (3rd ed.). San Francisco, CA: Berrett-Koehler. [Print].

Owen, H. (1987). *Spirit: Transformation and Development in Organizations.* Potomac, MD: Abbott Publishing. [Print].

Owen, H. (2000). *The Power of Spirit: How Organizations Transform.* San Francisco: Berrett-Koehler. [Print].

Owen, H. (1999). *The Spirit of Leadership: Liberating the Leader in Each of Us.* San Francisco, CA: Berrett-Koehler. [Print].

Owen, H. (2008). *Wave Rider: Leadership for High Performance in a Self-organizing World.* San Francisco: Berrett-Koehler. [Print].

Patterson, K., Grenny, J., McMillan, R., & , A. (2002). *Crucial Conversations: Tools for Talking When Stakes Are High.* New York: McGraw-Hill. [Print].

Pollack, S, & Fusoni, M. (2005). *Moving beyond Icebreakers: an Innovative Approach to Group Facilitation, Learning, and Action.* Boston: Center for Teen Empowerment. [Print].

Ragsdale, S., & Saylor, A. (2007). *Great Group Games: 175 Boredom-busting, Zero-prep Team Builders for All Ages.* Minneapolis, MN: Search Institute. [Print].

Schwaber, K., & Beedle, M. (1996). *Agile Software Development Using Scrum.* Upper Saddle River, NJ: Prentice Hall. [Print].

Senge, P. M., Roberts, C., Ross, R. B., Smith, B. J., & Kleiner, A. (1994). *The Fifth Discipline Fieldbook: Strategies and Tools for Building a Learning Organization.* New York: Currency, Doubleday. [Print].

Senge, P. M. (1990). *The Fifth Discipline: the Art and Practice of the Learning Organization.* New York: Doubleday/Currency. [Print].

Seykota, E. (2005). *The Trading Tribe*. Incline Village, Nevada: Trading Tribe. [Print].

Sibbet, D. (2010). *Visual Meetings: How Graphics, Sticky Notes, & Idea Mapping Can Transform Group Productivity*. Hoboken, NJ: John Wiley & Sons. [Print].

Stacey, R. D. (2000). *Strategic Management and Organisational Dynamics: The Challenge of Complexity.* (3rd ed.). New York: Financial Times. [Print].

Thomas, D., & Brown, J. S. (2011). *A New Culture of Learning: Cultivating the Imagination for a World of Constant Change*. Lexington, KY: CreateSpace. [Print].

Vaill, P. B. (1989). *Managing as a Performing Art: New Ideas for a World of Chaotic Change*. San Francisco: Jossey-Bass. [Print].

Vogt, J. W. (2009). *Recharge Your Team: the Grounded Visioning Approach.* Westport, CT: Praeger. [Print].

West, E. (1997). *201 Icebreakers: Group Mixers, Warm-ups, Energizers, and Playful Activities*. New York: McGraw-Hill. [Print].

Whitney, D. K., & Trosten-Bloom, A. (2010). *The Power of Appreciative Inquiry: a Practical Guide to Positive Change*. (2nd ed.). San Francisco: Berrett-Koehler. [Print].

Zaffron, S., & Logan, D. (2009). *The Three Laws of Performance: Rewriting the Future of Your Organization and Your Life*. San Francisco, CA: Jossey-Bass. [Print].

About the Author

Daniel Mezick is a management consultant focused on culture, self-management and self-organizing teams. He provides consulting to leaders around the world and is a frequent keynote speaker at industry conferences including SouthBySouthwest, the Global Scrum Gathering, and other Agile conferences.

Daniel is the formulator of the Open Agile Adoption, a repeatable method for creating rapid and lasting culture change in your organization. The Open Agile Adoption method employs many of the patterns and practices found in this book. Open Agile Adoption forms a complete system for encouraging and guiding intentional and designed culture change. It leverages the power of invitation, Open Space, game mechanics, storytelling and more. You can learn more at OpenAgileAdoption.com.

Dan's organization New Technology Solutions provides culture-design consulting and training and to businesses of all sizes that are seeking more business agility.

New Technology Solutions provides:

- Culture analysis, culture design, and implementation assistance;
- Executive coaching;
- Training and consulting in the Open Agile Adoption culture-change method;
- Training and coaching for Agile teams;
- Business agility coaching for executives, directors and managers;

- Webinars and courses on The Culture Game, Open Agile Adoption, and other cultural design topics of interest to business enterprises.

Daniel Mezick is available to address your group meeting with keynote sessions, seminars and workshops. Call or write to arrange speaking and consulting engagements.

You can reach Daniel as follows:

Web: http://newtechusa.net

Phone: 203 915 7248

Email: dan@newtechusa.net

Twitter: @DanMezick

This page intentionally left blank for Reader Notes

This page intentionally left blank for Reader Notes

Made in the USA
Lexington, KY
22 May 2015